FROM THE FAT
OF OUR SOULS

COMPARATIVE STUDIES OF
HEALTH SYSTEMS AND MEDICAL CARE

General Editor
John M. Janzen

Founding Editor
Charles Leslie

For a complete list of titles in this series, please contact the
Sales Department
University of California Press
2120 Berkeley Way
Berkeley, CA 94720

FROM THE FAT OF OUR SOULS

*Social Change,
Political Process,
and Medical Pluralism
in Bolivia*

Libbet Crandon-Malamud

UNIVERSITY OF CALIFORNIA PRESS
Berkeley   Los Angeles   Oxford

University of California Press
Berkeley and Los Angeles, California
University of California Press
Oxford, England

Copyright © 1991 by The Regents of the University of California

Library of Congress Cataloging-in-Publication Data

Crandon-Malamud, Libbet.
    From the fat of our souls: social change, political process, and
medical pluralism in Bolivia / Libbet Crandon-Malamud.
        p.   cm. — (Comparative studies of health systems and medical
care)
    Includes bibliographical references and index.
    ISBN 0-520-07011-9
    1. Aymara Indians—Medicine—Social aspects.   2. Medical
anthropology—Bolivia.   3. Social mobility—Bolivia.   4. Social
classes—Bolivia.   I. Title.   II. Series.
    F2230.2.A9C73   1991
    615.8'82'0984—dc20   90-37178
                                                              CIP

Printed in the United States of America

1   2   3   4   5   6   7   8   9

To
JAIME
and to
ANNA and JON
who make every morning
the beginning of a new adventure,
to
NATHAN ROBISON and BERTHA CARTER
whose adventuresome spirits
have in significant ways,
improved the world,
and to my father,
DR. JOHN HOWLAND CRANDON
who, having practiced surgery for
some fifty years, might say
this book is really common sense

Contents

Preface

This book is about opinions, rumors, gossip, and strategies concerning illness and health care, among and between Bolivian Aymara and mestizos, Catholics and Methodists, in Kachitu, a rural town on the altiplano, witnessed between 1976 and 1978. It is an argument for medical pluralism, not for medical, but for political reasons. Deriving from research that asked why people choose different or multiple medical resources, its thesis is that they do so for nonmedical reasons. It builds upon an idea originally proposed by Paul Unschuld (1975), that people use medicine as a primary resource through which they get access to secondary resources, particularly where multiple resources exist and choice between them becomes socially and politically significant.

Primary resources are, like capital, fungible. They can be used to acquire something else or transformed into something else. Secondary resources are those things acquired or created through primary resources. Health is one of many secondary resources that medicine as a primary resource can obtain for the sick, but the sick are not the only beneficiaries of medicine as a primary resource. Through medicine, physicians acquire economic power and prestige; insurance and pharmaceutical companies accumulate capital. The argument presented in this book is that, where medical pluralism exists, the principal secondary resources for which medicine is a primary resource are social relations and material resources that permit social mobility. Medical pluralism facilitates the permeability of ethnic and religious boundaries as well as movement across class lines because, as people talk about medicine, they are also negotiating a redefinition of their own identities.

This book is not about medical symbols or healing per se, but rather about social information expressed in medical ideologies and its use in social reformation. It is about the historical context of medical ideologies, the interpretations of history they express, and the medical discourse they define. It is about the dialogues that draw upon that discourse and the social implications of those dialogues.

The reinterpretation of history in medical ideology produces metaphors that are deployed in contemporary dialogue to effect social consequences. The consequences of these medical dialogues, particularly for social mobility, render them, and medical ideology, and thus medical systems themselves, primary resources.

This book, therefore, entails an additional argument as well: that ethnic boundaries in highland Bolivia are in fact markers of social class if social class is defined in terms of relations of production and ensuing access to power (Wolf 1982). In Bolivia ethnic boundaries are fluid and crossed regularly in spite of their castelike characterization and the use of racial metaphors. Everyone in Kachitu, regardless of ethnic identity, shares confluences of the same culture, specifically interlinking social relations through which passes a grammar of symbolic images and metaphors, including medical ideology. These images and metaphors are used and manipulated in medical dialogue to situate individuals in social classes at a point in history in which severe economic contraction or peripheralization has convoluted relations of production and in which individuals can be simultaneously situated in different class positions.

The notion of upward mobility of Indians into "national" or ladino culture in Latin America has been described in the anthropological literature at length, but it has been predicated on the concept of cultural pluralism (Furnival 1939, 1948), in which culture is inherently phenomenological, and it presumes only upward mobility out of Indian ethnic enclaves into the national culture (e.g., McVay and Vogt 1988). By redefining culture in material terms and recognizing ethnicity's relationship to social class in Latin America, the politico-economic nature and fluidity of boundaries within a single culture—in which Indian and mestizo understand quite well the dialogue that expresses mutual animosity—become visible.

The notion of ethnic boundaries as fluid and synonymous with social class in Bolivia is not novel (Albo 1972; Kelley 1977; Leons 1978; Murra 1980). However, in Kachitu, both upward and downward mobility occur. Both are possible specifically because the boundaries that define Aymaraness and mestizoness, and even membership in the Methodist church, are masks for social class. In much of Bolivia, the very content of ethnic identity and religious affiliation is ambivalent and constantly negotiated; this was true even before the revolution of 1952 destroyed the social structure established by colonialism. Contrary to the conceptualization of the Indian as marginalized from the wider system and of ethnicity as evidence of disarticulation with that system (Friedlander 1975), the Bolivian Indian is essential to the wider system. The Methodist church has also had a significant economic and political impact in Kachitu which is expressed in medical dialogue. This book, therefore, is also a historical analysis of contemporary social strategies in the village of Kachitu in Highland Bolivia. These contemporary social strategies are embedded in the development and reformation of social class and its meaning in the idiom of a cultural pluralism that in fact does not exist.

This research took place over eighteen months and was supported by a grant from the Organization of American States. I did not do it alone. My daughter, Anna Crankshaw, enjoyed and suffered the full two years that we lived in Bolivia. Before moving out to Kachitu, we lived and worked in La Paz for five months. Because of Anna, who was a beautiful, friendly, and sensitive little girl, I was given access to far more confidences than I would have been proffered had I been either a single woman or a man. Motherhood proved to be a wonderful asset to the anthropological endeavor. The adjustment to such an extreme cross-cultural experience was often very difficult and demanded an enormous amount of courage and strength from an eight-year-old, but it was always extremely rewarding. To honor it, Anna agreed to illustrate this volume.

"Kachitu" is not the real name of the research site. I chose the name because William Carter employed it when he wrote his master's thesis in the 1950s at Columbia University about the same site. The names of most, but not all, of the "cast of characters" have been changed as well. Anyone who in any way could be offended or hurt by this volume has been disguised. Several, however, should be recognized and honored: Dr. Frank Beck, the first missionary physician in Kachitu; Bertha Garcia, the first nurse in Kachitu and later wife to William Carter; the Robisons, one of the first families of missionaries who changed the scope of the mission from an evangelical crusade to a constructive, educational, and medical community activity. The names of historically significant figures are also, of course, their own.

Acknowledgments

These few pages are the most difficult of the entire book to write. I cannot possibly take total credit for the work described in these pages, although I do take total responsibility for it. It is the product of the greatly appreciated help, assistance, and support of virtually hundreds of people who let me into their lives, put up with my requests and needs, and responded with love and enthusiasm.

John Janzen saw the glimmer of something worthwhile in a rough draft, which he encouraged me to cultivate. His editorial suggestions and enthusiasm kept me alive. Robert Murphy labored through the first production, a second attempt, and the third draft, when he had other, far more pressing things to do. His invaluable guidance always raised my spirits and fired my enthusiasm while simultaneously doing the reader an immeasurable service. Perhaps he understood that the seeds of this research first emerged from the excitement his *Dialectics of Social Life* inspired in me almost twenty years ago. More than anything else in anthropology, that book helped me realize the significance of the fact that rarely do people mean what they say or say what they mean. That social law is the basic assumption of this book and perhaps the most notable difference between this book and those works in medical anthropology which apply positivist models and rely heavily on survey data.

Chris Leonard and Dan Moerman are those magnificent friends everyone wants, and I am lucky enough to have them. When I wrote drivel, Chris would come over with a bottle of wine and gently tell me so. Dan fervently persuaded me to make several alterations that saved the reader unspeakable pain. Joseph Bastien, whom I didn't even know well at the time, went out of his way to carefully read the manuscript and make detailed comments and suggestions. When I got stuck on a conceptual problem, Lambros Comitas consistently and patiently held my hand as I waded through it, prodded me when I needed it, and pulled down references from here and there to guide me when I was lost. I am also grateful to Todd Theringer and to Marilyn MacArthur. Barbara Price read and reread, inspired, and promoted my work with the animation of a true benefactor.

In the spring of 1987 when I had to finish the first draft, Tessy Siegel, the WID/POP officer at USAID, Tegucigalpa, invited me into her home for a month to enable me to do so. She let me raid her refrigerator, drink her booze, and wreak havoc in her home office. Robert Markens, my research assistant at Columbia University, spent a whole summer putting appendixes together from my obscure and often illegible field notes. Victoria Brown, my second research assistant typed the final draft. For their inestimable friendship, support, prudent council, and trips to the Chinese takeout, I am blessed and deeply grateful.

When the final draft was complete, I timorously gave it to my father, a surgeon with a very different worldview than that of an anthropologist, particularly a medical one. He painstakingly contemplated every word and concept. His improvements on the manuscript are not only profound, but brought two fields together, and two people. The gracious and meticulous editing by Linda Benefield and her gentle counsel were simply outstanding.

I am indebted to the Organization of American States for financing the research and to CIES Fulbright for allowing me to return to Bolivia for two weeks in 1987 on the tail of another project. Back in 1976 my great friend Betsy Dirnberger performed a little pecuniary wizardry to ensure that Anna and I would never be wanting financially in the field far from home.

The Instituto de Antropologia in La Paz gave me permission to carry out the research. Jere Haas, on a National Science Foundation grant, brought me to La Paz as a research assistant, which gave me the time to adjust to life at 13,000 feet and look for an appropriate research site. I chose Kachitu after consulting with Judith-Marie and Hans Buechler, Bertha and William Carter, Phil Blair, and Nathan Robison, whose assistance helped me initiate the research, carry it out, and analyze it in the light of their constant feedback. They were, as my daughter used to say, awesomely generous and kind with the time and care and attention they gave me and this work.

This work is grounded in the intellectual and emotional support that allowed me to develop as an anthropologist. That support came from my mentors, to whom I am grateful not only for their guidance in this work but for my career: Sylvia H. Forman, John W. Cole, Kay Warren, Joan Koss, Joan Ablon, and Margaret Clark. Years later, Paul Unschuld's ideas and gentle discussions with me about them lifted me out of a murky mire in which I found myself and led me to the central thesis of this book.

I went into the field with my daughter, Anna. She was eight years old when we arrived in Bolivia and ten when we left. As a mother and daughter in a foreign country for two years, we needed a social infrastructure in the city. In La Paz, the hospitality extended to us by Jorge, Lynne, and John Velasco; Rosemary and Frank Kimball; Winn and Dianne Crowther; Beverly and Carlos Olivares; Teresa and Tom Nelson; and Ronnie Ibatta provided us with the perennial support that is essential to a mother-daughter team. A very special thanks I extend to Bertha Carter, who gave me moral and physical support at a critical point in my research when I found myself involved in Gonzalo's serious illness. For assistance, service, and relief during that same episode I also thank Mrs. Paul Boeker, wife of the U.S. ambassador at that time, the American Women's Club in La Paz, and Dr. Jorge Velasco. Coco Velasco and Bertha Carter, in fact, saw me and my daughter through several illnesses of our own and gave valuable advice on my medical data.

I also give a special thanks to Rosemary and Frank Kimball and to Jean Mead-owcroft, who contributed materially on my behalf to the well-being of my village.

Many of the ideas I ultimately determined to be of major significance were those developed after long, stimulating discussions with Dianne Crowther, Nor-berto Rocha, Nathan Robison, Dr. Gregorio Losa Balsa, and Bertha Carter. Federico Aliaga also generously provided me with microfilming in the field.

And then there are the people of Kachitu. They tolerated my constant ques-tioning and my cultural naiveté. They invited me into their homes and fed me. They cured me when I was ill. They cared for and loved my daughter. They took interest in our welfare and shared interests, celebrations, and intimacies with us. And they actively helped me gather my data. To say my indebtedness and grati-tude to them is profound is to understate the truth.

Finally, I want to thank my daughter, Anna, for accompanying me and shar-ing the delight, adventure, and mystery of Bolivia. She made the entire two years a pleasure, even during the most difficult moments. To honor the Kachituños, she agreed to illustrate this book.

Cast

PROFESSIONALS IN KACHITU

JOHN HERRICK first North American missionary in Kachitu.

THE ROBISONS one of the first missionary families in Kachitu.

DR. FRANK BECK first Methodist missionary physician in Kachitu during the 1950s and 1960s.

DR. MAURICIO SABAS the town doctor in 1976 and 1977.

DR. HIPOLITO TALLACAGUA missionary-trained, Aymara physician serving briefly in Kachitu in 1977.

DR. ALEJO ACIETUNO replacement for Sabas and Tallacagua in 1978.

THE REVEREND ANGEL the Methodist minister.

FATHER CHRISTIAN the Catholic priest.

MESTIZOS

DON RAFAEL SALAZAR El Corregidor 1936–1944.

DOÑA VICTORIA CASTELLANO owner of the town *pension*.

DOÑA ANTONIA DE VILLAZON a poor mestiza who washed linens at the hospital.

DON LORENZO VILLAZON her husband, a rural schoolteacher.

DOÑA LEONORA DE UGALDE a poor mestiza whose daughter was the only vecina to join the Methodist church.

DON VALENTINO UGALDE her husband.

DOÑA ELSA DE NESTARES another poor mestiza.

DON RAFAEL NESTARES her husband.

COLONEL JUAN CARLOS CORDOVA first vecino in Kachitu, and direct descendant from the last reigning Inca.

DOÑA MIRIAM an elderly member of an old vecino clan.

DOÑA TERESA CORDOVA granddaughter to Colonel Juan Carlos, and town aristocrat; she also manages the town archives.

DON ASCARUNZ Doña Teresa's husband.

DON ALEJANDRO CORDOVA Doña Teresa's father.

DOÑA MARIA DE LA PAZ Doña Teresa's sister.

DOÑA LOURDES Doña Teresa's other sister2.

DOÑA ANA a mestiza neighbor.

DOÑA SOÑA ROMAN a socially self-exiled mestiza.

DOÑA SOÑA ROMAN'S HUSBAND the town curmudgeon.

DOÑA MARGARITA GARCIA VIUDA DE BILIS small landowner who rents out a room to the Aymara Bonifacia and her two boys Oldemar and Bartolo and who rents a small parcel of land to Renita's father, Norberto, who is also Aymara.

JUDGE DON JUAN MARQUEZ VASQUEZ judge in the 1930s, '40s, and '50s, and head of the vecino effort to oust the missionaries.

JUDGE RICARDO MARQUEZ his son.

DOÑA EVA DE MARQUEZ Judge Ricardo's widow.

LUIS MEZA her current husband.

GLADIS her eldest daughter.

MARISOL her second daughter.

PELUQUILLA PAUCARA the town crazy lady.

GONZALO one of her three sons.

MARIO one of her three sons.

DANERI one of her three sons.

DON MAGNO her alcoholic husband, long since passed away.

AYMARA

SEFERINO QARURU campesino from Chojña Kanata trying to join the Methodist church.

EULOGIO AÑAGUAYA head of the local campesino movement; once a Methodist, he prefers Aymara campesino identity.

EUSEBIA POMA campesina in Kachitu.

EUGENIO CALLISAYA campesino from Chojña Kanata.

PORFIRIO MONTORO aspirant to be a mozo in a North American household and speak English, he is ostracized by the town; he serves as my research assistant.

VICENTE CALLISAYA his father.

JULIA his aunt and Vicente's sister.

GENARA his aunt, and Vicente's other sister.

SERGIO Genara's son.

PRIMITIVA MAMANI VIUDA DE YANIQUE old blind lady.

BONIFACIA VIZCACHANI landless Aymara who rents a room from Doña Margarita Garcia viuda de Bilis.

BARTOLO her mischievous son.

OLDEMAR his mischievous brother and her other son.

RENITA AYLLASU a young Aymara woman looking for a husband.

NORBERTO her father.

MARIA her daughter.

TEODORO APAZA the corregidor.

METHODIST AYMARA

NOEL PEÑARANDA first Kachituño to convert; invites Herrick and Beck to Kachitu.

CLETO ZAMBRANA requests mission school in Chojña Kanata.

EUSEBIO PANDO campesino turned schoolteacher.

FRANCISCO APAZA first Indian head of the Evangelical Commission in Kachitu in 1949.

MARIANO MAMANI first Indian head of secular activity in the Methodist church in Kachitu in 1949.

ABELARDO ZUIDENA hospital chauffeur.

FELIPE APAZA head nurse at the hospital.

EMILIO ORDOÑEZ town baker; richest man in Kachitu.

ENRIQUE ORDOÑEZ his son.

IRIS QUISPE part-time nurse at the hospital.

PEDRO QUISPAYA Iris's husband and one of nine men who collectively own a tractor.

MERCEDES ALARCON a friend to Renita.

DR. GERONIMO TALLACAGUA graduate of the Methodist school and winner of a scholarship from the church.

INTRODUCTION
Locating a Theoretical Perspective, or How the Physician, the Preacher, the Peasant, and the Khan Achachi Came to Terms with One Another

Even the staid, imperturbable, American-educated Methodist pastor conceded that malignant spirits, or maybe enchanted incarnations, prowl in and around Chojña Kanata. The settlement of Chojña Kanata lies on the shore of Lake Titicaca on the Bolivian altiplano and is a half-hour walk, or about three miles, from the municipality of Kachitu. Kachitu qualifies as a social oasis on the vast, high, desert altiplano of Bolivia because, unlike Chojña Kanata, it is considered a veritable center of modern life: it can boast of a Catholic church with a full-time priest, a Methodist church, a hospital, a municipal building, a grammar school and high school designated by the national government as urban, a Sunday market, and a director of criminal investigation—called a DIC—who devoted himself wholeheartedly in 1977 to the fine art of inebriation. On the rare occasion that a crime occurs, one goes to the town seer, who acquired his clairvoyant powers in a malarial fever in the lowlands during the Chaco War. He is definitive evidence that the magic of medicine, disease, and illness plays a major role in the social and political life of Kachitu, in spite of its "cultural superiority" over Chojña Kanata.

In the late afternoon the walk from Kachitu to Chojña Kanata, past barren hills, the occasional mud-brick housing compound, and a few bleak stands of eucalyptus trees, is cold and brisk. The cold becomes bitter after the sun goes down over Illampu, an immense, glacier-covered peak of the Andean *cordillera* looming 10,000 feet above the expansive void of the altiplano. Frigid winds sweep down from the cordillera, cross the lake, and blast the emptiness of the plateau, silencing life in their wake. On this great plain two-and-a-half miles above sea level lives a phantom called the khan achachi who feeds on meat and alcohol and gifts it demands from the local people. If a man ignores the khan achachi, it feeds first, as a warning, on that man's crops, and then if that person does not respond, on his children, then on his wife, and finally on the man himself until the family has been eliminated. Many people on the altiplano take the demands of the khan achachi very seriously.

On May 18, 1977, the sunset over Illampu consisted of brilliant reds, oranges, and yellows. The mountain, a silent monument, lay shrouded in its own shadow. Though several hundred square miles were visible, I could see neither human nor animal, and the only sound was that of the wind in my ears. The sun set on a horizon of desolation. The wind swept down and blasted against my body as night descended, and on the road from Kachitu to Chojña Kanata, I figured there was a good possibility of my freezing to death before I reached the haven of Seferino Qaruru's home, in spite of my down parka, alpaca sweater, and long underwear. Seferino's mud-floored, thatch-roofed, windowless adobe hut was a dark mud cube in which the door must remain perpetually open to permit light and ventilation. Seferino's wife, barefoot and holding onto her shawl with one hand, led their cow and a few sheep to a small corral. She then joined her sister, her husband, and her mother-in-law, with whom she shared the one-room home, and the Methodist preacher and me.

We got on our knees on the mud floor. The preacher put his hands on the heads of Seferino and his wife and said, "Dear God, bless this couple and this household. Keep them from harm and illness. Make them, their fields, and their animals fertile. Help them stay in the path of righteousness. Give them the strength to believe in your almighty power, and to turn their backs in disbelief on the khan achachi."

Seferino had been sick for many months. His sickness followed the deaths of all three of his children. Their deaths followed the death of most of their livestock, which followed three years of crop failure. Although his neighbors warned Seferino that the cause of his misfortune was his refusal to feed the khan achachi, he turned to the physician for help.

The physician, Dr. Mauricio Sabas, first diagnosed pneumonia, then tuberculosis, and when Seferino did not respond to either treatment, Dr. Sabas, with Seferino's encouragement, turned to the preacher, the Reverend Angel. Reverend Angel advised that the answer to Seferino's problem resided in faith.

Seferino desperately wanted the doctor and the preacher, both authorities and employees of the Methodist church, to find the solutions to his problems, but he was not unheeding to the wisdom of his neighbors. Several days before my visit to Chojña Kanata, the neighbors' theories had gained a leading edge in Seferino's mind, yet he still refused to pay the khan achachi. Seferino desperately wanted to join the Methodist church. Such membership, however, would require that he renounce belief in the khan achachi and all supernatural beings except God. Fearing death, Seferino had returned once again to the Methodist clinic. Dr. Sabas, unable to identify any pathology except anemia, placed him under intensive care—such as it was (and still is) in that tiny, understaffed, and poorly supplied hospital.

On the eve of his second night at the clinic, a neighbor came up with yet another possible solution: several sticks of dynamite. Seferino, with all the agility of an inspired man, abandoned his bedpan and intravenous solution. He ran to Chojña Kanata and to the altar for the khan achachi which his grandfather had built more than forty years before in order to feed the phantom and keep it at bay. Seferino blew up the altar, and with it, he hoped, his obligations to the khan achachi. In spite of the church's disapproval of any acknowledgment of the khan achachi, Pastor Angel persistently visited and observed prayer, and Seferino welcomed him, probably in part because he was not certain that the dynamite would be effective. He had never before heard of this particular innovation. But Seferino also appreciated the attention the pastor bestowed upon him. It made him feel important, and closer to membership in the Methodist church.

In this case of Seferino's illness, three very different people with different interests and from different social classes and cultural groups, with different goals and parameters informing and limiting their strategies and decisions pertaining to health care, accommodated each other in order to pursue some element of their interests which was embedded in Seferino's situation. Seferino's quest for a cure, and Sabas's and Angel's therapeutic administrations, were informed by political, economic, and social considerations which in turn defined their perceptions of medical efficacy. A closer look at Seferino's, Sabas's, and Angel's differential interests in the case, and their therapeutic actions, reveal conflicting dimensions of "the quest for therapy," and how the evaluation of what is medically effective is subordinate to the social context in which it is perceived.

SEFERINO, THE CAMPESINO

Seferino is a *campesino*,[1] or Aymara peasant, whose family has tilled land in Chojña Kanata for as many generations as he can remember. Before the Bolivian land reform of 1953, Chojña Kanata was a free Indian community. At that time, half of the population of the canton of Kachitu, and half of its land, fell under the domain of haciendas. Indians within that domain lived under the tutelage of the hacienda owners—*hacendados* or *patrones*—and the *mestizo*[2] managers they employed, and the Indians' legal rights were virtually limited to those of serfs.

In contrast, the residents of free Indian communities enjoyed freedom from such masters: one's time and labor belonged to oneself and one's family. However, these communities were heavily taxed, and conditions inhibited, even prohibited, Indian participation in entrepreneurial activity. Hence, during the 450 years during which such laws pertained, from colonial times until the revolution and land reform, the men in free Indian communities like Chojña Kanata turned to the mines to earn cash to pay their taxes, and both men and women frequently traveled to lower altitudes to increase their resources through sale of their labor or trade. It is reasonable to assume that some of Seferino's ancestors lived in Chojña Kanata, working the mines and making seasonal treks to the lowlands, since at least the sixteenth century.

When Seferino and his wife married in 1973, they inherited the land they presently occupied in Chojña Kanata from Seferino's grandparents. The grandparents had, however, abandoned the land long before the land reform. Although it was rich and bordered the lake, the need for cash to pay heavy taxes forced Seferino's grandfather to leave the community annually after harvest to work in the mines and to trade in the lowlands, leaving Seferino's grandmother alone for months at a time.

During the 1970s, Seferino also left his wife alone at home while he went to La Paz, Bolivia's capital, and to the lowlands to trade his unskilled labor for cash, following the precedent that has at least 500 years of history in the rural highlands. At the Reverend Angel's request, Seferino explained to me the details of his grandparents' encounter with the khan achachi, their resultant misfortunes, and the source of the misfortunes of Seferino and his family, even though he simultaneously claimed not to believe in the khan achachi.

During one of his grandfather's absences, said Seferino, his grandmother began to have dreams in which admiring men visited her. One admirer courted her for many months. In her dreams they had sexual relations. Eventually the grandmother discovered that she was, in very real fact, pregnant. In fear and shame she retired from social life and sequestered herself indoors, refusing even her own husband entry into the house, and forcing him to stay with his parents nearby. When the moment of her delivery arrived, she gave birth to a childless placenta. A red dog, said Seferino, came to the door, entered the house, ate the placenta, and left. No one knew the dog nor has seen it since. To prevent further disaster, the grandparents built an altar to the khan achachi and gave it gifts until they were able to abandon the land.

In 1973, Seferino's relatives and neighbors warned him of the obligations the khan achachi demands from anyone who lives on the property, and they urged him not to occupy it. He ignored this advice, he said, because he and his family had become involved with the Methodist church, and the church claims there is no such thing as a khan achachi. Seferino reasoned that if the Methodists were right, his own life would benefit. Almost all the Methodists in Chojña Kanata and in Kachitu are materially better off than their neighbors. The local Methodist church controls the clinic and the high school in Kachitu. Virtually all entrepreneurial activities in Kachitu are owned by present or past members of the Methodist church, and they have friends in La Paz and in the United States who are often useful.

More immediately, Seferino could not afford to buy other land. The land of his inheritnace was Seferino's only capital. Only fellow villagers in Chojña Kanata would have any interest in buying it and none of them would consider it because of its association with the khan achachi. The land also had its benefits. It had good soil and bordered the lake. Many of the neighboring villagers were Methodists and the church in Kachitu was only a half hour's walk away. Hence there were great advantages for Seferino if he could disbelieve in the khan achachi, particularly if, as a result, the khan achachi would actually go away. Therefore Seferino accepted his inheritance, burned the altar where his father's mother had paid the khan regularly after her peculiar delivery, and planted eucalyptus trees in its stead.

In 1974, while Seferino was absent on one of his periodic trips to La Paz, his wife "began to be visited in her dreams by admiring men. Over the next three years, the crops my wife and I planted failed. Most of our livestock died. We lost all three of our children before their first birthday. In 1977 I, too, fell ill." Upon finishing his story, Seferino buried his face in his hands and said to Pastor Angel, "Your Reverend, I am working very hard to not believe, but my wife, she is having more difficulty not believing."

"You must help her to not believe," replied Angel.

Though Dr. Sabas twice failed to cure him, first of pneumonia, then of tuberculosis, Seferino persisted in his belief in Sabas's medicine. Seferino also persisted in his trust in Reverend Angel and was grateful for his attention, particularly when everything seemed to be going wrong. Nevertheless, Seferino never failed to remain alert to the advice of his neighbors. While he was more or less successful in not "believing" in the khan, he "knew" the phantom to be effective. To "not believe" does not preclude that the khan achachi exists. In his need for a pragmatic solution, Seferino reserved the right to allow that anything might be possible. Yet when he thought he was dying, Seferino chose medical care that had so far been totally ineffective, but that was defined by a philosophy, a social context, and a political position within the canton of Kachitu with which Seferino wished to associate himself. That is, there is no evidence in this case that Seferino returned to the clinic for medical reasons and much to argue that he returned for social ones.

THE DOCTOR

Dr. Sabas was a mestizo from La Paz who had completed all the medical education available in Bolivia: six years of training after high school. There are no internship or residency programs in Bolivia. Hence, medical specialization is taken in the United States, Europe, Japan, or other countries in Latin America. Sabas chose an

Eastern European country where he studied internal medicine for three years. One component of that education which deeply impressed Sabas was its emphasis on social awareness. Sabas devoted a great deal of attention to studying the links between health and poverty. He returned to Bolivia with less enthusiasm for curing with the scanty diagnostic and therapeutic resources available in Kachitu, than inspiration to free its Indians from the bonds of poverty in the presence of which no amount of Western medical knowledge could resolve the health problems that plague Kachitu.

Dr. Sabas's foremost goal was to help the Indians. To his mind, working for the Methodist church was the most effective vehicle through which to accomplish this. It is one of the very few organizations that serve the Indians in the countryside.[3] Since the 1970s this local church has been controlled by the campesinos themselves, rather than mestizos and foreigners, although it is subordinate to the mother church in La Paz. Furthermore the Methodist church's social and philosophical orientation is progressive, unlike the Evangelical movement throughout the rest of Latin America. In Kachitu the Methodists pay as much attention to Paulo Freire's *Pedagogy of the Oppressed* as they do to the Bible.

In a romantic fervor Sabas determined that Aymara was the first language in human evolutionary history. He referred frequently to a book that said so. He made effusive overtures to socialize with the campesinos, such as learning a few words of Aymara and tapping time to their music. In his more pragmatic but still inspired moods, he tried to organize an adult night school, a fisheries cooperative, and other ventures predicated on betterment through cooperative effort, but to no avail.

Much of Dr. Sabas's inability to help the Aymara might have been related to his inability to speak their language and his high standard of living relative to the campesinos. He resided in a house designed and built by the Methodist missionaries from the United States who first brought the church to Kachitu. It has two stories, wooden floors, indoor plumbing, a fairly modern kitchen, and an electrical generator; it could serve a middle-class family in Los Angeles. With a European wife and their two children, Sabas was not in a position to live like the indigenous population without heavy cost.

Sabas's material well-being did not reduce his desire to help the poor, but he gradually discovered that his ability to make a personal, substantial contribution to the Aymara on the altiplano was more limited than his aspirations. The only medical doctor in Kachitu, which had a population of 16,000, not including the province to the north which had no doctor at the time and also relied on Kachitu, Sabas was supplied with a closet full of drugs that had all surpassed their stipulated shelf life by at least five years and supported by a faulty generator to run his equipment and a truck that frequently broke down. Sabas discovered that he wasn't helping very much.

Sabas's only guaranteed strategy for being in any way effective lay in his gaining the campesinos' confidence. Their confidence was predicated on his respect for the Aymara. His need to demonstrate his respect impelled him to acknowledge the legitimacy of their medical world view, most of which differed radically from his biomedical training. Seferino was one possible convert to Sabas's economic schemes to revolutionize the countryside. Seferino was a seed in Chojña Kanata where, given the high percentage of Methodist church members, Sabas as staff at the Methodist clinic, might finally get a sympathetic audience. However, it became clear that Sabas was not going to gain Seferino's confidence by dispensing medical care. Consequently, when Seferino did not respond to his treatment, Sabas acknowledged that perhaps there was something beyond his biomedical powers, something inherent in this Aymara world, which he couldn't touch and which must be respected. To pursue Seferino's case he turned to religion. Being born a Catholic mestizo in La Paz, he confused Aymara medical belief with Catholic cosmology. Unaware that the khan achachi is not the Christian devil, he requested Pastor Angel to perform an exorcism, overlooking the fact that Methodists do not believe in the devil[4] and do not perform exorcisms.

THE PREACHER

The Reverend Angel was delighted to oblige. He also was born a Catholic mestizo from La Paz and saw in the Methodist church the possibility of social change in Bolivia: national development through the betterment of the campesinos through education, health care, and economic organization. Being the pastor, married to a mestiza from the city, and with several children, he also lived in a two-floored, wooden home provided by the North American missionaries for the preacher in residence. He at least spoke Aymara. Nevertheless, he was having a difficult time being accepted by the local Aymara. They refused his authority. Since he was neither campesino nor from Kachitu, they disputed his ability to speak for them. They resented the mother church in La Paz sending outsiders to assume authority that they felt should be in the hands of their own local members. Instead of improving the lot of the Indians as he had intended, Angel frequently found himself defending himself and his ideas. When the doctor called upon him to help Seferino, he was grateful to respond. The immediate need as he saw it was to maintain Seferino's confidence in him and in the church while he maintained his own integrity to church doctrine, even though no explanation or resource presented itself to help Seferino that was more effective than the belief system surrounding the khan achachi. On one hand, if the pastor had adamantly denied the khan achachi, he might have made Seferino feel foolish and resentful, and have lost a potential ally. On the other hand, if he could somehow encourage Seferino's suspicions about the khan achachi without himself acknowledging the phantom, he could relieve himself and Dr. Sabas of responsibility for alleviating Seferino's problems without alienating Seferino from their advances. Angel told me:

> Many years ago, when Christ first came to earth, the air was filled with evil spirits. Christ had two means with which to rid the world of these spirits. First he did not believe and tried through the strength of his belief to rid the world of the evil spirits. But the people continued to believe, and the evil spirits did not go away. So Christ tried a second way: he did believe, and in his belief he performed ceremonies against the evil, and in this way was able to begin to rid the world of evil spirits. Likewise I must say that I can only help if I accept what you believe. This is how I approach my people here in Kachitu.

He did not stop there, however, but continued mixing scientific, Christian, and magical Aymara images. The emphases are mine:

> Once there was a girl somewhere around here, living all alone during the Chaco War. A soldier was passing through and stopped by to visit with her, and she became pregnant. During her pregnancy her behavior changed. She began to act NEUROTIC. She didn't want to see anybody. When she delivered, the midwives came to help her. And they tell that the girl gave birth to a ball of fire. The Khan Achachi came, put out the fire, and left. IT COULD HAVE BEEN THE DEVIL OR SOME MANIFESTATION SENT BY THE DEVIL. It has several bodily forms it can take: sometimes it has a donkey's head with huge eyes; inside its head is fire so that its huge eyes glow like coals. It floats in the air
> and has a comet with a long tail and it visits where it will. IF IT VISITS YOUR LAND YOU MUST FEED IT; burn mesas and comida, a llama fetus, pigs, potatoes, oca, guinea pigs, and other foods, and make challa with alcohol and wine. When it visits these places, if people do not feed it, it makes the family sick. It destroys their crops and kills their animals. One can tell when the Khan Achachi kills an animal because it dies with a green spot on its skin. THE ILLNESS THE FAMILY GETS VARIES AND DISAPPEARS IF THEY BEGIN TO FEED THE Khan Achachi.

After struggling in Kachitu for several years, Angel himself was having difficulty "not believing."

THE OUTCOME OF SEFERINO'S CASE

As a result of Seferino's case, Sabas made changes in hospital policy that permitted greater interaction and collaboration between indigenous medical healers, called yatiris, and the clinic personnel. These changes were reversed by one of Sabas's successors, an Aymara in the process of turning Bolivian elite, who had his own strategies and problems, which are analyzed in chapter 7. They were later reinstituted when the hospital administration came under the control of the local Aymara Methodists in 1983, after an argument over the issue with a North American missionary physician and several mestizos. The argument was resolved in the Aymaras' favor when they tried to burn the North American physician's house down, stole his jeep, and threatened his life.

Acknowledgment of the value of indigenous medicine at the hospital under Sabas and his successors reinforced the legitimacy of the yatiris' abilities and gave them greater influence—social, political, and economic as well as medical—within the social world of Kachitu. As is demonstrated in several of the case studies in this book, yatiris are able to translate their medical legitimacy, obtained in this post-colonial, twentieth-century town in a Third World country trying to develop, into local political power. Political power is defined here and will be demonstrated throughout this book as the ability to modify the behavior of others and enforce, through either social or supernatural sanction, a monopoly of opinion. Sanction distinguishes political power from influence. Sabas's shift in ideology and change in hospital policy had broad and long-term implicatons in Kachitu. It positively affected the political power of yatiris and moderately increased his own influence among the Aymara (but not among all mestizos) in Kachitu.

The Reverend Angel incorporated more and more Aymara belief into Methodist doctrine and encouraged indigenous leadership at his own expense. The local church, including the administration of the clinic and controlling influence on the board of the high school, was securely in the hands of the local Aymara Methodists by 1979, the year that Seferino joined the Methodist church. Unlike the earlier missionaries from the United States, the local Aymara Methodists see indigenous beliefs, such as the one about the khan achachi, not as medical heresy but as cultural heritage that should be preserved. The Reverend Angel's endorsement of those beliefs, therefore, had implications for the content of the cultural identity of the Aymara Methodists. This element of their cultural identity has political ramifications because it is used to differentiate these Methodists as Aymara from the mestizo population as evidenced when the Methodist Aymara hospital administration insisted upon institutionalizing the use of Aymara medicine in the hospital.

When I left in 1978, Seferino's wife was pregnant again. But in 1983 and 1984, drought destroyed more than 90 percent of the altiplano crop. In 1985, massive flooding raised the lake and eliminated hundreds of thousands of acres of agricultural land, including Seferino's. The lake is expected to recede to its pre-1984 level no earlier than 1990. Meanwhile, economic and political disasters related to the sudden rise of the cocaine economy in 1980, the closure of the mines in 1987, massive unemployment, and unprecedented inflation made starvation chronic for the first time in Bolivia's history. As a member of the Methodist church, Seferino would no longer have had to concern himself with conflicting beliefs, had his economic and political aspirations not been destroyed by these disasters. By the time of my return to Kachitu in 1987, however, Seferino and his wife had disappeared into the slums of La Paz.

THE SIGNIFICANCE OF SEFERINO'S CASE

The almost inevitable student response to the recapitulation of Seferino's case is to ask if the dynamite worked, and what was really the cause of Seferino's misfortunes. "Hey," they say, "what REALLY happened?" or "What did he *really* suffer from?"

Unfortunately these questions place us squarely within a conceptual construct that leads to decision-making and explanatory models such as those that have been used by Cosminsky and Scrimshaw (1980), DeWalt (1977), Kleinman (1980), and James Young (1981). They seek to solve the problem of Seferino's medical symptoms and confine us to the assumption that when we know the medical answer, we will resolve Seferino's problem. The implication that there is a single correct answer assumes that the answer will affirm which is the most effective medical system. Allan Young (1982) has argued [5] that such questions and such decision-making and explanatory models do not address the political and economic contexts in which medical decisions are made. Furthermore, they construct patient and healer as Rational Man in the classical economic sense, looking for medical efficacy as understood in positivist, or scientific, terms. Indeed, Seferino's problem wasn't solely medical, nor did he see it as such. Furthermore, a number of contexts besides the purely medical affected the thinking of Sabas, Angel, and Seferino. Such questions and conceptual constructs also do not address the total outcome of Seferino's, Sabas's, and Angel's medical decisions, which affected many people besides Seferino. If the anthropological and medical significance of the case is greater than Seferino's medical symptoms, we need to ask questions and employ a conceptual model appropriate to the nature and scope of the larger issues, which appear to be the nature of medical pluralism and the use of ideologies. The broader and thus more accurate question to ask, then, is how Seferino's choices of action were informed, and what the consequences of them were, not only for him, but for all parties involved in the case. Contrary to the assumption behind the question "Did the dynamite work?" Seferino entertained at least two conflicting etiological theories about his own illness simultaneously. By 1977, the physician and the preacher had also shifted their own medical beliefs, though this was not because empirical evidence demonstrated the superior efficacy of Aymara medical practice to exorcise the khan achachi.

Part of the significance of Seferino's case is that Seferino, Sabas, and Angel shifted their medical beliefs because by doing so, they could obtain desired resources. These resources were not only medical, but economic, social, and political as well. Sabas was able to change hospital policy and thereby gain greater influence over the local population. Seferino's medical strategies brought him closer to Angel and hence to the Methodist church and to the economic benefits he surmised could accrue from membership in it. Yatiris were able to appropriate political power through changes in hospital policy pertaining to the dispensation of therapy. Indeed, all parties involved in the case reaped the rewards of resources obtained through medicine, with varying degrees of success. Seferino's case thus illustrates how we, the anthropological observers, can conceptualize medicine as a "primary resource" through which one can gain access to other "secondary resources," a conceptual model first suggested by Paul Unschuld (1975). Primary resources are, like capital, fungible. They can be used to acquire something else or transformed into something else. Secondary resources are those things acquired or created through primary resources. This model is predicated not only on the assumption that ideologies are conditioned by material conditions and class relations, but that individuals select from them and use them to accomplish their own ends. Thus, the use of medical ideology in the analysis of Seferino's case, and throughout this book, is not Parsonian, Marxist, or Harrisian, but conceives of the individual as a conscious actor who often maintains what we as outsiders might consider conflicting ideologies.

Employing this model, we can understand the total outcome of Seferino's case—the effect of all medical decisions made in it—by tracing why Seferino entertained several medical models simultaneously, why Sabas and Angel shifted their own medical beliefs, and what were the consequences of this seemingly irrational use of ideologies. By asking why people entertain various medical beliefs and why they choose different medical resources, we can understand medical behavior and medical pluralism.

Of further significance is that the outcome of Seferino's, Sabas's, and Angel's involvement was a change in social relations that significantly affected the whole community of Kachitu. Most of the literature in medical anthropology which addresses social relations demonstrates how medicine reconstructs[6] within the medical context those social relations that pertain outside the medical context (e.g., Frankenberg 1981). They argue that the hierarchy of medical care reproduces the social hierarchies found in society at large in order to render dispensation of such care more efficient. The case of Seferino demonstrates, and this book will discuss, how, within a medically plural environment, medicine restructures (Comaroff 1980; Taussig 1980; Crandon 1987) social relations outside the medical context.

In the Seferino case, all three parties shifted their beliefs in order to accommodate each other within a particular sociopolitical and historical context, in which all three parties had specific goals and limitations. As a result, by May 18, 1977, at least three social relationships, as well as the boundaries between cosmopolitan and indigenous medicine in Kachitu, had changed because of Seferino's illness in Chojña Kanata. By examining not only the case but the context in which the parties operated, and the anatomy of their strategies which extends beyond their medical interests, we are able to trace and understand the shifts in the medical or medically related beliefs entertained by the actors involved in the case. These shifts were not limited to the case itself. They ultimately affected medical ideology and social life in Kachitu, in Chojña Kanata, in the other surrounding communities (*comunidades*), and throughout the entire canton that the municipality of Kachitu serves.

CHAPTER 1

Medical, Ethnic, and Religious Pluralism in Kachitu and the Cultural Identity Crisis

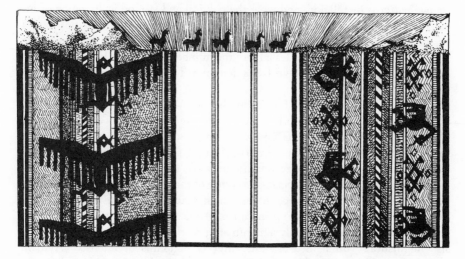

I was a graduate student looking for a research site. I had an eight-year-old daughter and a mission to study the use of indigenous and Western medical systems. In those days (1976) the latest word on the subject was rational decision making: Western medicine was often too costly, too unavailable, too invasive for a lot of Third World people. We were dealing with the revelation that people use more than one medical system at the same time. We were just becoming aware of the fact that, contrary to assumptions that Western medicine would eventually eclipse all other medical systems, what we now call alternative medical systems were thriving, even proliferating. We hadn't yet accepted the fact that they are thriving in the very centers of "rationality": Western Europe, the United States, Japan. The works of Margaret Lock, John Janzen, Paul Starr, Charles Leslie, Jean Comaroff, Ronald Frankenberg, and other ground-breaking authors hadn't yet been published or were just coming out. The term "medical pluralism" wasn't yet in use. Anthropologists, particularly those working in Latin America, such as George Foster, Horacio Fabrega, Benjamin Paul, and Irwin Press, were busy defending the use of non-Western medicine as the product of cultural logic and pragmatic choices in difficult situations. I sat on the crest of a generational transition wondering why, in anthropology, we were not giving medicine the same holistic treatment that we were giving to exchange patterns or religion, and what the political and economic dimenion of indigenous medicine and "dual use" (of indigenous and Western medicine) [1] might be. I also sat on an uncomfortable board that served as a seat on a bus with no shock absorbers, along with at least twice the number of people it had a capacity to hold, heading for Kachitu where I was determined to answer the latter question myself.

Anna and I were heading for Kachitu because William and Bertha Carter had recommended it. They had worked there some twenty-five years earlier with the Methodist mission that had set up a clinic and a school for the Indians. Surely, they said, there would be a lot of yatiris, Aymara seers who divine through coca leaf, and maybe cure too—they weren't sure. The clinic, the school, and the fact that most people would speak Spanish because of the presence of the school, made Kachitu sound like a good place. I was a high-strung mother, a veritable hypochondriac, and with good reason. In La Paz, Anna and I had already suffered typhoid and paratyphoid, and only a month after receiving our TPT shots too. I was also linguistically untalented at best. After two months of intensive Aymara lessons, I would stare blankly at my Aymara teacher while Anna, humiliatingly agile with languages, doubled over in laughter at my pronunciation. Kachitu sounded safe.

On the other hand, Kachitu sounded dangerous. I was foolish to take my daughter there, said a number of physicians we had met in the five months I adjusted to Bolivia by working as an assistant on Jere Haas's high altitude adaptation project in La Paz. Indians would never tell me anything, let alone accept me into their community, they said. I believed this was a reasonable possibility. The Aymara had a reputation at that time of being the nastiest folk in ethnographic literature. They were, I was advised, genetically coded to lie, steal, and stab me in the back. I would do better to ask the physicians themselves, who knew a great deal about Indians, having employed them as maids all their lives, they said.

Sitting on that bus, with a blond, green-eyed child on my lap, and maybe two hundred eyes focused on us, my heart pounded with excitement, muffled by painful self-consciousness. After leaving the center of La Paz, the bus began to climb the sides of the city in a slow ascent to the alto where the road to Kachitu begins. As we climbed higher and higher, and the mountains that form a wall to the east of the city loomed larger and larger, and the depth of the narrow valley in which the city sits grew more and more profound, the bus began puffing and wheezing and choking and gasping. There is a 3,000-foot drop in the city itself, the highest city in the world. It had taken me several months to learn how to breathe and walk at the same time. I suspected I would have to learn again before we got to the top of the city and onto the altiplano, where the vast majority of Bolivia's rural population lives.

As we climbed, housing construction grew poorer and the climate colder. Sidewalks and fruit trees and balmy breezes and cafes and cotton dresses and jackets and shoulder-length curls gave way to barren dusty mud streets and frigid winds, dark holes in brown adobe windswept buildings where people huddled drinking hot *mate de coca*—coca leaf tea—and warming their hands, full "pollera" skirts, bowler hats and alpaca caps with ear flaps, and ponchos and braids. Even the language switched from Spanish to Aymara. I felt terrified and exhilarated at the same time. Cresting the rim of the city, at 13,000 feet, the vast stretch of the altiplano lay before us, a totally new world.

The trip from La Paz took three hours that first day, but often, during the following eighteen months, it took up to two days depending on whether or not the lake had risen, the campesinos were on strike, or a coup had imposed a national state of siege, not to mention the state of the truck we managed to get a ride in or the weather. Kachitu turned out to be an almost treeless, mostly brown adobe, small town about one hundred miles from La Paz and 13,000 feet above sea level, some five miles from the shores of Lake Titicaca on the Bolivian altiplano, exposed to the wind at the mouth of a wide river valley. Here the population had, for hundreds of years, herded sheep, sown their crops, plied small trades, supported their church, traded at the Sunday market in the town square, and gotten as drunk as possible at the annual fiesta. They indeed had a school and a clinic and resorted to several medical systems. They tentatively welcomed me and Anna, allowed us to move in among them, accepted our bizarre ways, gradually grew concerned about us (and occasionally, due to my ignorance, alarmed), and fêted our departure eighteen months later. Since the revolution of 1952 and the land reform of 1953, however, they had been facing a cultural identity crisis. And as I found out, one way they try to resolve this crisis is through gossip, opinions, and decisions about health and medicine. Thus began my education in medical pluralism as a mechanism of economic and political proportions for identity negotiation and social change.

Kachitu serves as the center, or *municipio*, for a canton, throughout which 16,000 Aymara are disbursed in thirty-six comunidades. For them, Kachitu is the religious, educational, judicial, and regional political center. Kachitu itself, however, has a population of approximately a thousand persons, who fall loosely into

three broad groups, which are defined in religious and ethnic terms by the indigenous population themelves: Aymara Indians (also called campesinos), Aymara
who have become Methodists, and mestizo. Initially they appeared to correspond
to different cultural groups that correspond to M. G. Smith's notion of cultural
pluralism (1965, 1984) and Furnival's concept of economic pluralism (1939, 1948).
Certainly many mestizos would argue the point to their own advantage, particularly when engaged in medical dialogue. Mestizos and Methodists can distance
themselves from campesinos by eschewing Aymara medicine. Three different
marriage and settlement patterns, economic activities, and political orientations
distinguish three distinct groups, they argue, when it is in their interest to do so.
Upon closer examination, however, these apparently neat structural differences
become ephemeral and are displaced by the question of why the distinctions exist
at all, and with so much ferocity in certain circles in town.

THE MESTIZOS

Approximately one-third of the town's population are Catholic mestizos who, before the 1952 revolution and subsequent land reform, dominated the Aymara in
the canton socially, juridically, politically, and economically. They form a group
that they consider to be racially distinct. Since their arrival in Kachitu at the turn
of the century, they have referred to themselves as *vecinos* to support this conjec-
ture and with it, control Aymara labor. At the turn of the century they established
the Kachitu *vecindario*[2] composed of mestizo elders, which ran the town and comunidades around it. Hitorically Bolivian mestizos tried to emulate the life-style
of the elite, whose interests they served in the countryside until 1952. But in the
early nineteenth century, the forefathers of most Kachitu mestizos were themselves Indians, although everything possible was done in the twentieth century to
hide this fact. And today, since 1952, Aymara have moved into town, particularly
Methodist Aymara, and they dispute the definition of the term *vecino* in order
to claim for themselves a position in contemporary Kachitu society. What had
emerged as a locally powerful social class in the first half of the twentieth century
has, since the revolution, become fragile and impoverished or abandoned. After
1952 those Kachitu mestizo vecinos who could do so fled to La Paz and elsewhere,
although they still maintain ties with those who remained in Kachitu. For those
vecinos who remain, the glory of prerevolutionary life is over, as everything,
particularly interethnic relations and hence the mestizos' source of income, was
changed by the events of 1952 and 1953. Currently they are trying to avoid slip-
ping into complete poverty in a contracting national economy that turned its back
on the altiplano after the revolution.

This segment of Kachitu society is, more than anything else, disgruntled. They remember how much better life was before 1952. They reflect that the best of their class are gone. The good days are over, and with them have gone decency, morals, manners, appropriate behavior, leadership, authority, wisdom, the educated, and most other valued dimensions of social life. Divided and at varying degrees of economic survival, they form several social classes with different political and economic interests. Mostly they teach school or run small stores, all of which sell the same things, and remember better days. The poorest affiliate themselves with Aymara, lending a hand in agricultural labor, bartering spices for their agricultural resources, and trying to overcome old antagonisms. A few are interested in the Methodist church.

Kachitu is five blocks wide and seven blocks long. In the center of town is a square and in the center of the square is a park with a bandstand, a few eucalyptus trees, and some shrubbery and flowers that the mestizos are very proud of. The disgruntled, somewhat tattered, and self-appointed aristocrats spent fifty years hunting down resources to build that park, which they saw as a tangible sign of progress and which would therefore, they thought, link them to urbanity, education, culture, and the rest of the world.

At the end of the nineteenth century, their predecessors mobilized Aymara Indian labor to pave the square. To them a paved square was a tangible sign of the presence of aristocratic society, and thus, they thought, it would link them to the national elite in La Paz. Paved in different colored cobblestones and rocks, organized into designs and dates and the names of the Indian communities that did the work, the elaborate composition of the pavement is truly an indication of the power that mestizos had over the local Aymara, and of the labor they could mobilize at the turn of the century. Today, most of the color has worn off the cobblestones and the design is barely perceptible.

In the center of the northern border of the square is the Catholic church. The church was first erected in the seventeenth century and decorated with European tapestries, paintings, and elaborately dressed statues. But over time, particularly during the twentieth century, most of these treasures were stolen. Consensus has it that several of the priests took these things with them when they left, in exchange for the numerous offspring they left behind with the young mistresses who were willing to help make these priests' stays in town comfortable. This consensus must be significant as it is one of very few in Kachitu.

In the early 1970s a major debate raged in town between two factions of mestizos.[3] One saw Kachitu as a vulgar, parochial backwater inhabited by swains, yokels, boors, and uneducated social riffraff; the other saw Kachitu as a historical monument to a dramatic and glorious history that was played out right there in the center of town by their very forefathers. The subject of the debate concerned the value of the few relics that remained in the church. The former group was all for cleaning out the church and ridding the town of moth-eaten trash; the latter claimed the relics were the town's valuable estate and should be restored. In the end, nothing was restored or thrown out except the thatch roof, which was replaced with corrugated tin.

The statue of La Virgen de la Candelaria that still graces the altar compensates, however, for the town's losses by performing miracles. There is consensus in town over this too. Her eyes have been seen to come alive and glow on special occasions, a sign that she is powerful and should be respected and revered if she is to perform her duty to the town as its patron saint and keep Kachitu free of disease and pestilence. Reverence is shown through fiestas sponsored by the most prestigious of the town's residents. As there is no consensus over who are the town's most prestigious residents, how to elaborate the fiesta and who gets to control it are major sources of conflict and a focal point of the manipulation of medical ideology for social, economic, and political ends.

THE AYMARA

Approximately another third of the town's population are agriculturally based Aymara. The Aymara are campesinos, or land-based Indian peasants who also form a distinct ethnic group that were, until 1952, dominated by the mestizos and often complain that they still are. Until 1952 the Aymara were confined to either heavily taxed free Indian communities or to haciendas; thus those over thirty years of age usually did not speak Spanish in 1977. Until 1952 they formed the heart of the Bolivian economy by laboring in the mines and the agricultural fields and performing personal services (pongueaje). Such labor was controlled by the elite, who mostly lived in La Paz or elsewhere, but supervised by mestizos. From the Aymara point of view they gained little by the revolution except the ability to tell their mestizo oppressors to go to hell, which was, in itself, no small gain.

Many of them moved into Kachitu from the haciendas before the revolution, accessing land through campadrazgo, or fictive kin ties with mestizos. Others moved to town after the land reform to claim land on its outskirts which was confiscated from the mestizos. Currently they are doing the same thing their ancestors did for thousands of years: tilling the soil. Most keep to themselves, working hard, burying half their infants,[4] bartering at the weekly markets. A few are more politically active, particularly in the campesino movement, which, on this part of the altiplano, consists principally of mobilizing, through promises of favors, as many followers as possible to "confront" the political machine in La Paz, a symbolic action at best.

Eulogio Añaguaya once belonged to the Methodist church but identifies himself now as an Aymara campesino. He has been the president of the canton's campesino union since the revolutionary days of the 1950s when the union was genuinely effective. Today he augments his agricultural activities by being the doorkeeper of the grammar school, and thus, unlike most other Aymara, he has a dependable access to cash. With his accumulated capital, he would like very much to sponsor the town fiesta that honors the Virgin, an "obligation" that "burdened" only vecinas before 1952. But control of the fiesta is now in the hands of a few Kachituño mestizos who live in La Paz and manipulate fiesta sponsorship to generate a profit. They won't let Añaguaya play. In turn he blames them for the droughts of 1983 and 1984 because the Virgin insists the fiesta be in the hands of the local Kachituños. Thus, just as before the revolution, the Aymara are excluded from most political and entrepreneurial life; through medical metaphor, they ascribe this fact to mestizo domination.

THE METHODIST AYMARA

A final third of the town's population are Methodist Aymara who converted after the arrival in Kachitu of the mission in the early 1930s. They attended the Methodist mission schools and became literate. They listened to the Lord when he said through the missionaries that entrepreneurial activity was good. For more than forty years they have received all the ideological and economic benefits that entailed. Politicized and educated, they actively and regularly participate in the cash economy, unlike the campesinos and many of the mestizos in Kachitu. By the 1970s Kachitu's commercial class consisted virtually exclusively of people who were, at least at one time, Methodist Aymara, though many have left the church. They also monopolized local administrative and political positions when the revolutionary government threw all the rural mestizos out. They are politically conscious of their Aymara ethnicity. They are proud and jealous of their church, their school, and the political power they have been able to acquire through their organization as an educated religious community. All remain related to the soil and its cultivation. They have become the economic backbone of the town.

Today these three groups exist in a tumultuous world that emerged in 1952 from a 400-year history of asymmetrical relations of dependency and exploitation between two ethnically defined groups: mestizos and Aymara. The 1952 revolution offered promises to everyone. Most have never been fulfilled. It enriched a few, impoverished others, confused ethnic divisions, and multiplied class distinctions. By the late 1970s, as social divisions multiplied, the content, meaning, and significance of mestizoness, Aymara Indianness, Catholicism, and membership in the Methodist church were being culturally redefined within an environment of political and economic instability and radically changing social relations. The resulting confusion has left Kachitu politically charged. In Kachitu, and throughout the altiplano, resources are scarcer than they have ever been in Bolivian history. Inflation in 1985 reached the highest known inflation rate in recorded history of the world outside a war economy, with the exception of the Weimar Republic, until Argentina and Nicaragua threatened to surpass it: 25,000 percent in 1982. In that year, the second most expensive national import was paper currency. National political power has always been and remains unstable. The United Nations states that its figure for Bolivia's infant mortality rate, 138 per 1,000, is "unreliable." No one in town has a secure present, and all face a precarious future. Both regional and national forces have divided the town's population into competing and conflicting domains and cheated them out of the possibilities of collaboration and unity. In the search for scarce resources, including political security, Kachituños negotiate the very content of ethnic and religious identity, the rights and privileges thereof, and, among those whose lives are the most precarious, maintenance and even access to ethnic and religious membership. In this way people and groups compete for scarce material and nonmaterial resources, including power.

THE CONCEPT OF A SINGLE CULTURE AND THE CULTURAL IDENTITY CRISIS:
The Use of Ethnicity to Mask Social Class and Voice Resistance

Ethnic differentiation between Aymara (and other Indian groups), mestizos, and "whites" on the altiplano was, for 400 years, described as if defined in terms of race.[5] In the 1930s the Methodist church emerged as a new and significant social distinction in Kachitu. Today Kachituños profess that both ethnicity (as race) and religion are the significant markers of social differentiation. They argue that mestizos and Aymara have different customs. Indians speak principally Aymara; mestizos speak Spanish in public, except when they don't want physicians from La Paz, missionaries, and visiting gringos to understand something. Methodist Aymara assert that they maintain specific philosophical orientations, political positions, and economic interests that distinguish them from everyone else. These descriptions, however, do not accurately reflect historical and ethnographic data. The mestizos, for example, have fabricated genealogies that give them Hispanic ancestors. In Kachitu, both ethnic and religious distinctions, and the notion of cultural pluralism—groups with different social and cultural origins (Furnival 1939, 1948)—are problematic.

If following, say, Weber (1961 : 306) or Smith and Kornberg (1969 : 342) or A. Smith (1981), subjective assertions are combined with the objective criteria of common origin, history, and culture to define ethnicity, the category of ethnicity breaks down in its application to these three groups in Kachitu: all three speak fluent Aymara, share much of the same history—although sometimes different sides of it—and, it will be demonstrated in chapter 4, a common origin. If we move from the abstract notion of culture as symbolic systems of meaning (Geertz 1973) to a concrete concept of it as enduring representations in thought and practice (Coombs-Shilling 1989 : 26–27), we embed culture in the social world. If we further acknowledge that some people form their lives around resistance to those representations they inherit, we can further say that the entire population of Kachitu, and of Bolivia as well, regardless of ethnicity, shares confluences of the same culture.

If we treat the Aymara as an ethnic group defined by its minority status in the national economic and political structure (Wagley and Harris 1958 : 10) and, following Bonachich (1972) we apply principally economic criteria to locate ethnicity in Kachitu, what emerges approximates social class for two reasons: considerable movement takes place between the three groups, and their relative access to political and economic resources has constantly changed over time.

The notion of class, however, as "common shared interests and life chances, by virtue of their position in the system of production and in the political structure" (van den Berghe 1983 : 222) contradicts the very activity that goes on in medical dialogue in Kachitu: by virtue of their similar positions in the system of production and in the political structure, everyone in Kachitu has different interests, aspirations for different life chances, and strategies to change their position in the system.

Only the more limited material definition of class according to relationship to the productive process and consequential access to political resources (see Rebel 1989) can accommodate the Kachitu population. And when applied in historical perspective, this more limited definition exposes ethnicity as a mask for social class and a mode for the expression of resistance to oppression, entwined in constant negotiation over the meaning of cultural identity (and, of course, its material foundations): a means to maintain a specific class structure. Following Fredrik Barth (1969) and Abner Cohen (1969, 1974, 1976, 1981), ethnicity emerges as an

adapted strategy in social group interaction. It is very much "a mask of confrontation" (Vincent (1971 : 10; 1974).

Membership in the Methodist church emerges in the twentieth century as
yet another metaphor for social class. If we interpret Kachituños to be distinguish-
ing themselves by masking social class and voicing resistance with diverse elements of a single but complex culture, the political and economic significance of
medical dialogue in this medically plural environment emerges: medical dialogue
can be used to both redefine the content of ethnic and religious identity, and to
create alliances across boundaries that are, in fact, permeable, and effect changes in
social class—to redefine cultural identity.

Thus what appears as cultural pluralism or even several cultures dissolves
into a single complex culture: a web of interlinking social relations through which
pass, or which employ, a grammar of symbolic images and metaphors. As so defined, culture is composed of dialectical elements that the local people refer to in
oppositional ethnic and religious terms in order to define and redefine ethnic and
religious affiliation and thus social-class membership. Using the cultural grammar, people use and manipulate symbols and metaphors, including medical ideology, to situate individuals within different classes in the social order. The use of
culture is thus formed by social class. But on the Bolivian altiplano, a periphery
experiencing severe economic contraction, several modes of production inter-
twine: both barter and cash economies coexist; mercantile and capital markets appear and recede. Thus individuals may be placed in more than one class position
simultaneously, a situation that further demands negotiation of the meaning of
ethnic and religious affiliation: negotiation over cultural identity.

This book, therefore, will contend that the content of ethnicity and religion in
Kachitu are in dispute because they are essential threads of the same historical
cloth. Indianness is essential to mestizoness. Without the Catholic church, Meth-
odism as it pertains in contemporary Kachitu would not exist. All four are embedded in a larger, politically and economically hegemonic system to which Kachitu is
peripheral, powerless, and subordinate.

These two ethnic groups were clearly demarcatable in Kachitu before 1952
and were, before the arrival of the Methodists in the 1930s, inextricably bound
together under the Catholic church and regional economy in a relationship of mutual dependence and antagonism. This relationship was characterized by asymmetrical access to political power and economic and juridical resources that were in
the hands of the vecinos who, in turn, held that power in behalf of the elite in La
Paz and deployed it in their interests. Mestizos and Indians (and the elite for that
matter) shared certain elements of ideology, but maintained other differential elements that expressed their ethnic distinctiveness and mutual antagonism. Through
confluences of shared culture both groups survived on the labor of the Indians,
and they shared the same medical ideologies. In the 1930s Methodist missionaries

from the United States arrived in Kachitu specifically to wage war against that very relationship, and they drew their converts from people who were dissatisfied with it. Since that time, however, a promising revolution and its aftermath have left the altiplano of Bolivia in a contracting economy and marginalized Kachitu even further. Today as Kachituños struggle to exist, the very boundaries between ethnic and religious groups are vague, and old markers of identity have lost much of their meaning. A shift in affiliation and even in membership from one group to another is often made. In dispute is not so much ethnicity or religious affiliation, but the meaning of diversity within a single political and cultural history. Within this historically defined cultural identity crisis, Kachituños try to negotiate their way to power, resources, and security through medical dialogue. Through its facility as a primary resource, medicine helps create and regulate power within and between class relations.

MEDICAL PLURALISM IN KACHITU

In and around Kachitu, three types of medical ideologies and resources can be delineated as available to the local population. Cosmopolitan medicine[6] is dispensed at the local twelve-bed Methodist hospital by a physician in residence when there is one, and by two to four hospital auxiliaries trained by a North American missionary doctor named Frank Beck. Today they may dispense therapies deriving from Aymara medicine or from *medicinas caseras*, which are popular household remedies, as well as pharmaceuticals.[7]

Dr. Beck was the original missionary physician in Kachitu and the first missionary physician in Bolivia. Since his death, occasional missionary physicians have temporarily replaced him in Kachitu, but the attending physician is usually a Bolivian medical graduate fulfilling his year of work in the countryside as required by Bolivian law (the *año de provincia*) and as approved by the church board in La Paz. Those selected are usually, but not always, Methodists.

Aymara medicine is dispensed by a number of indigenous healers, or yatiris, dispersed throughout the thirty-six comunidades that fall under the auspices of the municipality of Kachitu. Yatiris diagnose ultimate cause of illness (what social or natural disturbances or supernatural entity is responsible for it) through divination of coca leaves; they also diagnose immediate cause by more pragmatic means of observation. Supplication of the supernatural is employed in tandem with herbal and other natural and chemotherapeutic curative therapies. Their curative therapies frequently make use of pharmaceutical resources.

Medicinas caseras is dispensed by the layperson—usually mothers—in the home. It consists of a heavy dose of Galenic medical theory[7] from Spanish colonial heritage including the concept that all ingestible things are either hot or cold, Aymara beliefs and practices including ancestor worship, appeal to non-human entities, herbal remedies, and Catholic moralism, as well as pharmaceuticals acquired at the clinic. Its status as the principal resource employed underlines the heavy emphasis on individual access to medical knowledge in the minds of the Kachituños.

The boundaries between these three medical traditions, however, are not always clear, as resources and ideas are appropriated by each domain from the others. That is, in Kachitu, the various medical systems are not closed and independent of the other medical systems, as they are within the medical pluralism analyzed by Janzen (1978) for Lower Zaire, or like those decribed by Nall and Speilberg (1967), Paul (1955), and Press (1969) for Latin America. The concept of medical systems as closed systems is also implied by studies of indigenous medical systems for Latin America (e.g., Fabrega 1972; Oblitas Poblete 1963, 1969, 1971; Press 1971; Sharon 1978), although questioned by scholars on African and Asian systems such as Comaroff (1980, 1981), Unschuld (1975), and Farquhar (1987). The exchange that takes place between systems as evidenced in Kachitu is corroborated by the works of Joseph Bastien for Bolivia (1987a,b) as well as Press in Colombia (1969, 1971). Such exchange may be ubiquitous, as it is the logical outcome of the embeddedness of systems within their cultural contexts, overlooked because of the boundaries that studies in contrasting medical systems artificially set up for purposes of clarity. One aspect of this exchange was evidenced in the shifts in medical beliefs that took place in the case of Seferino. Another is revealed in the negotiation of the content of ethnic and religious identity—the redefinition of cultural identity—that takes place in Kachitu as a means of defining social relations and social class, which in turn often provides access to resources. Maria's death is a case in point.

AN EXAMPLE OF HOW ETHNICITY, RELIGION, AND MEDICAL PLURALISM INTERACT:
Shifts in Medical Beliefs and the Deployment of Medical Metaphors to Define Social Relationships

Maria died in 1978 after a short illness. She was the daughter of Renita, an Aymara campesina who initially assumed that her child was suffering from an illness that the doctor could not cure. Her economic situation, like that of most people in town, was precarious. She had insufficient means to adequately feed herself and her two children. She had no cash whatsoever and no kin nor compadrazgo[8] ties that could bring her cash without straining several households severely. Consequently, like most people in town, Renita chose first to try all possible medicinas caseras before approaching the services of either yatiri or physician. The case of her daughter Maria's death and the events that led to it demonstrate both how others expressed their own ethnic and religious identities through diagnostic opinions and the limitations and possibilities of strategies that those identities define.

Renita was twenty-three and in the market for a husband when her child died. She lived mostly with her parents as the eldest of seven living children. Three others had died. The family owned a bit of land in a nearby comunidad, but it was not big enough to produce all the necessary food for such a large household. Renita's father, Norberto, rented two small rooms in Kachitu. The family lived in one and Norberto did what little blacksmithing business he could drum up in the other. They also rented a small chacra, or field, from Doña Margarita Garcia viuda de Bilis with the little money the blacksmithing brought in. Yet they still ate little. Renita was encouraged to marry to reduce the number of mouths to feed (and thereby improve everyone's nutrition). It was hoped that a marriage for Renita would also prove sufficiently lucrative to abolish her need to inherit a portion of Norberto's land, and leave thereby larger portions of inheritable land for the six remaining children.

Renita had indeed tried to find a husband. According to Aymara custom, she had lived with a potential husband in the state of trial marriage. Aymara couples live together for a year or more before an official wedding lest the couple prove incompatible or one partner infertile,[9] and Carter (1977), Bolton (1972), and Bolton and Bolton (1975) have described this as a lengthy, multiple-step marriage contract. This custom strikingly differentiates Aymara from mestizos, who follow the Catholic proscription of the elite which values female virginity at the church wedding. The economic advantage of the Aymara custom for an agriculturally based population with no cash income underlies its significance for class, regardless of ethnicity (Stinson 1978, 1980, 1982, 1983). Renita's first potential husband proved incompatible and the relationship was dissolved, but the union produced a child. Shortly thereafter Renita was courted by a second potential husband. This man told her that he was married to a woman in La Paz and would not leave his wife. Unfortunately, by then she was pregnant with Maria. Although this man did send small amounts of money to help with Renita's expenses, she still had to forage and raise the children by herself in her parents' household. Renita's efforts, then, had increased the number of mouths to feed in the household from nine to eleven, rather than decrease that number to reduce the family's economic burdens. At twenty-three, Renita was friendly, kind, and eager to laugh in spite of her difficult and precarious position. She was hopeful of her domestic abilities and anxiously looking for someone with whom she might share them, as her own and her children's future depended upon her finding a good husband.

Little Maria developed a cough and then a fever. Renita and her mother concluded because it was summer and Renita had kept the child in the sun as she worked their field, and because there was, after all, a fever involved, that the illness was due to excessive heat, or *calor*. Therefore, they administered *medicinas caseras: mates* (teas) that were *fresca* (cold) to offset the heat. But Maria's condition grew worse.

Renita became more worried, feared that Maria had lost her soul, her *ajayu*, and called all over the house and the fields for it, but the ajayu did not return. Soul loss is a belief shared by both Aymara and Hispanic folk medical traditions, but Renita's inability to locate Maria's soul within her shadow identified this case as strictly Aymara. Renita looked at the child's shadow, saw that it was missing its "fuzzy" part and thus her ajayu, and concluded the situation was hopeless. "My Maria's shadow lost its fuzzy part," she sobbed, and she took the child to a yatiri. The yatiri read the coca and determined that it was Maria's fate to die. There was nothing to be done. That night, Renita was visited in her dreams by *achachillas*, Aymara spirits who live in the mountains. They told her that because Maria was such a beautiful child they were taking her to bring up themselves, and that they would take good care of her. Thus Renita resigned herself to the inevitable.

Meanwhile Doña Antonia intervened. Antonia is a mestiza and was Maria's godmother. She is also the daughter of a hospital auxiliary, long since dead. He had worked with Dr. Frank Beck. Indeed, it was her father's job at the hospital that had brought her family to Kachitu. She, however, remained Catholic like her mother, and married Don Lorenzo, of the once prestigious Villazon family of the Kachitu vecindario. These days, however, Antonia, Lorenzo, and their four children could not make ends meet with Lorenzo's rural schoolteacher's salary. Thus they were poor and ashamed. But Antonia was familiar with cosmopolitan medicine, a knowledge in which she took pride, especially when her husband sent home insufficient money and the other vecinos began to shun her. Like some other vecinos in Kachitu, Antonia did not express her ethnic identity in anticampesino terms. She conversed at length with Renita about multiple cases of soul theft her own children had suffered, and tried to illustrate a difference between that diagnosis and Maria's condition.

Antonia fed her children by trading with campesinos, thus transforming her compadrazgo ties with them, and with Renita in particular, from asymmetrical patron-client ties, through which mestizos "traditionally" exploited the Aymara, into reciprocal exchange relations in an attempt to maximize her returns in a postrevolutionary setting; now that mestizos had lost their superordinate position in town, they could not so easily extract resources from Indians, particularly if the mestizo was poor, with no social power to offer in return. She also begged and borrowed from more economically secure vecinos until they finally refused her credit. These strategies reduced her social status as a vecino among members of that ethnic group. The mestizos disapproved of her intimate relations with the Aymara and her open expression of her own poverty.

Antonia's cosmopolitan medical knowledge, though not always accurate, was a reason for pride in her education, rather than a social statement of cultural superiority. If she had to beg, she at least had *some* education, which is more than many other mestizos could say.

If Maria died, Antonia, as Maria's godmother, would be required to buy new burial clothes and contribute to the funeral refreshments, a considerable expense. The death of a godchild also meant the end of a potential tie that might bring in resources in the future. Hence, when Renita brought Maria to Antonia's house to express her anxiety and concern, Antonia recognized the symptoms of pneumonia, knew Maria could benefit from antibiotics, and pleaded with Renita to take the child to the clinic.

Convinced that her child would die and knowing she would have to beg for money to pay for such a visit, Renita hesitated agitatedly. Obviously Renita still hoped that Maria would take a turn for the better, but in her mind such hope lay in the possibility that the achachillas would change their minds, rather than that the diagnosis was wrong. Her economic situation, however, and the pressure another child would place on the household encouraged the achachillas *not* to change their minds. Antonia went to great pains to convince her otherwise. Her argument was based upon diagnosis: she did not suggest that the yatiri was useless or superstitious, but rather that the yatiri might have been wrong. Indeed, had Antonia insisted that soul theft was an illegitimate diagnosis, she would have risked offending a campesina with whom she had established important reciprocal economic relations and therefore did not have the social legitimacy to insult, and who had an emotional and economic investment in the decision of the achachillas. Renita saw Antonia as a friend, not a social superior in ethnic terms.

Renita finally agreed to go to the clinic but by that time "the illness had become too severe and the child too weak" for direct administration of penicillin, said Dr. Acietuno, who had recently come to Kachitu after Dr. Sabas resolved to wage his war against poverty through journalism rather than medicine. Acietuno explained to me that he had given penicillin to another infant in a similarly advanced state, and when the child died later that day, he had faced accusations of ignorance and even murder. Therefore, having diagnosed pneumonia, he gave Maria some cough medicine and told Renita to return in the morning, when he hoped the child would be "strong enough" to begin a series of penicillin injections.

After Renita returned with Maria to Antonia's home from the clinic, however, the child lay on the bed breathing laboriously with her eyes unfocused and rolled up in her head, and later that afternoon she died.

As Renita's family did not have a yard, the wake was held at the home of a Methodist, Mercedes. The individuals at the funeral participated as they would never have done before 1952. Present were vecinos, Methodists, and campesinos, all drinking from the same bottles and socializing within the same social space. Everyone sat about sipping soup and eating the funeral meal, which included that rare item meat, served only on such solemn or special occasions. Renita and Antonia could not afford much, however, and the company shared the sparse bones of a few guinea pigs. The guests drank alcohol and beer and chewed coca while they said their last good-byes to Maria, paid their respects, comforted the bereaved, and swapped opinions on the cause of death.

The company made a concerted effort to get drunk to commune in the solemnity of the occasion and to ward off the achachillas, the khan achachi, and other entities that might inflict illness or steal souls from the present company, they being particularly vulnerable in their state of sorrow. Everyone drank to excess, including Mercedes and other guests who were Methodists. By drinking together they agreed to participate together in intimate fellowship.

Renita's father, Norberto, was slouched in the corner drinking and crying, and enjoying the attentions of his young son, who tried to humor and quiet him when his wife occasionally told him to shut up. Frequently he turned to the Methodists and to me, saying, "Señora, there are times when drinking is a good thing." His own grief, and his need for support and reinforcement, exceeded that of Renita who, perhaps because of her youth, saw neither so many aspects of the tragedy nor such effective means to gain attention as did her father. Renita was also too busy serving the funeral meal and drinks to express much sorrow and grief.

And as the alcohol flowed, people discussed their opinions of why Maria had died. Renita, the other campesinos, Antonia, and Doña Leonora de Ugalde, the only vecina in attendance besides the godmother, Antonia, made diagnostic and etiologic statements that had more social than medical significance. Some agreed that Maria had suffered pneumonia, but most felt she had lost her ajayu. Leonora, a mestiza with an interest in the Methodist church, was quite adamant about her own opinion.

Unlike Antonia, Leonora did not have compadrazgo ties with Renita. Though she was poor, she and her husband were trying to survive in the old prerevolutionary vecino manner as if nothing had happened since 1952. They were too old then to adopt new economic, political, and psychological strategies. And they were not doing well. They maintained a small store and Don Valentino was assistant to the *corregidor*, the local dispute resolver, but these activities were not lucrative and meat never appeared on their table. Valentino was an alcoholic and drank up most of the cash they got. Often he was physically debilitated for weeks on end after a severe drinking bout. Leonora wrote in 1980 to inform me that he died of liver poisoning. She found no reason to resort to metaphorical etiologies on his behalf.

"Yes," said Leonora, "certainly the child lost her ajayu, but it is the Devil who came and stole it, not any achachillas!" Just a few weeks back, she recalled, when Maria first became ill, she had fallen off the bed. The Devil had been hanging around the house, waiting for just such an opportunity, because Renita was not married to Maria's father. Had Renita been a Methodist, she would not have been living in sin. Methodists do not suffer these illnesses because the Devil does not lurk about their homes, she continued. The Methodist church is a protection against such evils, and Methodists are favored by God. That is why they don't live in sin, don't have extramarital or premarital affairs, especially when there are children involved, explained Leonora. In tears, Renita snapped back that the child had died becaue they had arrived at the hospital too late.

Leonora herself was not a Methodist. Her daughter and son-in-law, however, were the only vecinos in town who were. But Leonora's daughter was young. The daughter's husband was well educated and from out of town and had a post at the village high school. They belonged to a new generation and would probably move away from Kachitu. It was a much more difficult proposition for Leonora to join the church, being a vecina and surrounded by only Catholic social equals.

The next day, Leonora explained further that Maria's death was ultimately Renita's fault for not being a Methodist; that the child's ajayu had been stolen by a *bichu*, a small animal that travels about at night, which was given the opportunity for soul theft when the child was frightened in an enchanted place, specifically the bed. When I asked if beds are usually enchanted places, Leonora exclaimed that they certainly were not. Maria, she said, slept with her mother! And her mother, continued Leonora, was not in the grace of God.

But Antonia and Leonora were members of the vecino class and each had chosen a different economic and social strategy since the 1952 revolution stripped them of their superordinate positions. These different strategies permitted them to perceive of themselves and their own ethnic and religious identities in different ways. These differences were expressed in their opinions over Maria's illness and death. On Renita these two choices of identity had differing impacts, and all three individuals negotiated their varying identities with one another before and during the funeral.

Antonia's adoption of equilateral economic exchange with some campesinos, including Renita, led to her interactions with Renita as a social equal, in opposition to the values held by other vecinos, including her own husband and Leonora. Antonia nevertheless felt comfortable with physician care, though uncomfortable with her own ethnic peers. She proposed physician care to Renita in an expression of egalitarian friendship and not as an expression of social differentiation. At no point did she deride Renita's faith in the yatiri, in part because Renita had in the past helped Antonia search out the services of a good yatiri for her own children. The cultural statements exchanged between Renita and Antonia are expressive of identities that each accepted in the other.

Leonora, however, used the issue of Maria's death to differentiate herself from the ethnic and religious group (but actually social class) that Renita represents. Unlike Antonia, Doña Leonora tried to maintain the economic strategies and ethnic identity that had been successful before the 1952 revolution. Her children, however, forged a new cultural identity for themselves in the Methodist church, and while Leonora recognized their new approach, she herself could not follow them. To do so would have been to isolate herself from her social peers; as a member of an older generation, the option of Protestantism was closed to her. She expressed in her diagnosis of Maria's death a mixture of Aymara and Methodist doctrines: she proposed soul theft but in Protestant terms, therefore not aligning herself with either group. At the same time, however, she disassociated herself from Renita in terms expressive of ethnic superordination. That is, Leonora allowed that Renita's diagnosis was partially correct: Maria died of soul theft. But by mixing Aymara medical beliefs with Methodist doctrine, she inverted the concept of exploitation inherent in soul theft into a condemnation. Leonora claimed that Maria died because Renita's bed was an evil place, and it was evil because Renita is a campesina. Leonora was squarely acknowledging that because Renita is Aymara, she is therefore of lower socioeconomic class than Leonora. As an old vecina, Leonora was poor, almost as poor as the Aymara—hence her anxiety. Aymara-turned-Methodists had all done well socioeconomically, especially since 1952, and were therefore in a higher economic class than Leonora.

Renita, however, did not accept Leonora's opinions and rejected her expressions of the social relationship between them. To oppose Leonora's image of campesino identity, Renita resorted to cosmopolitan medical ideology, claiming Maria died because they arrived at the clinic too late. The issue, therefore, was not an interpersonal one. Leonora did not accuse Renita of irresponsibility nor did Renita interpret her statements as such. The issue was one of identity, and a definition of that identity.

Today in Kachitu there is a widespread consensus among the three contemporary social groups about the general content of all three medical ideologies, even though these three groups stand in different political and economic relationships to each other. There is no consensus, however, about the employment of these ideologies either among or between groups. Members of all three social groups—mestizos, campesinos, and Methodists—resort to all three medical traditions and systems, but at different times and to different degrees. The reinterpretation of elements of medical ideologies and the competition to monopolize the town's consumption of them so as to restructure social relationships is a grammar underlying this apparent chaos which makes it comprehensible. Hardly passive recipients of ideology, Kachituños actively—even aggressively—employ the most contradictory elements of different ideologies that they can think of. As they discuss and debate what they and their neighbors suffer from, and as they draw upon three medical traditions and resources, they are also saying something about themselves, the person they are talking to, and the person they are talking about. They are saying something as well about the social relationships between these individuals. Medical dialogue is an idiom through which people express values (Comaroff 1985; Douglas 1966; Frake 1961; Taussig 1980; Thompson 1979). Discussion and debate is an attempt by individuals to control the consumption of opinion. He who ultimately controls the consumption of a diagnostic opinion in a medical debate in Kachitu reinforces or alters his relationship to the others involved in the debate. Through such debates, social relationships are either reinforced or restructured. Membership and meaning shift. It is through social relationships that individuals gain access to resources, including both material goods and power. If differential use of these medical resources stems from their efforts to constantly negotiate new meanings of identities and restructure social relationships in order to gain access to resources, the logic behind the process of choice can be delineated.

In this environment, as everywhere else, the available medical systems serve extramedical functions. Healers and physicians and medical groups try to resolve disputes, maintain social control, direct political power, and serve as the basis upon which allied services accumulate wealth and capital and generate political power. But medical ideologies as expressed in day-to-day dialogue also generate power for the patient, healer, and community members at large.

In this study, the focus on diagnosis is not limited to that established by a therapy management group of close kin such as the groups Janzen studied among the Kongo (1978 : 4), which in Kachitu reality do not exist, but rather to the diagnostic opinions expressed by the patient, his or her family, neighbors, relations, various healers called into the case, and all other members of the town. The patient or kin may not agree with the town consensus, or the town may be in disagreement over the diagnosis. A therapy management group may actually emerge and determine ultimate treatment in a case. It is in the domain of public diagnosis, however, that negotiation and competition over the consumption of an opinion takes place.

In order to identify the incremental steps involved in the dialectics of daily life which take place in medical dialogue, one focus of this analysis must be on the individual within a complex context that Kachituños define as ethnically and religiously plural, but which is analyzed in terms of class within a coherent cultural environment. This study is not an analysis of the ideologies in and of themselves, but of how and why individuals employ elements of all available medical ideologies to effect changes in social relations. Nor, contrary to most contemporary Andean ethnography (Abercrombie 1986, Allen 1988, Poole 1984, Rasnake 1989, Sallnow 1987), is it focused on the formation of ideology for solidarity, resistance, and accommodation of an ethnic group to hegemonic forces; although solidarity, resistance, or accommodation may frequently be the objective of medical dialogue. Rather, it focuses on the interstices and junctions, joints and hinges, margins and frontiers between nebulously defined groups. Here individuals make choices and generate strategies for solidarity and resistance, for mobility and immutability, accommodation and empowerment. Through this narrower focus on individual actions, the dynamics of medical pluralism and how it is embedded in a sociopolitical context become visible.

When medical pluralism is looked at from this perspective, several other processes become visible. The explicit assumption that defines this perspective is that medical systems, medical practitioners, and the population served operate and coexist within a political and economic context. Consequently the degree to which both cosmopolitan medicine and indigenous systems operate within historical and contemporary, national and international, contexts must also be clarified in order to understand their value as a primary resource that facilitates negotiation of cultural identity and thus alters social relations and creates access to secondary resources.

An accompanying community focus also elucidates the penetrability of the boundaries between the three medical systems. Boundaries are in fact fluid, as economic, political, and historical contexts change. From a community perspective and focus on dialogue and individual activity, therefore, the small changes that take place in medical ideologies over time become visible. Medical ideologies emerge from this perspective related to their historical, social, and political contexts as politically empowering, and the degree to which transformations of medical ideologies take place in order to accommodate history become evident. The patient suddenly emerges from this complex, constantly changing, and politically charged situation as a kind of decision maker that most scientists want to avoid: he is not Rational Man looking for medical efficacy; rather, he is a social and political animal who at times may be looking for meaning through efficacy which becomes a validation of some sociopolitical or economic proposition, but more often is looking for efficacy through meaning in a sociopolitical and economic context. This view also explains how the patient, and even the healer, can maintain contradictory ideologies at the same time.

CHAPTER 2

Working in the Field

When I began the fieldwork in Kachitu in February, 1977, my intention was to investigate the historical, political, economic, and social conditions that lead to what I assumed would be differential use of available cosmopolitan and indigenous health-care resources. I determined to discover what resources were available, how people used them, and why they made the choices they did. I had construed these three questions as three dimensions of anthropological knowledge about medical pluralism. The specific and immediate problem to be addressed, however, was quite one-dimensional: how to collect information. This was a population that, Tschopik (1947, 1951) informs us, is very suspicious of outsiders, particularly, I feared, of gringas, especially ones who asked insufferable questions, as I would.

November 10, 1977: I make a large batch of stuffed cabbage on my kerosene burner on which I cook breakfast and dinner. My intention to do all my own cooking evaporated months ago with the discovery that it takes forty-five minutes to boil anything at 13,000 feet and that there are simple ecological reasons why women here on the altiplano spend most of their time cooking. Anna and I have decided to take lunch at the local pension, which exists solely to feed the schoolteachers who reluctantly come out from La Paz to staff the grammar school, the occasional traveler, and us. The owner refuses to serve breakfast or dinner, however, because she has her own family to take care of.

Since we have no electricity, I keep meat on the hoof and learn how to slaughter, with the help of the Kachituños and much to their amusement, or I bring llama and beef back from La Paz once a month and hang it outside to dry in the crisp wind and intense radiation, or we go vegetarian. The only things that grow in Kachitu are tubers, grains, and haba beans, which limit a gringa's conception of a vegetarian diet. Sunday market in town brings campesinos up from the lowlands to sell all kinds of vegetables, but by the time leafy vegetables arrive after a day's travel on someone's back, they are somewhat wilted. Several days later they are brown and limp. So tonight I make stuffed cabbage out of wilted cabbage and ground llama meat hung outside for three weeks.

As usual I make a large batch so I can give most of it away as gifts of appeasement and lures to extract information. I give some to the three nuns, the first ever to work in Kachitu. They belong to a German order and the two young novices are Bolivian mestizas from Oruro, while the nun in charge is German. She lives up to my stereotype of stern German authoritarianism. She doesn't like it here very much, particularly because the Kachituños drink during fiesta, which she sees as a sign of the Devil who, she complains, continues to live among these people in spite of her efforts. I note that she doesn't associate with Seferino, Dr. Sabas, or the Reverend Angel. She confines herself to the parish on the main square where she looks after the two young novices. She is harsh with them, and she is suspicious of my request to copy the church archives.

From the recently constructed warm and tidy room the nuns live in, I cross the church patio to the tattered thatched-roof adobe apartment built in the 1800s and maintained by the community for the padre. The thatched roof leaks, the apartment is in disrepair, and Padre Christian has recently castigated his flock for their lack of attention to his living conditions. Inside, ancient dusty books are scattered everywhere, covering even the miserable pallet on which he sleeps. He speaks five languages and knows more social science than I do. Grinning and twinkling his eyes at me, he is delighted to get some stuffed cabbage, although he reminds me a tad sternly, as he always does, of my promise to send copies of my research results to the community. Though he is kind to me, he secretly harbors his suspicions about my abilities to commit cultural imperialism. Father Christian is to me an enchanting enigma. He seems to live with no creature comforts whatsoever, except for a snappy down parka and a pair of sunglasses. He was highly educated in Europe, is an adherent of liberation theology, and is an Indian from Achacachi. He reflects that it is this very enigma—all these characteristics in one person—that distances him from his parishioners and inhibits the roof repairs.

I also give some stuffed cabbage to the campesina Eusebia Poma, who doesn't know what an anthropologist is, but figures I, like all non-Indians, she says, will take advantage of her. She says I am going to take the information back to the States—which are someplace north of Peru—and make a lot of money off it, and she is tired of being exploited.

I had intended to give some of the cabbage to the old lady with the failing eyes who lives across the street from me: Primitiva Mamani viuda de Yanique. I figure she is close to 100 years old, for she remembers *caudillos* (regional strong men) who roamed the area in the late nineteenth century. Being penniless, she lives on the charity of the town. The nuns and Eusebia, however, have taken more than I had anticipated, and if I give some to the old lady, I'll have none left for me and Anna. I decide not to give her any. As it turns out, however, she sees me pass by and stops me in the street. I ask about her eyes and she complains in Aymara. She speaks only Aymara. I speak only Spanish. For nine months now we have been conversing with each other. I wonder if we really understand each other. It is clear, however, that she knows when I have food, and how to get it. With great difficulty and greater dignity, she walks through my door almost daily, sits down at my table, gives me an update on her eyes, and waits to be served something to eat.

Tonight she complains about the pain (I think) and I offer to bring her aspirin. She agrees that would be a constructive way to spend my time and makes a pointed gesture in reference to the stuffed cabbage. Genara, another campesina who moved to Kachitu before the 1952 revolution and subsequent land reform, from a hacienda where she had been a serf, either overhears or smells the stuffed cabbage, and steps up. She is sick too, she says. I assent to visit her with some aspirin in the evening. She doesn't move and continues to stand there expectantly. I add that I will bring some stuffed cabbage too. She smiles and moves on. I wonder what Anna will say when I serve her canned vienna sausages and canned sardines for dinner for the fourth time this week.

Genara is a healer[1] but like Eusebia Poma, is not inclined to tell me about it. She has already appropriated the llama I inherited from a North American family in La Paz. When I bring the aspirin and stuffed cabbage, I ask her again to teach me what she knows about illness and healing. Tonight she agrees and says I should come the next night around six. The next night around six I arrive at Genara's compound of adobe and thatch huts that house her and her animals. I am armed with Porfirio as translator, and three eggs. Porfirio is her godson, or *ahijado*, and he is also my assistant because I was his godmother, his *madrina*, for his high school graduation. That means he is obligated to both of us.

She refuses to see me, saying she is very angry and has a headache. I give her the three eggs anyway, wish her well, and turn to leave. She is pleased with the eggs and grudgingly concedes to explain that I am going to take the knowledge that she gives me back to the States and make a lot of money with it, thereby exploiting her knowledge. I ask her if she would like some aspirin for her headache. She thinks that might be worth trying, so I go home for the aspirin. When I return, she agrees to teach me some small thing that she knows if I come tomorrow night around six. She tells Porfirio to collect specific herbs for the lesson. The next night I arrive at six but she is not there. She hasn't returned from the fields with her animals. I go home, try again at half past six, and open my door to try yet again at seven when I see her coming up the street on her way to my house—empty handed. She tentatively sits down at my table with me and Porfirio. I make tea and offer her a cigarette. She smokes none but she pockets about ten to take home. She says the stuffed cabbage I gave her made her sick.

When she talks, she looks directly at me, even though Porfirio is translating, and she corrects my pronunciation. She says she doesn't want to teach me how to cure *los locos* (craziness) because people will talk and might accuse her of witchcraft. We tell her no one has to know. She concedes and agrees to come Monday to teach me, and she lets Porfirio know that I should offer her dinner next time.

THE FIRST DIMENSION OF INQUIRY

Not until after she was certain that I knew my place and would both behave and reciprocate appropriately, did Genara attempt to teach me what she knew. She gave me a recipe to cure *kustipa*, a deadly condition that befalls one who is drunk and falls asleep in the sun (at high altitude, dehydration can be a serious problem). She taught me how to call a lost soul, and eventually she even taught me how to cure los locos. Then, when Porfirio fell ill, she showed me how she treated those illnesses caused by phantasms such as the *kharisiri* and the khan achachi.

I did not know, however, to what extent Genara's knowledge reflected that of the rest of the population. Press's work in Bogota (1969, 1971) led me to suspect that mestizos might concur to some extent, but Taussig's treatment of ideology among Bolivian mine workers (1980) suggested the Aymara and mestizos might provide different versions of similar ideology. Thus after I had exhausted the inventory of nosological categories in Kachitu, I undertook a long and exhaustive scheduled interview with thirty-eight yatiris, campesinos, Methodists, upwardly mobile but Catholic campesinos and vecinos. I asked them to explain etiology, symptomatology, and treatment. Assuming (incorrectly) that my own disaggregation of "magical," "psychological," and "natural" ideological elements would reveal divisions along ethnic and religious lines, I analyzed the data accordingly. What I discovered was consensus, which forced me to question the ethnic and religious categories with which I came armed into the field. Thus my first research dimension—what medical resources were available—required a fourth dimension of investigation on ethnic and religious history.

THE SECOND DIMENSION

The second dimension was how this knowledge within a context of medical pluralism is deployed; how people choose one procedure over another, particularly
when options are available from three different medical systems each claiming to
be the appropriate cure. Following earlier studies, I assumed medical classifications
had social values (Frake 1961), that those social values affected social relations both
within and outside the medical context (Ehrenreich and Ehrenreich 1978; Ehrenreich and English 1973a and b), and that such effect could both support the politics
of hegemony as well as act as a medium for struggle against it (Comaroff 1980,
1981, 1985; Taussig 1987). Thus, as medical resources were deployed, I paid attention to all dialogue and activity surrounding them, to who said what and how they
structured their conversation, and not to the patient-client relationship alone.

What I learned from Genara about this dimension, I learned because we both
became involved in Porfirio's illness, and I spent several days and nights in her
household. I witnessed her discussions with other people and with Porfirio, her
arrivals at decisions, her responses to other suggestions that were presented,
her post-illness evaluation, and what other related concerns she associated with
the event. I also witnessed other people's response to her, what they said to one
another when she wasn't present, and how they evaluated the event and her treatment of it. Through her life history and theirs I was able to partially reconstruct
the logic behind her choices and changes in decisions. I repeated this procedure
with every illness that occurred during our seventeen months in town, collecting
many pertinent data at the gossip corner when references to individual illness
events arose. With medical histories, I reconstructed past major illness events by
discussing them with everyone in town who would talk about them. Although all
these illness events were correlated with the records at the local hospital and, in
two cases to be discussed, with appropriate records from public hospitals in La Paz,
the significant data were collected in interviews, as people from every ethnic and
religious category reflected on the significance of each event. Through their life
histories I partially reconstructed the logic behind what they saw as significant.
Missing still was the historical context that could clarify their logic.

THE THIRD DIMENSION

Hence, a third dimension of anthropological knowledge about medical pluralism is
to what social, political, and economic processes Genara's choices, their logic and
their history, were related. I did not fully understand Genara's treatment choices
for Porfirio until I had reconstructed the history of Kachitu, ascertained the economic and political dynamics of the town, and understood what, exactly, the Ka-

chituños, and Genara and Porfirio in this case, were doing in this cold, windswept, and almost forgotten part of the altiplano. To achieve that I took a census; followed disputes; copied the DIC's (the resident policeman's), the judge's, and the corregidor's records; gathered historical data from informants and from the *Junta de Vecinos* (a sort of town council) records; copied the local Catholic church archives back to the sixteenth century; and microfilmed the entire body of correspondence and records of the Methodist mission. These data allowed me to discern the political dimensions of town behavior, reconstruct its economy and government since the turn of the century, and trace shifts in political power. This last analysis was rendered more accurate by a spacial analysis over time of individuals and what politically significant actions they had performed (or committed). Thus I was able to locate the logic of Genara's choices and everyone's evaluation of them within a reconstructed social and historical context. And I learned what I learned from everyone else in town, in pretty much the same way.

THE FOURTH DIMENSION

These data allowed me to pursue a fourth dimension of research: the relationship between medical beliefs and ethnic and religious history. Following Foucault's and Sahlins's analyses on the reproduction and transformation of ideologies in their historical contexts, I analyzed the medical ideologies and the discourse that emerged from medical pluralism. To do so I analyzed the medical ideological options clarified in the scheduled interview in light of the local and national history from which they emerged. These two analyses revealed that the migration of the mestizos into Kachitu in the latter half of the nineteenth century, the rise of the Methodist church in the first half of the twentieth, and the consequential development of class were responsible for what people in town expressed as cultural pluralism, and they linked the data on behavior and gossip to medical discourse as a mechanism to reproduce and transform social relations.

WHY KACHITU

I chose Kachitu for this study because of its medical and self-proclaimed cultural pluralism. Cultural diversity, I thought, would permit a broader and deeper analysis of multiple medical resource use than does a single-classed, an ethnically distinct, or a religiously homogenous population. What unfolded was cultural homogeneity and the manipulation of medical ideology to mask social class with ethnicity and religion.

COLLECTING THE DATA

The primary data were gathered through participant observation and extensive and repeated interviews. I requested permission to work in Kachitu from the village corregidor, his two assistants, the president of the Junta de Vecinos, the judge, the DIC, the doctor, the pastor, the head of the Methodist high school, and Eulogio Añaguaya, head of the inactive peasant union. This took some time, as I had not realized permission was needed from so many people, and I found myself offending someone every time I attempted to initiate my work. Cautiously, Anna and I moved into a house that had been built by a *preste*, or fiesta sponsor, some years earlier to hold a fiesta and which had stood empty since. As a woman and most significantly, as a mother, I was welcomed into confidences and conversations and was subjected to advice and concerns that might not have been proffered had I not been a single person of either sex. Yet because I was a gringa and an anthropologist, and because I also had possible access to USAID project funds and other desirable resources upon occasion, I was accorded, for the most part, the respect and consequential access to local civic and political domains and to male conversation that usually excluded women.

Many of my data were collected in the daily rounds of household and hospital visits; attendance at school, church, and town meetings; attention to gossip; helping out in work; and generally making myself visible asking a lot of questions, which upon occasion made informants tired and exasperated. From the beginning of my stay in Kachitu I was explicit about the general nature of my work there. I explained my interest in medicine and history and tried to incorporate the townspeople as much as possible into the research effort. While I often engaged in defenses of indigenous medicine and apologies for the cosmopolitan variety, and while I also exposed my appetite for gossip and discussion, I did not specifically discuss my hypotheses, for fear that doing so would prejudice my data collection. I was aware that my voracity for rumor, scandal, slander, and politics, accompanied by my vulnerability to "collaboration,"—to getting talked into paying for refreshments, events, and things—made me a secondary resource, as Porfirio's father, Vicente, demonstrates in chapter 6. This was both boon and affliction: while it facilitated my data collection it rendered many data suspicious and subject to evaluation in light of this reality.

Having heard of my interest in indigenous medicine, a yatiri from one of the outlying communities agreed to teach me his art and make me a yatiri, "so that Libbet will return to the United States to practice and make a lot of money." I have always regretted that there has not been more truth to the various hypotheses in Kachitu concerning the relationship between my work and money.[2] This yatiri spoke only Aymara and relied on his cousins who live in Kachitu to translate, with the aim of gaining a little profit for himself and for them through their combined efforts. I eventually found this unsatisfactory because he seemed to be teaching me what most townspeople also knew. I consequently searched for other translators, who had to be satisfactory to both myself and the yatiri, and for other yatiris. Through my neighbor's concerns for my own and my daughter's welfare, I eventually gained access to a yatiri who cleansed my house of evil spirits, read my future in the *coca*, and intervened on my behalf with the supernatural to bring my daughter's father and grandmother to Bolivia (the yatiri's suggestion) and to secure a job for me for the month of September of 1978 (my request; both of these events occurred, although it wasn't the job I'd had in mind).

As my friendships grew, I gained access to more yatiris, more townspeople, and more intimate and significant conversation. Friendships grew in part because I shared my food with them, drank with them, and "collaborated" with them by being godmother for their children and subsidizing just about everything from children undergoing their first haircut to shirts for the football team and iron inlays for the windows at the high school.

While there are about 1,000 people in Kachitu, its significant population is not confined to those people whose homes are within the physical limits of the village. Relations of Kachituños, principally those who are Aymara, include friends and relations who live in the outlying communities around Kachitu, particularly if they are Aymara recently migrated from the community to Kachitu in a move of upward mobility. Some community members pass a lot of time in Kachitu, particularly Methodists whose members have established compadrazgo ties with the Kachitu mestizos by asking them to be godparents at births, baptisms, first teeth, first haircuts, and all the other occasions that permit it; though few if any mestizos initiate contact with the Aymara in the communities, including their godchildren, or ahijados. The ambiguous boundaries around Kachitu that these relations create meant that my activities were scrutinized by many more people than those whose friendships I was able to cultivate. Some people whom I did not know except by face suspected that I was a communist, which meant to them that one day I would take from everyone half of everything they had. This led to hostile relations but great data collection as rumors spread, my friends defended me, and medicine became a primary resource for me. Others figured I was in some way connected with an evangelical group. Initially this made for friendly relations but poor data collection, as these people treated me like an authority and were thus closemouthed about anything even remotely interesting. This situation improved when it was determined that, with evangelical connections or perhaps something even better, like ties with USAID, I, too, could be a primary resource. Still others, mostly people with whom I did not become good friends, did not care what I did, but figured that whatever it was, was exploitative of them, would give them nothing in return for their information, and would bring me a lot of money once I got to the States with it. My only recourse was to offer the Kachituños what services I had.

Hence I dispensed a few free drugs (eye drops, aspirin, medication for dysentery and other innocuous items), taught English to the children, taught English and anthropology at the high school, established networks with USAID for grant money, played godmother for almost everything, bought a lot of beer, cooked a lot of food, and in other ways extended myself as I could.

I spent many hours with a variety of women poring over herbs in their yards, in the hills, or at the market. When we did this at the market, my inquiries and obvious lack of medical education provided free public entertainment and thus prejudiced the data collected there. Yet it expanded the data and the very categories of analysis as this public spectacle inspired veritable orations of herbal erudition, aroused envy, and incited controversy, dissent, and even confrontation that I tried to quell, after selfishly amassing and savoring all I could, by "collaborating" with several rounds of beers.

Whenever anyone was sick I visited daily to observe the processes and progressions of curative treatments and to offer my services. Because illness focuses people's attention, I hung out at the centers of gossip to see what others were saying about these people. Finally, when I was sick I suffered the ultimate in participant observation through the generous concerns of my neighbors who subjected me to a variety of diagnoses and curative treatments. I consider myself lucky to have been sick only twice in Kachitu.[3]

The greatest difficulty I had in collecting such data was verifying information, particularly that pertaining to reconstruction of the past, or to opinion. Invariably, answers to these types of questions differed each time I asked them. Lest they suspect I doubted their word, I occasionally cultivated a self-image of disorganization and difficulty with the language to permit me to repeat the same question over and over. In this way I collected as much information about individual experiences, medical ideology, and case studies as seventeen months permitted, and made myself a reputation as the town comic.

Through these techniques I did uncover two other medical traditions that are not prevalent in town, although elements of these traditions are incorporated into the Aymara medical tradition and into medicinas caseras. These are the traditions of the Kallawayas and of Hispanic folk belief.

Kallawayas are an Aymara group of medical men from remote mountain towns in Provincia Batista Saavedra, such as Curva and Charaasni (e.g., Bastien 1978, 1979, 1987; Losa Balsa 1977; Oblitas Poblete 1963, 1969, 1971) who practice an ancient and impressive medical tradition that, say Kachituños, requires the use of its own language by its medical practitioners. This knowledge is passed down from father to son. Practitioners wander throughout the Andean region, east to Brazil, and north, even perhaps into the United States, to practice and trade herbs from their remote environment for other medical resources. Occasionally a Kallawaya practitioner comes through Kachitu. His practice is seen as distinct from that of yatiris and of medicinas caseras. Nevertheless, many cures, both magical and natural, require an item or two from a Kallawaya. The actual relationship between the Aymara and the Kallawaya medical traditions has not yet been analyzed. Gregorio Losa Balsa (1977), when talking about the Kallawayas, refers to their tradition as the Aymara tradition. In Kachitu, however, the Kallawaya tradition is understood as a highly specialized, complex, and somewhat standardized tradition of which the Aymara tradition, practiced by yatiris, is a simplified folk version. Bastien's material strongly and unmistakably supports this position and implies that a Kallawaya might be offended if he were addressed as a mere Yatiri.

Hispanic folk medicine consists of those concepts that are related to homeopathy and humoral theory, including hot and cold theory. *Susto, envidia, empacho,* and other illnesses common throughout Latin America are examples of Hispanic folk nosological and etiological concepts. They are often presented in a moral form through Christian metaphor. Blind men sit on the steps of the cathedral in La Paz and tell futures that are based on one's past behavior. The term "Hispanic folk belief" brings nothing but puzzled looks from Kachituños because these etiologies are merged by them along with indigenous herbal knowledge and Aymara medical concepts into medicinas caseras. Soul loss and other ailments treated in the home fall into the category of medicinas caseras, until they become serious. Magical causes of illness, such as witchcraft or *la viuda* (the enchanted widow), are lumped together with similar Aymara phenomena, such as the khan achachi. As there are many Spanish translations for Aymara terms, this merging of elements of Hispanic folk and Aymara medical traditions does not seem incongruous.

After I had been in the field about six months and felt somewhat secure in the little rapport I had made, I collected kinship data and undertook a series of structured questionnaires on nutrition, marketing, social status, capital accumulation, disputes, world view and religious beliefs, and health. Administering these questionnaires, together with the scheduled interview on nosological, etiological, and therapeutic knowledge, took many hours and required numerous trips to each informant's house, along with a substantial outlay of gifts: beer, coca, candy, bread, meat, potatoes, and various concoctions based on gringo recipes intended to be intriguing. Particularly popular was the soy sauce I carried to mask the occasionally novel and curious if not inexplicable fare they offered me—though inevitably I became a devotee as I became accustomed to it.

Only one household, with which I had had no previous social contact, refused outright to give me information. Others put me off. People responded to most of the questionnaires as contrived, artificial situations that made them self-conscious and led them to give me answers they suspected I wanted to hear. I suspected that the questionnaire designed to elicit nutritional information was entirely useless; people told me they ate what they had seen me eat. They would admit their poverty only when we were relaxing, maybe drinking and complaining about the world market, neo-imperialism, and other forces they felt victimize the rural mestizo and campesino, or when the company present had decided that the gringa was going to "collaborate" on something. They would not admit such poverty when the anthropologist might be scrutinizing it or comparing it with other neighbors' property. Consequently I find that my data of most value is that which derived from extensive conversation, often taken with the pen in hand while someone tried laboriously and often patiently to make me understand what they were trying to explain. Kachituños rather enjoyed my picking their minds for history, understanding, and wisdom, which questionnaires, especially those that ask about one's daily activities, do not do.

When I became well known in the village I would take an idea and go from house to house with it. I spent a week trying to reconstruct the history of the fiesta system, for example. And at one point I tried to do a network analysis, inquiring about best friends, advisers, and people with the most prestige. The answers to these last questions were the beginning of my insight into the ethnicity crisis: with few exceptions no one had any best friends or advisers except their parents and siblings, and those with prestige had left town after the revolution of 1952, with the exception, of course, of the informant to whom I was talking.

Intimate discussions about stressful problems and appropriate behavior revealed that Kachituños look inside themselves for strength as much as toward friends and family; that there is little consensus on appropriate behavior; and that life for the Kachituños is a hard and lonely experience in an unpredictable world in which everything can go wrong and little goes right. This insight greatly increased my appreciation for these Kachituños who, by all local standards, let me into their lives against their better judgment and planted a fear that there might be some truth to their criticisms of me; the idea of exploiting these profoundly wonderful people had become to me intolerable.

CHAPTER 3

The Historical Context from Which Kachitu Medical Ideology Emerged

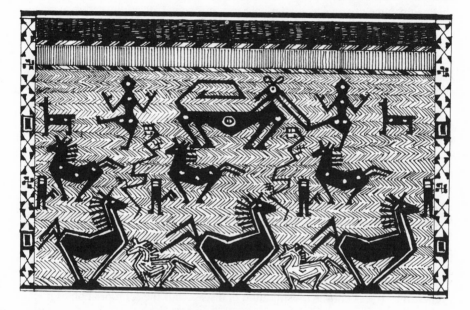

FOUR METAPHORS

Four themes consistently appear in discussions about medical etiology and diagnosis in Kachitu: insatiable hunger (like that of the khan achachi), the vulnerability of subordination (as in Maria's loss of soul to the Achachillas), victimization, and exploitation. As metaphors, they are the dimensions that Kachituños draw upon to create meaning out of the world around them. As concerns, they are the principal preoccupations of Kachituños: they emerged from historical circumstances and concrete events.

Considerable work has been done on the relationship between the perception of illness and historical context. Michel Foucault's anatomy of madness (1965) places the variations of its perception within their historical contexts to expose its cultural construction. The image of the ship of fools as a vessel for social exclusion and spiritual reintegration—evidence of God's omnipotence—which pertained at the end of the Middle Ages, shifted at the dawn of the age of reason to that of the follies of vice and unreason. Two hundred years later, in the nineteenth-century Victorian asylum where psychotherapy was born, the mad patient emerged as reason-able and thus subject to authoritative management by fear through guilt.

Susan Sontag's study of the metaphors of tuberculosis and cancer (1977) refers to the relationship between conceptualization of these diseases, and political economy. She sketches the nineteenth-century portrayal of tuberculosis as the product of limited energy expenditure and elevated creative sensitivity, the romantic metaphors of early capital accumulation, and the twentieth-century portrayal of cancer as the product of repression (insufficient investment) and energy out of control, the metaphors of advanced capitalism.

Foucault's intent was to reveal the cultural construction of illness and its consequential social and political implications; a dialectical interplay among political economy, world view, and the perception of madness reinforces and restructures each one. Building upon Foucault, Sontag's motive was to expose the inauspicious effects of the mystification of illness, particularly of "master diseases," on the fortification of asymmetrical social relations: menacing illnesses we don't understand are pregnant with metaphorical potentiality and thus service hegemonic interests of political economy. Analysis of the Kachitu data on the extraction of values and images from historical context, and their application to illness to render it comprehensible, traces not the mystification of disease, but the appropriation of metaphors to restructure social relations. In Kachitu, etiology is a metaphor for history, and use of Kachitu's metaphors in medical dialogue is an attempt to change history.

These metaphors are bandied about by Kachituños in dialogue to make statements about the ill, the audience, the opinion holder, and the relationship between the three. Deriving from the larger history of which Kachitu is a part, they are germane to the dynamics of social relations within contemporary Kachitu. History that impinged upon Kachitu constitutes the parameters around social relations and the contemporary identity crisis, and it gives the outline of meaning to the metaphors employed to change that history.

These four themes emerged from four integral components of the national political economy which have become entrenched institutions in Bolivian society. First, the notion of race has differentiated the elite (or "whites"), mestizos, and Indians to justify unequal access to political participation, the legal system, and economic resources—the very resources Kachituños try to obtain through medical dialogue. Second, unequal access led to the development of an irrational economy dependent on the wasteful exploitation of Indian labor and the allocation of greatest economic risk to the Indian population which, after 1952, shifted to include the rural mestizo on the altiplano as well. Third, the entrenchment of caudillo political structures and use of suppression to maintain civil order has inhibited effective political mobilization of the agriculturally based Indian population and the rural mestizo as social classes. Fourth, a consequential antagonism between Indian and non-Indian has expressed itself among the rural Indian population as aversion to non-Indians, and among the mestizos in the countryside as a terror of Indian retaliation. From these four historical processes, the four metaphors that are expressed in etiology, diagnosis, and medical dialogue emerged as salient to contemporary medical dialogue, and today these metaphors are persistent referents in the strategies Kachituños employ in that dialogue.

THE FIRST ENTRENCHED INSTITUTION: Race to Justify Ethnicity, and Ethnicity to Establish Class

The Spanish conquistadores effectively defined the meaning that social differentiation in Bolivia would take when in 1572 they executed the last Inca, Tupac Amaru, and members of the royal family, to secure political control over the indigenous population. Tupac Amaru was the son of Wayna Kapajj, last Inca to die while in power, and ancestor to Kachitu's town aristocrat, Doña Teresa. Doña Teresa is very proud of this fact, although she is a mestiza and believes that Indians are genetically coded to lie, steal, and stab one in the back.

Two very different roads to *mestizaje* in Bolivia's history illuminate the political motives behind the concept of race—an immutable social classification—to establish ethnicity, and the mystification of class—a permeable category—to permit the unbridled exploitation of Indian labor.

First, to insure Spanish control over the colonies, colonialists born in Spain were differentiated from colonialists' sons born in Bolivia—*criollos*—and had access to economic and political privileges lest they harbor separatist interests. The criollos, prohibited from political offices, indeed cultivated separatist interests and established among themselves caudillo enclaves that encased the altiplano in violence as they vied for power among each other and fought the crown for independence. Some made fortunes in the mines, staked out lands, and appropriated rights to Indian labor. Those unable to acquire wealth served the interests of those who did, and supervised Indian labor. These were further differentiated from the Spanish as mestizos.

Second, to insure its control over the local population the crown gave privileges to members of the indigenous aristocracy in return for loyalty and assistance in the maintenance of Spanish dominion over the Indian population. Indigenous leaders—caciques,[1] or *kurakas*—were given land and power that surpassed that of many products of Spanish-Indian unions, and thus had the legal status of mestizos *and* criollos. Social analyses of the relationship between kurakas, or caciques, and the crown have been written by Abercrombie (1986 : 24–101), Choque-Canqui (1978 : 28–32), Larson (1979), Murra (1978), Platt (1978b), Rasnake (1988), Rowe (1954), Spalding (1973, 1984), Stern (1982), and Wachtel (1977).

Criollos and caciques and their successors exploited their opportunities well into the twentieth century. People with power pursued political careers as caudillos to accumulate more of it. As these political careers were made and unmade, wealth was gained and lost in the form of land and control over Indian labor, and consequently influence. Thus "Indians" as an ethnic group within the Bolivian political structure were not descendants of Tupac Amaru's empire but that population whose labor was controlled by mestizos, criollos, and the elite. Individuals from all four groups who could do so sought their fortunes, moved from one part of the altiplano to another, fabricated genealogies, and crossed the ethnic boundaries pertaining to Aymara, Quechua, and mestizo "races."

The most successful became "Spanish elites." Simon Patiño, the great tin baron of the early twentieth century and the richest man in the world at that time, was born of a Quechua mother and mestizo father. Although he was rebuffed as a social equal by the Bolivian elite and removed himself in a huff to Europe and New York, his children were acknowledged as genuine representatives of the upper class. Thus Indians and criollos flowed into mestizo enclaves, and mestizos moved into Indian and criollo domains, according to their fortunes, and the most successful became white.

M. Rigoberto Paredes's *Los Siñani* (1968), a history of the town of Carabuco, not too far from Kachitu, vividly demonstrates the development of its local mestizo class as a rising Aymara aristocracy through the leadership of its caciques. And many of the characters in his history came to Kachitu at the turn of the twentieth century to take advantage of growing opportunities there, enter the local mestizo class, and establish a vecindario. These mestizos however, like the majority, were unsuccessful aspirants to *caudillismo* and the accumulation of substantial wealth. To at least establish or maintain themselves as mestizos on an auspicious route to gentility, they sought to serve the interests of the elite in the countryside. Thus arose the anthropological myth that mestizos are the despised class because they are neither white nor Indian (Carter 1958). In fact it was their limited access to land and riches, their subsequent inability to finance careers as caudillos, and the consequential limitation of their careers to overseers and managers of Indian laborers in the mines and on the haciendas which contributed to the mutual aversion of them by poor Indians and the elite alike. Membership in the mestizo class had no "racial" coherence from its very inception but was defined in cultural terms that were founded in economic and political circumscriptions. Ethnicity, which did not exist on the altiplano before the fifteenth century, emerged from those circumscriptions, and the four metaphors describe them from the Indian perspective.

The vast majority of the Bolivian population, however, remained Indian. Their constant revolts have been so extensive and the literature on them is so vast[2] that Leon G. Campbell (1979) has composed a review of primary and secondary source materials on the subject. It was upon Indian labor and resources that the social mobility of the rest depended. Until the 1940s, the racial boundaries of these ethnic groups were encoded in law under Spencerian evolutionary philosophy. Indian use of dress and language were restricted; their education was prohibited. When in 1931 the Methodists and Canadian Baptists established the first Indian school in Huatahata, some fifty miles from Kachitu, even proponents referred to it as utopian-socialist because it sought to educate Indians. Local hacienda owners and rural mestizos lobbied fiercely against it and had it closed down in 1943. On August 20, 1943, in defense of governmental opposition to the organization of unions in the mines after the December 1942 massacre at Catavi, Diomedes de Pereyra published in the *Commonweal* (August 20, 1943) an account of the "Bolivian Indian" as

> slothful and morose . . . [an addict] to coca, chicha and distilled alcohol. . . . He is aware of these consequences, yet, like the fatalist weakling that he is, he accepts them as the enjoyment most ready at hand to his futile and ephemeral existence. Psychologically, then, the Indian is an apathetic suicide, and it is not the farm owners or the mine operators who are responsible for his wretchedness. It is his bankrupt nature. . . . [H]e is a pervert, stultified of his own free will by two of humanity's most hideous vices: the drug habit and debauchery . . . [He] is a tumbledown, tottering specimen of humanity.

Opposed to unionization, he wrote,

> Rights can only emanate from the maturity of the workers in their social and industrial preparation, from attainments that will make them morally solvent and respectable. You can no more expect Indian workers (whose stage of development still places them in the category of embryos) to deal soberly with momentous questions escaping even the scope of high-minded people than demand of the infants in a kindergarten that they formulate their own nursery regulations. These Indian workmen whom the Republic so frivolously entrusted with boundless liberty, are constantly being agitated by utopian or opportunist politicians aiming

to import extremist patterns of dictatorships to their as yet patriarchal country. [These politicians are] would-be Lenins, Trotskys, or Stalins. . . . The large proportion of Indians in the population of the country has handicapped tremendously the half million white Bolivians scattered over a large, landlocked territory.

Within this ideological framework, patronage of the Indian was perceived as benevolent charity. The patron-client relationship of protectorate and dependency, of master and servant, that developed between the hacienda patron and his Indian laborers gave meaning to ethnicity in Bolivia, defined inter-ethnic relations, and became the model of authority justified by the notion of race, which in 1978 continued to pervade social relations that support the hegemonic political and economic structure. It defines the parameters of Aymara and mestizo world views and produces the four metaphors specifically in the context of Aymara-mestizo relations.

Elderly Aymara who lived in Kachitu in 1977 and 1978 would recall the hacienda life before 1952 with uncompromised bitterness and assert that they had to bend and kiss the feet, not only of the patron, but of all mestizos and whites as a form of greeting. Some said they had to share their brides with the patron on their wedding night, and that their fingers were cut off if it were discovered that they could read and write. Whether these tales are elaborations or evidence of common practice is not as clear as the nature of social relations between ethnic groups that such tales structure, even today. In 1978 work was still so hard, food still so scarce, and disease still so endemic as to produce a life expectancy of forty-seven years. Today peasant hunger is still alleviated by coca on the altiplano, much as it was during the colonial era when Indians refused to work unless the Spanish provided enough leaf. The structure of social relations between owner and laborer, elite and peasant, capitalist and merchant, politician and plebian, is described in terms of the four metaphors by mestizos and Indians alike, although in different contexts and with different applications because, in spite of the racial myth that masked their common origins and asymmetric dependency, they shared confluences of the same culture.

THE SECOND ENTRENCHED INSTITUTION

An Irrational Economy That Generated Insatiable Hunger

The economy that emerged from the colonial era was irrational: it inhibited internal capital investment, impeded technological advancement, particularly on the altiplano, and continued to do so through 1988 with no indication of change. The exploitation of Indian labor on the altiplano as cheap and unlimited was essential not only to the development of capital in the mining sector, to the clearance of virgin forest to make way for agribusiness (sugar and cotton; Gill 1987) and cattle in the lowlands, and to the cocaine industry, but to the development of prestige structures outside the capitalist sector altogether: to rural elite hacendados wealthy in land and Indians, who produced virtually nothing for the market. The employment of the four dominant metaphors in Kachitu medical dialogue is directly traceable to the effects of this irrationality on the indigenous population.

An Irrational Economy That Generated Labor

The Spanish crown originally established the system of *encomienda* throughout Latin America to entice Spanish settlement and loyalty in the New World. Key to this system was Indian servitude and labor. The resultant abuse of Indians by the colonists led the crown to replace that system with *repartimiento*, and eventually the hacienda system and pongueaje obligations that allowed landlords to demand rent from Indians in the form of labor and services, in return for Christian knowledge. For usufruct rights in Bolivia, hacienda Indians were responsible for all the patron's agricultural production; for the provision of seed for the following year; for animal husbandry, including shepherding, cleaning, and caring for the animals; for all domestic services within the patron's country estate and in his house in the city if he had one; for preparation of agricultural goods to be taken to market and transportation of the goods by mule or llama; for payment of the hacendado's taxes; and for any other services the hacendado wished. Indians not confined to haciendas lived in "free" comunidades subject to taxes paid in the form of labor in the mines. Unlimited free labor gave the owners no incentive to invest in fertilizers, irrigation, or other agricultural improvements or in modern mining equipment. The extent of abuse under this system has been written about at length in the literature on Bolivia,[3] not because it was unique by any means in the New World, but because it lasted so long, until 1952, without directly contributing to the accumulation of export capital. Although President Villarroel abolished pongueaje in 1945, the decree was never enforced and his execution put an end to the issue. In Bolivia, wealth was measured by land ownership, dominion over Indian servitude, and links to the mining elite.

In the nineteenth century, when the Central American indigenous population became essential to the production of coffee on *fincas* and haciendas, and in
the early twentieth century when it became essential to U.S. investment in fruit
on agribusiness plantations, the Central American equivalents of pongueaje were
displaced by absentee landlords, often in the form of international corporations.
Bolivia, however, continued to rely almost totally on mining until the 1950s, as it
had done since 1572 when Potosi became the principle source of currency in the
world economy, and "the treasure of the world and the envy of kings" was exploited by such extravagantly undisciplined and wasteful use of Indian labor that it
decimated the indigenous population (Barton 1968 : 122).

With free Indian labor until 1952, the hacendados and *latifundistas*, owners
of vast estates, had no incentive to invest their scarce capital in the intensification
of agricultural production. Because so little was being produced, agricultural goods
had a guaranteed market, and their prices remained high. Thibodeaux maintains
that hacendados artificially limited production in order to keep prices in the cities
high (1946 : 195–196). Given the absence of any marketing risk, the latifundistas
and hacendados provided their laborers with neither tools nor seed, and thus only
rudimentary technology and poor quality seed were employed. The limitations in
quality and quantity of production resulted in insufficient production to feed
Bolivia's increasing population, particularly in the urban sector, and agricultural
imports rapidly rose in the first half of the twentieth century to approximately one
third of all imports by 1950.

Thus while throughout much of the rest of Latin America, indigenous labor
(and slave labor until the nineteenth century) was involved in capitalist production
for the world market, most of Bolivia's indigenous population had been released
from direct articulation with the world market since the eighteenth century when
the Spanish withdrew its search for gold and silver essential to its own economy
(Stein and Stein 1970). The Aymara and Quechua who served as labor reserves
for mining, which produced at varying times 70 percent to 90 percent of the national income, constituted, by the twentieth century, only 3 percent of the Bolivian population. Until the 1950s Bolivia had no other source of national income,
was dependent on Indian agricultural production, and required a labor reserve for
the mines. The consequential critical need to control the indigenous population in
an unproductive agricultural economy led to the rigorous enforcement of a racial
basis of ethnicity in order to justify such exploitation. Tumiri Apaza (1978) discusses the continued irrational exploitation of Indian labor by the Bolivian government after the mines were nationalized in 1952.

Exploitation by race is a medical ideological axiom, an etiological principle on
the altiplano. It is expressed in multiple illnesses caused by the insatiable hunger
of noncorporeal entities like the khan achachi and the achachillas, who do not, like
microorganisms in cosmopolitan medicine, invade or infect, but eat the spirit or

soul or heart of—according to Aymara and mestizos alike—only Indians: only the subordinate are vulnerable.

An Irrational Economy That Limited Ownership of Land

Until the MNR (Movimiento Nacional Revolutionario) revolution of 1952, which put an end to the agricultural and mining elite and implemented a land reform, Indian communal land ownership was sacrificed to the exploitation of Indians as a labor reserve, the suppression of agricultural production to increase prices in the city, and prestige as the principal interest in land. As land was easily expropriatable on the foundation of race, the process of reversing the relationship between free and landless Indians began as soon as independence was declared from Spain. By the dawn of the nineteenth century the majority on the altiplano belonged to free, self-governing communities relegated to the poorest soils and divested of mechanisms that had stimulated surplus agricultural production in the precolonial era, of economic networks, and of rights to citizenship. They were vulnerable to the exploitation of hacendados, miners, government officials, and the army, without compensation. In 1846 a national census determined the rural population to compose 89 percent of the national population (Klein 1969 : 160) of which 23,107 were hacendados or patrones within 5,000 families; 261,468 individuals were free Quechua and Aymara Indians, and 360,000 were landless estate Indians who had lost their lands to the encroaching hacendados (Klein 1969 : 7).[4] Throughout the nineteenth century, these 5,000 hacendado families constituting 2.3 percent of the rural population aggressively implemented the Liberal laws defining private property as an absolute individual right. The goal of the Liberal reforms of the nineteenth century was to privatize land tenure, and their usurpation of Indian land has been recorded and examined by Tristan Platt (1982a). By 1900 free Indians numbered 250,000, and by 1950 a mere 140,000, even though the rural population remained around 70 percent of the national total during that time. Thus by the twentieth century most of the Bolivian population on the altiplano were landless and working on haciendas. The rise of the Kachitu vecindario rested on the last great surge of Liberal appropriation of communal Indian land.

On the eve of April 9, 1952, when the MNR revolution occurred, the rural agricultural economy was stagnant even though 87.2 percent of the Indian population was involved in agriculture. According to the 1950 census, 72 percent of the economically active population of Bolivia were engaged in agriculture and allied industries but they produced 33 percent of the gross national product. Only 2 percent of the total land area of Bolivia was under cultivation. The Keenleyside report of the United Nations Mission of Technical Assistance to Bolivia declared that "the land tenure system almost completely blocked the development of a progressive agriculture" (Goodrich 1971 : 8). That land was divided into 86,377 properties in what Klein (1969 : 394) has called "one of the most badly distorted land-ownership distribution patterns in Latin America."

Of these 86,377 properties, those consisting of 1,000 hectares or more belonged to 6.3 percent of the total number of landowners, yet their land covered 91.9 percent of the total owned property. Landowners, including free Indians and rural mestizos, who owned *minifundias*, or small landholdings of less than 1,000 hectares, made up 93.7 percent of all landlords and controlled 8.1 percent of the total number of privately owned lands. Burke, also relying on the 1950 census, confirms these figures: "Three-fourths of the country's agricultural population had no property rights. Although 30 percent of the total land area was classified as arable, only 2 percent was cultivated. There was also an inverse relationship between the size of holdings and area cultivated. While the smallest agricultural units cultivated 44 percent of their land, the largest estates, comprising 92 percent of all land, cultivated only 1 percent of their holdings" (1971 : 302).

This pattern of designed inefficiency had been paralleled in the mining industry until all but very low quality tin in the most poorly accessible veins had been exhausted by 1952. Hence the tin industry stagnated while the cost of production increased, and yet the national income remained more dependent upon tin than upon any other type of production. The consequences of this 400-year-old pattern of investment, or rather lack of it, encouraged the conservative middle class to join the revolutionary party of 1952, making the MNR takeover a relatively easy affair. Indeed, Bolivia's economic retardation had reached such critical proportions that the MNR's radical visions of social change appealed even to conservative elements.

Irrational Effects of the Revolution

The MNR land reform is the only comprehensive land reform in Latin America outside Castro's Cuba and Ortega's Nicaragua. However, the extent to which it constituted a radical change for the Aymara was tempered by the nature of the reform.[5] While the Aymara and Quechua did indeed get title to their land, this was, in most cases, all they got: title to the small plot they had been allowed to cultivate for their subsistence on the haciendas. Because on the altiplano population pressure was high to begin with, because the hacendados and latifundistas were allowed to keep some of their land, and because there were thousands of landless peasants waiting for land, there was, in fact, little redistribution, and precious little for everyone. In many cases the Aymara continued to work the hacendados' and latifundistas' lands and brought the owners' produce to La Paz until the plots became legally the Aymaras', or the Aymara gave such produce to the new revolutionary peasant *sindicatos*, or peasant unions, that levied their own taxes with their newfound power. Often the Aymara sold the land to defray expropriation costs.

In terror, many of the rural mestizos fled the countryside. The small entrepreneurs, shopkeepers, and middlemen who had lived off the Indians' small surpluses and exchanged produce between the countryside and La Paz virtually disappeared. The previous market structure collapsed. Decisions concerning crops, livestock, managing, and marketing reverted after the revolution to the individual Aymara. As a result, spontaneous markets for the Indians' small agricultural surpluses sprang up throughout the altiplano. Some, like the Saturday market that now meets at a crossroads just south of Kachitu and the Thursday market that now meets just north of Kachitu, established themselves as permanent marketplaces where the peasants could buy and sell and avoid the tax that mestizo-controlled municipios like Kachitu levied upon them (as they still do). Many of these markets grew into "urban centers." Peasants began to build houses in which to stay on market day. The first were built around town plazas in a strategy to become the vecinos and town leaders when they could afford to transform the market into a permanent settlement, as the rural mestizos had done before them in Kachitu. As the plazas were drawn up, there developed a need for town officials, truck and bus transport, and small shops and pensions, as well as opportunities for further commercial activity. Gradually, central institutions such as the National Confederation of Campesinos, sindicatos, schools, and most significantly, Protestant churches, also established themselves in these purely Indian towns. It is here in the social, political, and economic spheres of the rural towns that the revolution had its greatest impact, not in land nor in access to national political power.

Yet even these gains were restricted. In 1977, the price of food in Bolivia was kept artificially low by the government to favor the urban working classes, impeding any attempt by campesino food producers to accumulate wealth. A black market in industrial and commercial goods flourished. Agribusiness in the lowlands, particularly cotton, received government subsidies and boomed, while the campesino's agricultural economy on the altiplano was regulated and impeded by the government. The profit the average landed peasant could gain from the surplus from an average of ten hectares prohibited further investment in land. In Kachitu, the ubiquitous family cow that drew the plow in the 1950s when William Carter lived there had been replaced when I lived there by the foot plow. Most official positions in Kachitu and the other towns in the altiplano are not elective but delegated by political authorities in La Paz. Virtually no industry exists in Bolivia, and thus there is a very limited labor market in the formal economic sector for the unemployed population. Employment on the altiplano is limited principally to teaching school, which falls under the federal payroll, is poorly paid, and carries heavily sanctioned political strings with it.

The land reform hit the rural mestizos far harder than it hit any other group. Although they had never played a role in the national political sphere, they now were no longer even socially or politically superior to their Aymara neighbors. The revolution on the altiplano saw them as the opposition. There was no place for them in the campesino sindicatos set up by the MNR government which permitted only "true peasant types"—and only hacienda Indians at that.

In the years following MNR rule, the effects of land reform on the altiplano have been seen in a doubling of the population, presumably due to improved nutrition, increased income and economic opportunities, and decreased infant mortality. This in turn has led to greater intensification of land use where investment in terms of modern equipment and fertilizers has not occurred. Erosion and soil depletion and necessarily longer fallow periods have resulted. The size of the average private plot of land has decreased since 1952. Increased population, increased consumption, and a decrease in the amount of cultivatable land due to extensive agricultural practices has not permitted any sizable increase in cash income from the sale of agricultural produce (Burke 1971:315). In fact, Carter (1965:74–75) showed that the overall acreage allotment per household dropped. Furthermore, without investment and agricultural intensification, agricultural patterns on the altiplano provide virtually nothing exportable and therefore nothing with which to integrate the Aymara on the altiplano, and around Kachitu, into the national economy and life. Though they were promised participation in the national political order and economy in return for their support for the MNR revolution, the Bolivian Indians received little and the mestizos lost a great deal. Metaphors for insecurity and subordination, victimization and exploitation, which had previously been employed by the Indians and motivated movement into the mestizo class, were now appropriated by mestizos as inequality reemerged after the MNR Revolution more widely than ever (Kelley and Klein 1981). This was most evident in medical ideology when mestizos in Kachitu came down with illnesses to which only Indians are presumably vulnerable, and thus altered their social relations and negotiated a change in their ethnic membership or in the content of ethnic identity.

THE THIRD ENTRENCHED INSTITUTION: The Insatiable Hunger of Caudillos and Dictators and the Vulnerability of Subordination

Bolivian caudillismo deprived Indians of land and power while promising the very opposite. It is this irony, as much as the extent of exploitation it unleashed, that infused Bolivian history with the themes of hunger, vulnerability of subordination, victimization, and exploitation which dominate medical metaphor in Kachitu. In the twentieth century, caudillismo has been transformed into dictatorship, which has shifted the negative impact of these metaphors onto the rural Kachitu mestizos as well.

Caudillos are "strong men" who, through favors and violence, seize political power. In Bolivia, caudillos cultivated power domains through the manipulation of personal favors and loyalty, and they fought each other to expand their spheres of influence. This decentralized and competitive political structure was originally encouraged by the Spanish crown as a means of maintaining royal control over a strong-willed and independent-minded population far from Spain: rule by division. Within the broader parameters of independence in 1825, caudillismo flourished. Of Bolivia's nineteenth century, Carter once wrote, "for many decades it was a notable event for a Bolivian president to finish his term of office alive" (1958:39). Caudillos differed from dictators not only by the magnitude of their power and institutionalization, but by their ability to mobilize Indian support through patron-client relations. Caudillismo gave way to dictatorship when Indians as a social class began to oppose the state. Dictators inherited from their caudillo predecessors the unbridled use of force, which was facilitated by the importation of German nazi elements after World War II[6] and lubricated with North American economic pressures and International Monetary Fund restrictions throughout the twentieth century. As caudillismo had consisted of conical structures of power, Indians could ally themselves with mestizos and the elite until well into the nineteenth century. But since independence Indians have suffered dictators and caudillos whose principle interests have been to further disempower rural mestizos and Indians alike. They have destroyed rather than mobilized Indian power.

Unlike caudillos, dictators have increasingly needed legitimacy from neither the Indian nor rural mestizo sectors. Their rise has corresponded with a shift in national economic power from the altiplano to the Santa Cruz lowlands, and the exacerbation of an irrational economy on the altiplano. Dictatorship, however, has expanded the risk previously placed on the back of the Indian to presently include much of the rest of the population. Although Bolivian political structure has changed since 1825, it is still not unreasonable to conceive of Garcia Meza, the cocaine dictator of 1980 and 1981, as a modern caudillo. As of 1983 when Hernan

Siles Zuazo was elected to office, caudillos and dictators had ruled Bolivia 144 out of 158 years of national independence from Spain. Between 1825 and 1980, 154 years, Bolivia experienced more than 250 political coups, as caudillos vied for the presidency, 189 of which were successful. Between 1978 and 1983 eight men and one woman occupied the office of "president."

Caudillos and dictators have shared the view that the nation is their personal property and Indians a handy source of income, although an impediment to progress. Between 1864 and 1871 Mariano Melgarejo sold large tracts of national territory to foreign powers for personal profit, including 60,000 square miles of lowlands to Brazil in return for a medal and transportation rights on Brazilian rivers, and the entire Bolivian Pacific coastlands to Chile in return for half the revenues gained there. A century later little had changed. On October 8, 1980, Garcia Meza mandated the exploitation of semiprecious stones on land in La Gaiba near the Brazilian border which belonged to the Corporacion de las Fuerzas Armadas para el Desarrollo Nacional (COFADENA) by a firm known as Rumy Limited in return for 50 percent of all sales, which reverted to himself, Waldo Bernal, and Ramiro Terrazas, the other members of his ruling junta (*El Deber*, Santa Cruz, May 6, 1981). In 1981 Garcia Meza's foreign minister, Mario Rolon Anaya, was not indicted for withdrawing $87,000 from the Banco Central to buy a decorative glass cow from East Germany for the state university in Trinidad which the university had not ordered.

In 1866 when Melgarejo had emptied the treasury, he turned to the Indian in search of a source of income for his bankrupt nation: he declared all land occupied by Indians to be state property and mandated Indians to obtain legal title and pay a tax of from 25 to 200 pesos within sixty days, without which all land reverted to the state and was sold to "whites." That action deprived over 100,000 Indians of their land. In 1980, Garcia Meza took control of Bolivia with the support of Klaus Barbie and cocaine dollars (Dunkerley 1984:320), mandated an increase in coca production, and implemented an informal tax system for personal gain (*El Heraldo*, Mexico, August 14, 1980; *New York Times*, August 31, 1980; *Wall Street Journal*, May 8, 1981) which brought in revenues estimated to be as high as $8 million in 1981 when the value of legal exports was less than $1 million for 1980 (*New York Times*, August 6, 1982). Between 1980 and 1983 the treasury was empty on many occasions. Opposition by the Indian miners at Potosi, Huanuni, Siglo XX-Catavi, Corocoro, Caracoles, and Viloco was met with the worst massacres in Bolivia's mining history, in which there have been many. On August 4, 1980, after executing atrocities upon women and children, the government "disappeared" more than 900 miners (PADI 1981; Dunkerley 1984:295–296). To acquire revenue for the state in this grotesque economy, on January 9, 1981, Garcia Meza froze all wages, reduced subsidies on staple items (but not on bank loans for agribusiness in Santa Cruz), and nearly eliminated all social security and health benefits to decrease government costs at the expense of the campesinos, the rural mestizos, and the urban laborers. Dunkerley observes (1984 : 300) that, "while the other states of the southern cone had "Chicago Boys" of the Milton Friedman school, Bolivia's belonged to the Al Capone tradition."

Caudillismo often backfired and shifted national power from one elite sector to another, exacerbating conditions in the countryside. The War of the Pacific, in which Indians were virtually kidnapped and sent to the front, was a desperate attempt to regain the Pacific coastland of Antofagasta that Melgarejo had lost to Chile. Although Bolivia was defeated hopelessly in the first battle in 1879, my daughter Anna was taught to sing every morning as she entered school in 1978 a patriotic song about reclaiming the territory, and relations with Chile were suspended in that year over the issue. That war caused the first of several changes in elite class structure which eventually led to the MNR revolution. The defeat cost the nineteenth-century agricultural elite their legitimacy. They were displaced by a conservative silver oligarchy who lost their control to the tin barons at the turn of the century when the silver deposits were depleted. The tin barons, Patiño, Aramayo, and Hochschild, were themselves displaced by the 1952 revolution engineered by the MNR after the military defeat in the Chaco War, the near exhaustion of tin reserves, and an unrecoupable drop in the price of tin on the world market.[7] Until the arrival of the postrevolutionary generation of dictators, Rene Barrientos Ortuño (1964–1969), Hugo Banzer Suarez (1971–1978), and Luis Garcia Meza Tejada (1980–1982), each ascension to power relied to some extent on Indian support which, once power was attained, was betrayed.

The Liberal silver administrators (1889–1920) allowed the Aymara to believe that when they, the Liberals, gained power, they would return the lands appropriated by Melgarejo. When this did not occur, the Aymara around Achacachi revolted under the leadership of Temible Willke (pronounced Vilca) in 1899. They were, of course, unsuccessful. As a result, Liberal legislation affected the Indians and rural mestizos on the altiplano, particularly in Kachitu, in three ways: it promoted education for all except Indians; it opened the country to religions other than Roman Catholicism in 1906, allowing the Methodist church to establish the mission in Kachitu; and it promoted private property as an absolute individual right, opening Indian community lands. Thus the mestizo class of small landholders was able to establish itself in Kachitu. As a result, town markets expanded on the altiplano and a road network along with them. This market expansion further widened the niche for mestizos in Kachitu while it all but eliminated community-held, free Indian territory.

The rationale for this pillage was that the Indian revolts were quite the opposite of a pursuit of justice: a fanatical move to restore Incaic communism and exterminate all "whites." This was a classical nineteenth-century liberal attitude that I heard repeated in Kachitu in 1977 and 1978 when vecinos referred to the same "Indian Problem" that President Bautista Saavedra had addressed at the beginning of the century: he, the press, the intellectual community, and political commentary held that Indians had no legitimate ground for grievance against the "whites," and that their problems were self-inflicted: Indian communities, they claimed, reject all attempts at reform, impede progress, and maintain through collective ownership an inherited hatred for "whites," whom they falsely accuse of oppression and usurpation. Consequently free Indian comunidades and collective ownership should be destroyed in the name of progress.

Indian revolts have always been commonplace and still are, as Garcia Meza's regime confirmed. Relations with the United States have not helped. During the years of the tin barons Bolivia's economy persisted in a chronic state of crisis, and its dependence upon the United States grew to enormous proportions. Between 1927 and 1930 the prices for tin, the major source of income for the Bolivian state, plummeted. The annual monetary gain of tin exports was less than it had been in 1916 even though annual tonnage had doubled. In response Bolivia cut its tin production by two-thirds. The result of these efforts had no effect on the price of tin but impoverished the Indian workers in the mines and further decreased government incomes. The miners struck. The state responded militarily. The world depression took its own multifaceted toll. Internal turmoil kept the nation under a state of siege for more than three years. The economic crisis and foreign debt, mostly to the United States, increased to the extent that in 1926 the government's obligations represented 33 percent of the value of the national income for that year. Seen as shocking in those days, Bolivia's foreign debt actually surpassed the national income in 1985. With no flexibility in 1930, Bolivia defaulted on U.S. loans, which it would do again in 1985. As a result, the urban middle classes were willing to follow the elites and President Daniel Salamanca into the Chaco in the hopes that the war would alter Bolivia's fortunes. Indians, however, were not, and they had to be forced into service by military squads mobilized to hunt them down to serve as shock troops on the front lines. In the hot, thorny Chaco, with little resistance to malaria and no interest in the war, 50,000 Aymara and Quechua lost their lives.

Salamanca's caudillo approach to the war, and his defeat, transformed the Chaco into the turning point for revolution in Bolivia. To the front he sent the disfavored: Indians and assorted leftist idealists, and there they discovered each other. Those not eliminated mingled, developed revolutionary strategies, and emerged from the Chaco with the seeds of the MNR. When the armies returned home, social relations in Bolivia had been changed forever. The tidy constructed division between Indians and non-Indians, the alliance between the middle classes—the mestizos—and the elite, and the unity of the elite were broken. In

These gestures, however, were sabotaged by economic forces beyond COMI-BOL's and the MNR's control. As the tin barons had known for years, the rich ore had long since been extracted from the mines and additional exploration brought continuously lower-grade ore. The United Nations estimated that Catavi was by that time mining ore that contained only 0.8 percent tin (Goodrich 1971:7). The Korean War inflated the world price of tin to $1.90 a pound, at which point the United States, which had bought 80 percent of Bolivia's tin, refused to buy. Production dropped 60 percent, while the gross value of exports fell from $141 million to $65 million in the first seven years after the revolution. Inflation consequently became astronomical, the highest in the world at that time. It effectively wiped out the elite based on urban property, as well as much of the traditional middle class, and within twelve years helped destroy the MNR.

Thousands of Indian peasants from Achacachi, the capital of the province that encompasses Kachitu, played a significant role in the revolutionary coup for the potential such a revolution promised them. Consequently, when no land reform appeared, they joined a nationwide peasant revolt, throwing hacendados who had not fled off the countryside, burning and looting hacendado and rural mestizo property. In this chaos, the COB recognized the potential in radicalizing the revolution and aligning themselves with the peasants to gain control over them and thus of the MNR party. Through their civilian militia program they roamed the countryside to arm the peasants, encouraged them to take over haciendas, and organized them into peasant unions, or sindicatos. The sindicatos in turn organized themselves around caudillo caciques who controlled their domains almost as completely as small sovereign states. On the altiplano Achacachi became one of the two nuclei of these armed groups. There, earlier organizational ties with labor on the one hand, and with the Methodist mission schools in Huatahata, Huarisata, and Kachitu on the other, provided leaders.

The rest of the MNR tried to stifle the peasant uprisings and sent in police to defend the landowners and destroy the sindicatos. However, Paz Estenssoro was losing control in all areas. Without the elite, the major link that had held the bifurcated Bolivian social structure together was destroyed. With armed unionized Indians and the disappearance of the hacendado in the countryside, actual power over the altiplano ended up not in La Paz, but in the hands of the peasant caudillo caciques.

Under these circumstances it appeared advantageous to ride with the swell of the peasant revolt, bow to the inevitable, grant land reform and universal suffrage, and thereby gain peasant support. On January 9, 1953, Paz legitimized the peasant sindicatos and established a commission to study and advise on the form the reform should take. However, when he signed the land reform into law seven months later in the presence of 150,000 armed and cheering Aymara and Quechua campesinos in Uncia, the law simply ratified a fait accompli.

The law he signed, however, was hastily written in ninety days to appease the campesinos and maintain a semblance of order. It was fundamentally a liberal document based on Spanish concepts of individualism and private property and ignored indigenous concepts of land tenure and settlement patterns, agricultural practices, and economic needs. The fact that its thorough lack of attention to indigenous and ecological factors would inhibit production is secondary to its creation of the sindicato as the principal interface between the government and the campesino population, which still constituted the vast majority of Bolivia's population. Through this maneuver the sindicato simply displaced the hacienda as a mechanism of social control. Campesino caudillos shifted their attention to contention among themselves, disputes over land, competition over political favors, control over markets, and increasing their dominions: the land reform effectively neutralized the campesinos as a social class with any significant political power.

The neutralization of the sindicatos as a powerful representative of the campesino class (rule by division) was insured by its very structure. To combat the vacuum created by the disappearance of many mestizos, the landlords, and the hacienda system, and to organize the sindicatos and keep them out of the hands of more leftist groups, Paz Estenssoro established the National Confederation of Campesinos to represent the peasant in governmental affairs, the Ministry of Rural Affairs to coordinate the sindicatos, and the sindicatos to provide information, agricultural assistance, social development, education, credit, cooperatives, and technical assistance. Except for rural education, none of these services materialized. The conical structure through which information and services were supposed to flow, however, underwrote the further development of caudillismo on the altiplano. Through this structure, the power of the sindicatos was never centralized but atomized under the caciques. The amount of power each sindicato wielded varied. Many were consolidated, twenty or thirty into a "central" that officiated over them. Many did become nuclei of social, political, and economic organizations, especially in Achacachi, Huarina, and Huarisata. But this always happened under the leadership of local caciques who fought each other for power.

Probably the most powerful of these caciques was Toribio Salas, the cacique of Achacachi, who virtually controlled the entire department, including Kachitu. He had his own militia and barracks at a time when the national government had transformed the army into a construction crew. He monopolized force, levied taxes, bought more arms and ammunition, made laws, and punished transgressors. No comparable leaders or powerholders emerged from Kachitu, perhaps because Toribio Salas eclipsed them, perhaps because he put a stop to any potential competitors, perhaps because Eulogio Añaguaya was loyal to him for giving him a vast number of positions and titles to parade around Kachitu.

With their own armies, these caciques were the law on the altiplano and throughout the countryside, and immune to state law. They could block roads and thereby threaten La Paz with starvation. Hence they supported or threatened the MNR government as they chose. As a result, the National Confederation of Campesinos never became unified; it vacillated between powerful caciques, never projected a coherent political line, and never developed into an active institution. The power of the caciques, which derived from constituencies drawn from their personal, social, and compadrazgo ties, was based on their ability to reciprocate resources for loyalty and manpower. Much of their access to resources depended on their ability to mobilize a threatening body of armed Indians and manipulate the MNR government. Peasant dependence on the patron had merely been transferred to the cacique. Thus their structure was self-limiting. They remained a series of self-serving cells, which diverted peasant access to national political power granted through the universal suffrage law. Even such access was rendered irrelevant in 1963, when dictatorship indisputably reasserted itself in Bolivia: active peasant sindicatos on the altiplano disappeared and free elections along with them.

An Irrational Land Reform

The formation of sindicatos around caudillos was not alone to blame for the subversion of Indian participation in the national economic and political domain. The implementation of the reform itself stultified the development of any potential campesino economy. The majority of the MNR had wanted to give those Indians bound to a hacienda or latifundia legal title to their small plots but to maintain the basic traditional hacienda structure. The COB had pushed for complete expropriation without indemnification facilitated with twenty-five-year bonds at 2 percent interest, granting all land traditionally worked by peasants to the peasants, expropriating the majority of hacienda land and archaically run holdings for redistribution. But the law preserved all agricultural enterprises, holdings in which modern methods were being employed, and a portion of all landholdings, for the landowner. Size of holdings was presumably determined by ecological and demographic characteristics. In fact, most were too small for subsistence—the first flaw in the land reform program. In 1959, of the 64,280 units of property in the department of La Paz in which Kachitu sits, 45,281 were less than one hectare in size.

Second, each individual land title had to be signed by the president. Consequently most applications for title were blocked. It was not until 1968, when the Cuban revolution had encouraged the U.S. administrations during the 1960s to view land reform as essential to blocking revolution in Latin America, that actual transference of title got rapidly underway. The U.S. Agency for International Development (USAID) sent mobile brigades to Bolivia, handled land titles in Washington with an IBM computer, and thereby processed 360 to 400 per hour, rather than the previous average of 36 per day (Carter 1965 : 245).

Third, the amount of money the government set aside for agrarian reform was consistently one of the smallest items on the national budget: between 1954 and 1969, 1.5 percent to 2.0 percent of the annual budget was alloted to land reform. This not only limited activities but encouraged graft among employees, who earned scandalously low wages. Joseph Thome, consulting for USAID, wrote:

> The list of deficiencies is staggering: the Departmental Offices have no money for mailing case files to La Paz and must charge this to campesinos; [the Council] . . . has only two serviceable vehicles for the entire nation; and, as of August 31, 1966 [the Council] . . . has already used up 80 percent of its operating budget for 1966, which, among other things, means that it will not be able to provide any more paper, stationery or pencils to any of its 386 employees (1966 : 20).

Fourth, the law did not specify exactly how land should be divided beyond simply giving it to those who worked it. Consequently distribution tended to follow the old usufruct pattern, often giving to some peasant families several tiny plots scattered in a variety of different places, giving differential amounts to most families, and creating great disparities between holdings. This contributed to social stratification among the peasants themselves and discriminated against the masses of landless because those with more land could afford the legal costs of claim presentation. Bastien delineates the effects of the reform's lack of adherence to Andean land-use patterns as socially destructive (1978 : 32–34, 290, 35n).

Fifth, the law did not affect the free Aymara communities at all; free Aymara gained little from the reform, and they constitute half of the population within the canton of Kachitu. Futhermore they were not welcome in many sindicatos organized around caciques from ex-haciendas who controlled through personal power and loyalties.

Finally, the reform was disastrous for the rural mestizos, the Kachitu vecindario. Having no significant influence in La Paz, and only enemies among the region's caciques, they lost most of what they had.

The End of MNR Rule and the Peripheralization of the Altiplano

When the MNR first came into power in 1952, the exchange rate was 145 pesos bolivianos to the dollar (Pick 1971). By 1956 the peso had devalued to 16,000 to the dollar. With hyperinflation, food shortages were critical. The world price of tin dropped to 80 cents a pound; benefits to the mine workers brought cost of production up to $2.10 U.S. a pound. In the following thirteen months, the MNR government issued more currency than had been issued in the previous history of

the Republic. The middle sector took the brunt of this monetary policy and abandoned the MNR. In response the MNR abandoned its anti-imperialist national
independence stand and sought U.S. aid.

The Kennedy administration's Alliance for Progress sought a state capitalist
solution that historian Malloy criticizes as being based on the assumption of the
developing technocratic middle class which in fact did not exist in Bolivia (1971 : 43).
Analysts in New York traced Bolivia's economic problem directly to the miners to
whom the MNR had given concessions while the tin industry deteriorated, and
they advised that Bolivia's economic burden be shifted back onto labor to free the
elite classes to be more economically active. Labor retaliated with strikes, demon-
strations, and violence. In order to fulfill U.S. assistance requirements, Paz Estenssoro had to break the power of local bosses. To accomplish this he resorted to
military oppression, political exile, and peasant militias. He convinced the latter
that labor was communistic and would collectivize all that the peasants had gained
in the revolution. By 1966, peasant sindicatos had completely disappeared from
the altiplano. When Paz rewrote the constitution to allow himself to preside for a
third term, he had in fact made certain economic gains: self-sufficiency in rice,
sugar, and oil, all produced in the lowlands, not in the altiplano, had increased the
gross national product growth. However, he was opposed by almost every sector
and finally toppled by a military coup, thus bringing an end to MNR and civilian
rule. Through his policies, the focus of the Bolivian economy, especially in the
agricultural sector, had shifted to the lowlands where a colonization program was
established. Between 1952 and 1966, the United States poured more than $194 mil-
lion into Bolivia, in return for a reinstatement of the Bolivian army (rendered
more efficient with U.S. training in Panama); a retraction of the revolutionary
economic policy, particularly in the labor sector; and an invitation to foreign investment, especially in oil, particularly in the lowlands, and specifically in Santa
Cruz. The altiplano became the backwaters, the periphery of the Bolivian economy. As of December, 1988, no serious investment had ever again been made on
the altiplano.[8]

THE FOURTH ENTRENCHED INSTITUTION:
Mestizo-Aymara Antagonism and the Expansion of
the Category "Exploited Victim"

The 1952 revolution was not a complete revolution in the true sense of the word. While it destroyed the hacienda system and altered relations between Indian and non-Indian, it did not change that part of the economic landscape of the altiplano which consists of the principal factors that determine capital accumulation and flow of wealth. With changed relations among Aymara, the vecindario, and the Methodists, but no substantial gain for anyone and genuine losses for others, the significance and meaning of ethnic identity that pertained for more than 400 years is no longer valid.

The greatest benefit of the revolution for the majority of Kachitu Aymara campesinos has been little more than self-respect, although self-respect counts for a lot. In 1977 and 1978 the Aymara in and around Kachitu expressed a solid distrust of many of the Kachitu mestizos and, generally speaking, most non-Aymara. In fact, they were not particularly trusting of other Aymara who live outside their province. They expressed no confidence in the national political domain to represent their interests. In the 1978 elections they accused particular mestizos, and outsiders who came to witness the voting procedures, of mishandling the ballot box. They voted unanimously for Hernan Siles Zuazo, the principal engineer of the MNR revolution in 1952, but he was prevented from assuming office after winning elections in 1978, 1979, and 1980. Their distrust was well founded and coupled with a readiness to defend their interests. When Garcia Meza took over the government in 1980, and when Paz Estenssoro, once again voted president in 1985, reduced teachers' salaries to twenty dollars a month and implemented a campesino tax in 1987, the Aymara were quick to pressure the government and block the roads. Nevertheless, in Kachitu the arrival of the Methodists and the eventual campesino appropriation of the Methodist mission provided those Aymara who joined the church with more economic and educational resources than anything the MNR or subsequent governments have supplied or permitted. They express their distrust through medical dialogue. In the guise of etiological beliefs they often accuse non-Indians of abuse of power relations or accept them as copartners in the quest for autonomy and justice.

Contemporary Downward Mobility and the Cultural Identity Crisis

While the 1952 revolution had profound effects on all of Bolivian society, it affected most the rural mestizos who lost their local superior political and social position and the basis of their economic support through the land reform, thus destroying the foundation of a cultural identity that had supported them as a class in Kachitu since the end of the nineteenth century. Distinguished, exclusive, privileged, and coherent until 1952, the Kachitu vecindario has been none of those things since. In the twenty-five years following the revolution, the most prominent and educated vecinos in town invested their time and energy in the same Victorian notion of progress espoused by the Liberals in the early years of the century. They fought hard to make Kachitu a significant urban center and a participant in the benefits of the twentieth century. But receiving no response from the government, their efforts had little effect. By 1977 and 1978, what endured of the old mestizo vecino society remained ingrown and provincial. They had learned to share with the Aymara a lack of confidence in the national government as an institution serving their interests. The majority described their relationship to the Bolivian government in much the same terms the Aymara are said to have used to describe their relationship to the vecinos before 1952. As a consequence, the themes of hunger (for resources they no longer have), the vulnerability of subordination (now to the urban sector), victimization (to forces now beyond their control), and exploitation (by interests in the La Paz government that has neglected them) exacerbate the trauma of toil that Indians once performed for them but that they must now perform for themselves. These themes are the central metaphors running through their medical dialogue. They restructure Bolivian history as they are perceived to affect all Kachituños, be they mestizo, Indian, or Methodist Aymara.

The upward and downward mobility that resulted from 1952, from the Chaco, and from the Methodist mission resulted in a different set of identity problems facing Aymara and Aymara-turned-Methodist than that which the mestizos had and still have to confront. In 1977 and 1978, while all three groups undergo changes in cultural identity in the aftermath of the revolution, the polarization of Aymara and mestizos which developed over the past hundred years in Kachitu and four hundred years in Bolivia precludes a joining of forces of these cultural groups. It does not, however, preclude the abandonment of one ethnic group for identification with another by individuals in an effort to gain access to scarce resources, material and nonmaterial. The need to do so reinforces the legitimacy of the Aymara medical tradition and the nature of the complex of medical systems and beliefs in Kachitu. Indeed it has made medical pluralism a primary mode through which local political dialogue, which defines the content of cultural identity, takes place. The content of that dialogue and its meaning is embedded in the rise and fall of the vecindario and the emergence of the Methodist church as a significant institution, both of which are predicated on the ecology of dependency that has defined social relations in Kachitu both before and after the revolution.

In 1955, the Bolivian historian M. Rigoberto Paredes wrote the following about the province in which Kachitu is situated:

> Such is the geography of the famous and legendary province of Omasuyu. Its history is intimately linked with the political convulsions of the country, as no other province has spilled the blood of their sons so abundantly in the country's civil wars. From her womb emerged the most notable public figure in Bolivia's history. In the latter half of this century, however, her population has been reduced by emigration and her inhabitants dominated by alcoholism; it is now in a state of open decline. After so many years of fighting for improvement, it now experiences true regression.

CHAPTER 4

The Ecology of Dependency

To the southeast of Kachitu, agricultural fields stretch three miles to the lake and fifty miles beyond to the closest peak of the cordillera, broken only by occasional settlements. The cordillera, looming up like a jagged, snow-capped spine, stretches to the south until it disappears over the horizon, giving the impression that one could see forever if the earth were not curved. At this altitude, radiation is intense, the sun bright and hot, and the sky cloudless, but the air is thin, and the wind is cold and perpetual. One can get a radiation burn in the sun while a glass of water freezes in the shade. Sometimes when you walk away from the village and into those fields, you walk out into an absolute silence; the only sound you can hear is the wind whipping past your ear. Such moments give the illusion that the altiplano is so vast and empty that there is nothing to hear.

On the north side of Kachitu is an escarpment running east and west which forms a back wall for the town. A narrow path climbs the escarpment from behind the center of town and behind the Catholic church, switching back fourteen times upon its ascent to symbolize the fourteen stations of the cross, until it pauses halfway up at a statue of La Virgen de la Candelaria, the patron saint of Kachitu. Beyond the Virgin it turns northwest, eventually takes a right turn in a

71

narrow pass through the escarpment, and empties into the valley on the other side. From her vantage point on the escarpment, the Virgin looks out for the well-being of the villagers and occasionally performs miracles.

Often Anna and I would walk up to the statue to look down at Kachitu and beyond, to the lake and the vast altiplano. From here one hears the perpetual wind, as well as the sounds of Kachitu: the few oxen as they are led home to their corrals in the late afternoon; the grunt of pigs and barking dogs; chickens clucking as they are fed handfuls of grain; Don Abelardo yelling across the clinic compound to Dr. Sabas that he has finished fixing the generator so that Sabas can now take an X-ray; Genara calling to Porfirio that there is soup ready for him to eat; Bonifacia scolding Bartolo and his brother Oldemar for getting into mischief; Peluquilla, the town crazy lady, announcing from the town plaza, where she is harassing someone to give her food or alcohol, the details of the most recent indiscretion committed in town; and the low murmur of Doñas Antonia, Leonora, and Elsa as they sit at the gossip corner on the plaza after a long hard day, evaluating the details of Peluquilla's announcement. From the escarpment, the impression that the altiplano is empty dissolves into the realization that the altiplano has been a center of civilization on the South American continent for several thousand years. The illusion that one can hear nothing is transformed into the reality that, in fact, one can hear almost everything that goes on in Kachitu, even that which goes on behind closed doors.

SECONDARY RESOURCES: Kachitu's Political Economy

From Peluquilla's announcements and the corners of gossip spring discussions on the health of the day's miscreants, debates over what the sick are suffering from, and arguments about what illnesses will surely befall whom: medical dialogue. The real information being communicated in these dialogues, however, concerns each person's identity, as statements are offered like pawns on a chessboard, evaluated, subsequently negotiated, and perhaps consensus is formed, but more often, disagreement. The purpose behind such dialogue is to convince enough people of the validity of a particular identity that will have repercussions that benefit the speaker: the secondary resources for which medicine and medical dialogue are a primary resource mobilized to acquire. The infrastructure that delineates those secondary resources is, of course, the political economy of Kachitu.

Before 1952 the political economy of Kachitu was contingent upon a mode of production and vecino (mestizo) exploitation of it, the form and nature of which was delimited not only by the political and economic structure from which it emerged but also by the extreme altitude and desert climate that render the area incapable of self-sufficiency. In 1978 these limitations still fertilize the contemporary need to negotiate the content of cultural identity to which medical dialogue virtually devotes itself. The limitations are now, however, exacerbated by the altiplano's increasing peripheral status in the Bolivian and world economies in the postrevolutionary context.

The fact that Kachitu exploits an ecological niche that is not self-sufficient renders the area dependent on three other zones. Furthermore, the wasteful and

extensive agricultural mode of production implemented by the Spanish and aggra-
vated by the land reform reduced the fertility of the soil. Exacerbated by the desert
climate, these factors limited agricultural production to that which could be dried
and stored for lean years and inhibited experimental crops that might have improved local nutrition, reduced local dependency on other zones, or produced a
greater variety of cash crops. Since 1952 the peripheralization of the region has
reinforced the area's dependency on other zones and on primarily barter exchange
between them. Given the extreme vagaries of the Bolivian economy and the scarcity of cash in the post-revolutionary years, the availability of barter has proved to
be a blessing rather than a handicap in recent years. Before the revolution, however, these conditions permitted the development in Kachitu of the vecindario, the
recent demise of which led to the crisis over the content of cultural identity that
medical dialogue tries to resolve.

THE LIMITATIONS OF AGRICULTURE AND
ANIMAL HUSBANDRY IN KACHITU

Kachitu sits in a valley at the mouth of a river and therefore on relatively fertile
soil. Population pressure, however, is so great in relation to actual production, that
the hillsides must be cultivated. The hillsides are covered with the ancient crum-
bling remains of terraces built under Inca colonialism, since fallen into disrepair.
They attest to the potential for agricultural intensification, but this would require
resources far beyond those available to contemporary Kachituños. The faint outlines of their broken walls cast the same shadow of disintegrated grandeur and
decay that do southern mansions strangled under the prolific kudzu vines in a
Faulkner novel.

During the Inca Empire the investment required to intensify production was
provided in the form of state mobilized labor, the annual *mit'a* tax, which generated the manpower to build and maintain an extensive terracing and irrigation
system (Murra 1980). The Spanish who took control in the sixteenth century had
no interest in the intensification of agricultural production. The mode of production established under their colonialism was as extensive and wasteful as the Inca
system had been efficient (Rowe 1957; S. Smith 1977; Stein and Stein 1970;
Vargas 1979), and this mode continued under the hacienda system until the land

reform, which in turn did not provide means with which to intensify production (Browman 1980; Dandler 1969; Kelley and Klein 1981; Zuvekas 1977, 1979).

The privately owned plots disbursed among the campesinos by the reform are too small to provide more than subsistence without some capital investment. The campesinos had no access to credit. By 1977 Kachitu families' agricultural fields had to lie fallow for between five to seven years between crops. Fallow fields are used for grazing, but grazing causes extensive erosion, especially if by sheep. Alas, the escalating costs of animal husbandry on diminishing property inheritances has forced a shift from llamas and cattle to sheep.

Inheritance patterns that grant privileges equally to all children, mandated by federal law, exacerbate the problem. The subdivision of small plots renders each inheritance insufficient to support a family. Most families have more than two inheriting children, and as there is little major industry in Bolivia to which younger generations may turn in order to leave the agricultural sector, most of those children have no other means of making a living. A consequential but modest practice of favored inheritance engenders conflict and sorrow, while actual landholdings are diminishing in size.

Marriage joins property of husband and wife, but such properties are dispersed throughout the area, often miles from each other. The settlement pattern has become scattered with houses often several hours' walk from Kachitu or one of its comunidades. The amount of land, the quality of that land, the number of years it must lie fallow, the number of plots it is divided into, the distance of such plots from the homestead and from each other, and the number of days of labor that must be devoted to preparation for planting, maintenance, and harvest—all these factors differ for each family unit, leading to different labor strategies for each family and often exacerbating social relationships. Unlike other Andean communities or groups studied by anthropologists, such as Chuschi by Isbell (1978) or the Yura by Rasnake (1982, 1988), Compi by the Buechlers (1971) or the Laymi by O. Harris (1964, 1979), no ayllus or moiety organization helps to regulate inheritance and labor in and around Kachitu.

Without irrigation, chemical fertilizers, or cooperative labor such as the *ayni* system based on kin obligations which was broken down by haciendas around Kachitu, not much can grow at 13,000 feet above sea level in a desert climate. What does grow is put to extensive use. Kachituños cut thick clumps of sharp stiff grasses, scattered scrub, low woody thola bushes, and mosslike mounds of yareta with huge pulpy roots to use for fodder, thatch, straw for adobes, stuffing for mattresses, rope, baskets, tools, and tinder. What is cultivated is highly adapted to the constrictions of the mode of production, the climate, and patterns of exchange and is thus limited to varieties of tubers and grains which can be dried and stored for the winter months, for next year's planting, for lean years, and for trade in other ecological zones. In winter months potatoes are frozen and dried in the grass for about a week, trampled by feet to extract the moisture, and finally dried in the sun to make *chuño* which, before it is reconstituted in water, is as hard as rock and, freeze-dried, can be stored for years before it begins to disintegrate. There are, in fact, many ways to freeze-dry potatoes and other tubers which vary in taste and consistency, so that one may be offered a plate of chuño, *tunta,* and *caya* for lunch and think of oneself as lucky to have such diversity. The staple potato is augmented by the indigenous grain quinoa, famous for its high protein content of 12.3 grams per 100 grams edible weight. Only three of the crops introduced by the Spanish have been adopted in Kachitu because they alone can be dried and stored: barley, peas, and broad beans.

When the Methodists came in the 1930s, they resolved to improve the bleak diet and introduced a variety of vegetables: lettuce, onions, carrots, turnips, and cabbage. In 1977, a few enterprising individuals continued to grow some of these crops, but they require more care than the local population can provide. Those who grow them face a high risk of losing the harvest, and they must devote scarce agricultural land to crops that cannot be stored. Thus, for simple ecological and economic reasons, the missionaries' efforts to expand agricultural production failed.

To augment their meager agricultural production, Kachituños raise a variety of animals. Guinea pigs squeak as they peek out from under campesino beds. Vecinos give them separate rooms of their own. Yards are given over to the chickens. Pigs optimistically rummage in the gutters, particularly around the square, looking for banana peels and other refuse from Sunday market and passing litterers. Cows, oxen, and sheep must be taken out daily to graze and are therefore limited to those families with the manpower to do so: relatively well-off campesinos. Each family has a watchdog that is left to fare for itself and certainly never given any affection. The absence of a concept of dogs as pets makes them excellent watchdogs and hard workers, but it increased the Kachituños' suspicion that I lacked certain fundamentals when I made dog food out of cornmeal and table scraps and let my dog sleep on the end of my bed. It is a rare family in Kachitu that knows the concept "table scrap."

When William Carter lived in Kachitu during the early 1950s most families owned a cow or an ox. By 1977, there were very few cows or oxen in town, reflecting the inability of the reform to increase agricultural production while new economic strategies and the health care provided at the clinic have permitted the population to grow. Those families without a cow or ox must struggle with crude foot plows, which are now ubiquitous in Kachitu.

As with the indigenous plants, all parts of the animals are used. Sheep provide dung for fuel, hides for bedding, wool for textiles, fat for consumption, and meat to tranform into cash. The pig, which grows not much bigger than a beagle at this altitude and on a limited diet, is also reserved for cash and is consumed only at feasts and fiestas. In most cases meat is the only source of cash (besides eggs). Thus its nutritional value is secondary to its market value. Were it not for the fish from the lake, Kachituños would consume protein only a few times a year.

Animals pose problems. They are taken first to the fallow fields in the valley bottom to return fertilizer to the land. They eat through fields quickly, though, and must be removed to the hillsides where their grazing exacerbates erosion. Often the adults cannot watch the animals and tend to the fields at the same time, so they relegate the responsibility for the animals to young girls from six to fifteen years of age who might otherwise go to school.

Kachituños with land, then, must choose among conflicting strategies. Ecological factors encourage them to keep their herds small and their families large to insure a sufficient number of laborers (Stinson 1978). At the same time, the inaccessibility of needed cash pushes them to increase their herds. Yet when coupled with the land usage practices presently possible, the diminishing quality of the land, the ever-decreasing amounts of land, and persistent low yields, the nutritional economic conditions of the Kachitu farmers are increasingly inadequate for large families.

Kachitu is in an ecological zone that precludes self-sufficiency in food production and thus has always required trade with three other zones in a manner that corresponds relatively closely with the archipelago extended types (Brush 1976a, 1976b:150–151; Murra 1972). These three zones are the lake region, the puna, and the eastern slopes of the Andes.

THE THREE OTHER REGIONS ON WHICH KACHITU DEPENDS

The Lake

The vast Lake Titicaca lies southwest of Kachitu and teems with fish. Unfortunately many of the fish also teem with tapeworms.[1] The indigenous fish, *karachis*, *bogas*, and *ispis*, nearly disappeared during the first half of the century when the U.S. government introduced the salmon trout, or *trucha*, to encourage tourism. The trucha rapidly consumed the indigenous species until its own population was threatened. The indigenous species sprang back, though not to their previous levels, for the ecological balance in the lake had been redefined. By the 1970s a rare trucha brought a more handsome price than any other species, and consequently they were translated into cash rather than consumed. The mischievous Bartolo and Oldemar took good advantage of this and found at least one trucha a week, for which they charged me an inflated price, a finder's fee, and a delivery charge, plus a special tax for giving me first option. Anna and I ate a lot of trucha.

Fish is consumed almost daily in Kachitu. In the early morning, women who live near the lake disperse their men's daily catch from door to door. Both the protein and the iodine in fish, which prevent goiter which is endemic on the altiplano, contribute to Kachitu's attraction as a place to live. Fish in Kachitu have a guaranteed market.

The lake region also provides totora reeds that grow just off the shoreline. The coastal waters are marked off into big square fields of cultivated green reeds, the boundaries of which demarcate private property. The roots of the reeds are eaten. The stalks are used for fodder and for making mats, mattresses, boats, thatch, and ceilings, and are, therefore, indispensable.

Although the lake is very productive, it is also dangerous. Sudden gusts of wind frequently capsize the fragile totora reed boats. The cold water is lethal. The souls of the drowned menace Kachituños. The altiplano around its shores is so flat that a human is often the tallest object within hundreds of square miles and acts as a lightning rod during electrical storms that suddenly appear. Five people were killed by lightning while we lived in Kachitu. Occasional survivors are blessed with the powers of a yatiri. The khan achachi is regularly seen in the form of a ball of fire, and achachillas inhabit all the major geological formations, including the surrounding mountains, and the lake itself.

The Puna

Puna sits behind Kachitu where the altiplano rises toward the cordillera in the north and reaches an elevation of 17,000 feet. Here wander herds of llamas and alpacas. Small mining outfits with archaic equipment extract minuscule quantities of gold and silver, lead, zinc, and wolfram, which were sold to COMIBOL until it was dissolved in 1987 by Paz Estenssoro. Tiny enclaves of humans keep their lonely vigil in the silent, windswept emptiness. On market day these people bring llama fat and meat, hides, wool, rope, and dung to Kachitu and to other markets close by, where they exchange them for fruits and vegetables and coca from the eastern slopes, fish and totora from the lake, and quinoa, potatoes, tubers, and maybe a little employment from Kachitu.

While achachillas inhabit the mountains behind the Puna, the very isolation of the puna is its principal threat. Dangerous *anchanchus,* another type of noncorporeal entity, prevail there, making travel in the Puna without prudent circumspection perilous for Kachituños.

The Eastern Slopes and Valleys

Ancient paths pass through the puna and beyond to isolated mountain passes that cross the Andes at about 17,000 feet and then drop radically into the lush, semitropical, deep and narrow valleys on the other side. Here coffee, corn, coca, fruits, and vegetables grow abundantly. Local populations from here either carry their produce on their backs for several days to reach the markets in and around Kachitu, or, since the revolution and expansion of peasant transport, use trucks owned by enterprising *cholos*.[2] Due to political turmoil, weather conditions, the condition of the roads and the vehicle, and social obligations that keep drivers preoccupied, the trip by truck still takes two days.

The trip to the eastern slopes and valleys is long and dangerous. Not only are the trails and paths isolated, they are liminal as well, the netherland between tropics and tundra, and between *camba* (lowland people) and *kolla* (highland) cultures. Among them lurk hungry supernatural entities whose appetites for human spirit, soul, and life require the traveler to take serious precaution. The hot, humid climate and lush foliage at these lower altitudes—the valley communities at 6,000 feet and the lowlands in the Amazon basin—contrast sharply with the cold altiplano desert. Malaria and the incurable *chagas* disease are endemic. Much of the population speaks Quechua. While contact with camba and trips to the area are necessary and frequent, Kachituños are wary of the eastern slopes and valleys.

THE SIGNIFICANCE OF DEPENDENCY ON OTHER ECOLOGICAL ZONES FOR THE DEVELOPMENT OF SOCIAL CLASS AND THE MEANING OF ETHNICITY

At the end of the nineteenth century, the dependency of Kachitu on these three other zones contributed to the creation of a mestizo population in town, the rise of a vecindario enshrined in racial metaphors that controlled Indian labor and exchange and the development of social class. Fundamental to this development was a population movement stimulated by those laws passed by the Liberals between 1889 and 1920, which appropriated Indian communal lands throughout the altiplano and sold them cheaply to privatize them. The vecindario of today were aspiring rural mestizos and Aymara who came to Kachitu at that time to take advantage of opportunities the land laws made available. This land policy rendered Indian labor to the new landowners, which in turn, allowed the newcomers to transform themselves into the ruling elite of the municipio and thus of the canton. The nature and mode of exchange between the three zones permitted vecino control of exchange as well. Control of Indian labor and exchange both created the vecino class and served as its very economic and political foundation. As vecinos, many were able to cultivate professions: they occupied civil offices, studied law, and taught school. All opened small stores, or *tiendas*, that sold or bartered alcohol, magical and herbal medicinal items that supply the Aymara medical tradition, and staples in exchange for labor and agricultural produce from the Aymara. Most if not all of these mestizos, however, had been Indians before the move.

The revolution of 1952 destroyed this foundation and replaced it with new alternatives that serve the minimal economic and political interests of the campesinos by removing them from direct exploitation by the vecinos. The vecinos lost most of their land and the mechanism to control Indian labor. Many soon sold what land they had left for needed cash. When no longer fettered by vecino control, the rural market expanded, permitted Methodist missions, encouraged entrepreneurship, and stimulated the rise of a class of Indians which articulates with the cash market. The vecinos found no means to accumulate resources and power in the post-revolutionary rural countryside; they had no viable alternative to their old strategies except to migrate to La Paz. And for multiple reasons many were unable to successfully undertake such a migration. In La Paz many of Kachitu's most prestigious individuals were viewed as provincial philistines unable to compete in a complex urban environment.

Those vecinos who could not migrate remained behind in varying degrees of decreasing financial and political well-being. They were left with an inherited system of values and skills that were, and still are, no longer productive. Many shifted into poverty. Campesinos, in contrast, while poor by definition, had access to land and could participate in peasant barter exchange, which supported a subsistence standard of living. By the 1970s the contracting economy left those vecinos who remained in Kachitu with no margin of flexibility; they faced an immediate risk of impoverishment. The economy of the peasantry, however, only deteriorated by generation as landholdings diminished through inheritance. Indian barter exchange in the postrevolutionary economy provided the flexibility to withstand the constrictions and convulsions of the national economy, as it still does. The best possible adaptation for vecinos in the most inflexible economic situation since 1952 has been to gain access to peasant exchange on campesinos' terms, the exploitative terms of the old vecindario being no longer an option. Access to peasant exchange according to these new dictates of social relations is today a secondary resource that medicine as a primary resource is mobilized to obtain. Such access, however, has costly implications for vecinos, and the repercussions are severe.

The shift from control over Indian exchange to egalitarian participation in it

requires the adoption of egalitarian social relations with Indians, the very anath-
ema to prerevolutionary vecino identity, and precisely that which their forefathers
came to Kachitu to transform into asymmetrical exploitative relations in order to
accumulate wealth. Some vecinos maintain the comportment of superior social
standing that accompanies the ideology of vecino elitism and campesino subordination and repudiate the establishment of egalitarian relations with Indians, in a
high-risk and high-gain strategy to migrate to La Paz as members of the "privileged" classes. Based on patronage, this is the only path available to these Kachituños for entry into more powerful urban social circles. This strategy, however,
is also too inflexible to accommodate the downward mobility of those who choose
the alternative of adopting egalitarian relations with the Aymara Indians. It is
around this one issue, the insecurity of one strategy and the great social cost of the
other, that the crisis of mestizo identity revolves and it is this issue that medical
dialogue addresses. And most mestizos who try to establish egalitarian relations
with Aymara are landless or near landless widows or women with under- or unemployed husbands.

In 1977, Doña Leonora, her husband Don Valentino Ugalde, and their six
surviving children (she bore nine) live just off the square in a single room with a
tiny courtyard. Don Valentino suffers from an incapacitating liver disorder. He is
unable to withstand the rigors of living away from home most of the year to teach
school, but he picks up a little cash by serving as an assistant to the corregidor, Teodoro Apaza. His assistantship is a kindness extended by the corregidor.
Teodoro Apaza was born an Indian but is an aspiring mestizo now that he has a
Methodist education, has a house in town and a tienda, and was appointed to a
civil position by the higher authorities in Achacachi. His governmental salary and
income from his tienda augment his agricultural production, rendering Apaza materially well-off. He is fond of Leonora's husband because Don Valentino treats
him as an equal. Don Valentino is not ostracized by the other vecinos for this
behavior because Apaza is now, after all, almost a mestizo and the corregidor, and
the two, in their authoritative capacities, act as social superiors to the Indians,
though members of the vecino "lower class." They have some, though limited,
power.
    The income the assistantship provides Don Valentino, however, is minuscule,
and Doña Leonora augments it by trading spices and Aymara medicinal items for
grain and eggs in the Wednesday and Saturday markets near Kachitu and the Sunday market in town. Along with the Indian women, she sits on the ground with
her *aguayu*, or shawl, in front of her, half of which is covered with items to barter: bags of spices, llama fetuses, herbs, and items for yatiris to use to make
mesas, offerings to the spirits. On the other half of the aguayu are several grow-

ing mounds of grains and eggs that she receives in exchange. The larger percentage of these grains and eggs are Leonora's working capital. She takes them to La Paz where she trades them to women in the Indian market in La Paz for the items she sells. The remainder is her profit, and that which she uses to feed her family.

Doña Leonora and Don Valentino serve as a contrast with Doña Elsa and Don Rafael Nestares, who live next door to them, but on the square. They are trying to insure the move to La Paz for their two children (a third died in infancy). This has required the establishment of an extremely modest part-time residency in La Paz and the cultivation of compadrazgo ties with people there who will take in the Nestareses' children so they can go to school in the city. The Nestares family, however, has little with which to reciprocate such social favors. Their strategy is to try to bridge the urban and rural social worlds and serve as a funnel for the exchange of agricultural and social resources. To their urban friends they bring agricultural resources extracted from Kachitu Indians who are the Nestareses' *compadres* and provide them with agricultural goods as part of the obligations that accompany that relationship. This strategy is based, therefore, on asymmetrical social, juridical, and economic relations with the Aymara. The Aymara families who are their compadres benefit from this arrangement because the Nestareses can provide them with juridical protection, social ties, and hence an umbrella for possible economic endeavors in La Paz through their own social ties in the city. However, the Nestareses' social ties in La Paz are neither wealthy nor powerful. Likewise, their Aymara compadres are few, inherited from their parents, and reluctant. The strategy is sufficient but just barely, providing no room for error. Their hope is that their children will be able to go to the university or get good jobs because of their parents' investment in their urban education.

These two couples contrast with Doña Antonia and Don Lorenzo Villazon and their four sons (a fifth child died at birth, a sixth in her third month; Antonia also suffered a miscarriage). They own neither land nor tienda. Lorenzo is a schoolteacher, but a rural one who is therefore sent to another part of the country for most of the year and must spend half of his income ($35.00 of $70.00 U.S. per month in 1978) on his own upkeep. Doña Antonia washes sheets and towels for the clinic, originally at one peso per item. In 1978 the clinic was forced to make financial cuts and reduced her piece rate to one peso for every six items. On this income Antonia cannot feed her four sons. She initially tried to survive on credit from other vecinos, but her inability to repay strained these relationships. She turned, therefore, to the establishment of egalitarian social relations with some Aymara. Having nothing material to offer anyone in a compadrazgo relationship, she cultivates friends. With them she socializes and gossips. To them she offers her kindness, her friendship, and her medical advice. Her medical advice is valuable because she openly sympathizes with Aymara medicine, having suffered, she says, from many Aymara diseases herself. At the same time, she is familiar with cosmopolitan medicine, in part through her work at the clinic, and in part because her father had been an auxiliary nurse there. The most valuable resource she gives to her Aymara friends, however, and that which solidifies the relationship, is her rendering the usual asymmetrical relationship between vecino and campesinos explicitly and conspicuously absent between herself and her Aymara friends.

In precious moments, Don Lorenzo's admiration for his wife's independence, resourcefulness, and rebelliousness is conspicuous. But most of the time he is humiliated by her behavior. The other vecinos condemn Antonia for her associations. The woman from whom Anna and I rent our small house threatens us to prevent us from associating with Antonia. Many vecinos advise me to avoid her, allowing that I am too naive to know better. In Don Lorenzo's humiliation he publicly threatens Antonia, a strategy that saves him some dignity in public. He calls her a spendthrift, frequently threatens to bring home another wife, and taunts her with allusions to other lovers. Many vecinos approve on the grounds that Antonia deserves this sort of treatment. Antonia, however, can find no alternative for feeding her children. Lorenzo's acts to preserve his dignity cost her extreme anxiety as she does not know if he will ever feel obligated to carry out his threats. Often Antonia's anxiety is debilitating. An occasional dose of valium sometimes alleviates her "nervous attacks," but she finds that Aymara medicine is more consistently beneficial.

Antonia and Lorenzo Villazon, Elsa and Rafael Nestares, and Leonora and Valentino Ugalde are not living in the style their parents planned for them. Their parents' and grandparents' move to Kachitu at the turn of the century was explicitly made to avert poverty and humiliation. Ironically, their migration to Kachitu underlies the fact that vecinos and campesinos share the same cultural symbols and are not divided by culture but by class. Ethnicity is a mask for social class. The racial metaphor that supports it requires identities for each class that distinguish themselves by social opposition. As ethnic and social class boundaries become blurred under political and economic changes, so does the content of these identities. It is the content of these identities that is under negotiation.

THE RISE OF THE VECINDARIO

Several factors create the impression that the vecinos have lived in Kachitu since the beginning of time. Being a Kachituño is an inherent part of their identity. Migrants to La Paz are still considered Kachituños and have obligations to the town. Their superordinate status in relation to the Aymara, the myth of racial differentiation, and the display of ethnic boundaries imply permanence. The social ties that bound the two groups asymmetrically together for a hundred years were lifelong and inheritable over the generations. Yet until the nineteenth century Kachitu was in fact a free Indian community.

A story about the origin of the real name of Kachitu is quoted by Rigoberto Paredes in his *La Provincia de Omasuyu*, published in 1914, but it is also repeated by just about everyone on the altiplano. Perhaps they read the book. The story tells that the name is a contraction and hispanization of the names of two Aymara families who for many generations produced caciques who ruled the eastern and western halves of the area respectively. They were bitter feuding enemies and waged continual war on each other until the daughter of one family and the son of the other fell in love. Their marriage merged the two lineages, ended the feudal warfare, and transformed Kachitu into a coherent community.

Kachitu was established as a town in the eighteenth century and made the capital of the canton of Kachitu in 1790. This transformation made Kachitu the economic, political, religious, and social center for the cantonal population which, according to the 1900 census, consisted of 9,251 inhabitants dispersed throughout thirty-six haciendas and free Indian communities, now known as comunidades. The only history ever written about Kachitu forms a short chapter in the Rigoberto Paredes book. He cites the Kachitu population at 310 "urban inhabitants," making it a big town on the altiplano in those days. He writes, "the pueblo is identifiable by its repaired houses and painted walls that line the street," and refers to this condition as "relative progress." Indeed, the conception of "progress" as infrastructural maintenance and development rather than economic and socio-structural change is the predominant concept right up through 1978 when Anna and I left Kachitu. The synergistic factors that brought the new prosperity to Kachitu around the turn of the century and attracted the vecindario made this "progress" possible. Rigoberto Paredes says the population of Kachitu at that time was "poor and rebellious."

The first member of a vecino family to come to Kachitu was Colonel Juan Carlos Cordova, great-grandfather to Doña Teresa, the contemporary town aristocrat. Except for the Cordovas, not one contemporary vecino family name can be found in the Catholic church archives before the late nineteenth century. In the late nineteenth and early twentieth centuries, however, widespread violence and instability throughout the altiplano induced migration among those rural social segments that could afford upward mobility and caused the ambitious to move into new areas perceived to have potential. The Aymara were frequently rebelling against oppression. Huizer (1972) states that more than 2,000 peasant revolts over issues of land and labor occurred in Bolivia between 1866 and 1944 alone. Indians also fought Indians, as in the case of the feuding families of Kachitu. And vecinos fought vecinos as they followed different caudillos and vied for control of Indian labor and political power (Albo 1975). Most of the contemporary vecino families came to Kachitu during that time, most of them Indians presenting themselves in the guise of a mestizo identity, because Kachitu was then a frontier, abundant with opportunities. The series of laws that transformed Indian communal land into inexpensive private property stimulated in Kachitu a brief surge of commercialism because of the town's economically strategic location. Thus it permitted the move from Aymara to mestizo affiliation. Land, commercialism, and location that depended on three other zones permitted mechanisms for mestizo control over Indian labor and was thus an ideal place to establish a vecindario.

First, Kachitu is located both near the lake, and on its far side, on the lesser traveled road from La Paz to Peru. Relatively isolated, the road became the main channel for contraband from the north, thus contributing to the economic desirability of Kachitu.

Second, with the change in land laws, commercial establishments flourished. In 1889 the Cristy factory was incorporated and opened silver mines throughout the canton. Aymara in free Indian comunidades who needed cash to pay taxes supplied the mines with labor, while enterprising Kachituños supplied the factory with services. Although the Cristy factory underwent a rapid demise as the high-quality silver quickly gave way to antimony, which was too costly to mine, it was only one of ten mining companies operating in the region in the late nineteenth century. Together they employed 300 Indians at any given time. Mining production led to the construction of a mill along the lakeshore that was declared a minor port and therefore required mestizo administration and supervision. Almost all of these enterprises collapsed before 1952, but long after the Kachitu vecindario was well established.

These commercial activities needed services that a vecindario could supply. At the turn of the century Doña Victoria Castellano's father opened a pension where travelers could find meals and lodging. Members of the new vecindario opened a blacksmith shop, a tailor shop, and other "commercial" establishments while they set themselves up as mestizos eligible to supervise Indian activity. The mines, the entrepreneurs, and the large Indian population around Kachitu were captive customers for tiendas, a principal source of vecino income. Tiendas are small stores that uncompetitively sell the same things: magical items, candy, cigarettes, beer, alcohol and a purple liquid that is unconvincingly referred to as wine, bread, noodles, rice, coffee, sugar, soda, a few pharmaceuticals such as aspirin, and a small variety of tinned goods such as vienna sausages, sardines, and condensed milk. In the uncompetitive economy of the Bolivian altiplano a tienda did not generate a cash income, but rather controlled Indian labor. Their inventory catered to the needs of principally cashless Indians who bartered for the merchandise with their agricultural resources and labor. The right to barter with a vecino, and on the vecino's terms, accompanied a fictive kin relationship known as compadrazgo. The Aymara, both free and serf, patronized their vecino compadres' tiendas for all their consumption needs that they could not supply themselves, and the vecino compadres called upon their Aymara *ahijados,* or godchildren, for potatoes and quinoa, for labor at planting and harvest, and for loyalty and obeisance.

Also supporting these growing commercial establishments and the large number of free Indian comunidades was the Sunday market in Kachitu, the only market in the canton. Because free Aymara participated in trade far more often than did hacienda-based Aymara, and free Aymara constituted half the population of the canton, it was a big market. Once a vecindario was established in Kachitu, it levied a tax upon all market sales, thereby gaining financially as a town, and as a class, from all market exchanges. The vecindario was able to prevent the development of other markets and thus monopolized control over all market activity in the canton until 1953.

To fortify the growing vecindario, the Santa Lucia fair was moved to town in 1890 from a nearby hacienda where it had been celebrated since colonial times. The Santa Lucia fair is the biggest commercial event on the altiplano. It takes place in December, at which time traders from all over Bolivia supply the region with resources not indigenously available, particularly tools. It draws thousands of people from the northern altiplano and is therefore an opportunity to generate an income by serving food and drink in the tiendas. Until 1952 it was a highly lucrative event for vecinos to coordinate, manage, and tax.

Most of this trade and supervision were not based on a cash economy. Most of these people were illiterate. Exchange was primarily barter based on asymmetrical social relationships formed through the medium of compadrazgo.

Compadrazgo relations are negotiated dyadic relations between the parents of a child and another couple who serve as godparents to the child at birth, baptism, marriage, and other occasions (Stricken and Greenfield 1972). They are strategic relationships with exchange value, not simply a system established to look out for the well-being of children, in an environment in which nothing is obtained or exchanged, from potatoes to presidents, outside personal networks. Compadrazgo is the most convenient way to create such networks, which vertically cut across class lines shrouded in the metaphor of race, realized through rules of ethnicity, and sanctioned by law (Lavaud 1976, 1977). Lifelong and even inheritable, and requiring a series of exchanges to maintain and reinforce the relationship, the institution is a mechanism that redistributes resources. Thus compadrazgo ties are made on as many occasions as possible. Redistribution, however, is asymmetrical.

Besides the events of birth, baptism, and marriage, any other event in a child's life which requires the outlay of resources is occasion to establish a compadrazgo relationship. The *rutucha*, or first hair cutting, is a case in point. Ostensibly initiated to request godparents to cover the expenses of the event, the compadrazgo relations may last several generations. Material goods continue to flow from parents to godparents, while nonmaterial goods, such as protection, flow from the godparents to the parents to reinforce the relationship. The significant relationship is not that between child and godparent, but between parents and godparents, the compadres who are able to accumulate resources through the relationship. The nature of exchange, however, is not equilateral. It takes the form of patron-client relations in which the parents are the clients and donors of material goods, the godparents are patrons and donors of nonmaterial resources. Therein lies the mechanism by which self-proclaimed mestizos came to Kachitu, exploited Indian labor resources through the institution of compadrazgo, and established the vecindario.

At the first hair cutting, for example, which usually occurs when a child is a year old, the vecino godparents receive the Aymara child and the child's parents into their home and invite other guests, mostly other vecinos, for the event. The Aymara parents bring gifts to their compadres: potatoes, coca, fish, a sheep, and other items. Invited vecino guests bring a little cash. The child sits in the center of the room and the godparents, the madrina and padrino, give her or him candy and soft drinks to keep the child happy and occupied. Each guest then cuts a lock of the child's hair, makes a gesture to keep it for its sentimental value, and places some pesos in front of the parents in return. The godparents provide the other vecinos with beer to increase the vecino guests' generosity, and the Aymara parents with cane alcohol. The Aymara parents will repay this generosity by providing their vecino compadres with labor and agricultural resources throughout their lives.

The institution of compadrazgo was particularly potent in Kachitu because half the comunidades that pertain to the canton today were free Indian comunidades at the turn of the century. The ability of vecinos to control Indian production and labor through the institution of compadrazgo was thus another factor that made Kachitu attractive to an aspiring vecindario. Aymara on haciendas were given the legal status of serfs and were obligated to the hacendado but protected by him from state taxes and harassment. To the Indians, the hacendado was a patron. Those in free Indian comunidades were subject to state tax and free from obligations to the hacienda but bereft of the nonmaterial resources a hacendado might provide. They thus needed relationships with mestizos to get access to nonmaterial resources. As representatives of the state in Kachitu, the mestizos who took control of the canton were in a position to establish relations through compadrazgo with Indians from free comunidades which could provide the Indians with such resources in return for favors, and were thus structurally similar to those between hacienda Indians and hacendados. Compadrazgo relations funneled agricultural resources and labor from free Indian comunidades into the hands of the newly developing vecindario and were the key to local accumulation of wealth, to the control of the canton, and hence to the very foundation of the vecindario as a social class. Such control sanctioned domination of mestizo over Indian, granted enormous prestige, and provided the ability to tax the weekly markets and the annual Santa Lucia fair.

In Kachitu shrewd Aymara parents were careful to establish compadrazgo relations with strategic vecino families who could provide them with such nonmaterial resources as legal protection. The most valuable compadres were the corregidor, the judge, the wealthy, and vecinos who knew people in La Paz in high places. Meanwhile, the vecinos cultivated compadrazgo ties with their superiors in Achacachi, the capital of the province, and in La Paz to gain access to more powerful nonmaterial resources than those they controlled in Kachitu.

Teresa Cordova, town aristocrat and keeper of the town archives, and wife to Don Ascarunz, who practices law in La Paz, has more ahijados, or godchildren, than any other vecino in Kachitu: well over a hundred. Her family's larder is always full of potatoes and chuño, tunta, quinoa, and caya that their ahijados bring them in return for small favors and as an annual ritual acknowledgment of the relationship. Some of the potatoes and chuño left at the Cordova household are left by Aymara whose grandfathers were compadres to Colonel Juan Carlos Cordova almost a hundred years ago. In La Paz, Teresa and Ascarunz have asked doctors, politicians, and members of the military to be compadres for their children.

Compadrazgo was rendered as valuable and powerful as it was because of the myth of race that underwrote ethnicity. On its basis Indian social, linguistic, judicial, and political circumscription was defined by law. Indians were prohibited from participation in cantonal or national political and judicial decision making. Much of their ethnic identity was clear-cut, indisputable, and legally proscribed. Indian dependency on mestizos was incontrovertibly forced. Nevertheless sufficient movement from one ethnic group (social class) to another enabled the very development of the Kachitu vecindario that, through the myth of mestizo racial superiority, allowed the Ugaldes, the Nestares, the Villazones, and the other new families in town to appropriate control of the canton and its labor. In return for protection and access to social, political, and judicial resources that vecinos could provide with their civic positions and their own compadrazgo ties, the Aymara fulfilled all the mestizo agricultural needs and much of their domestic labor. Thus the vecinos were free to establish themselves as a class based on the exploitation of Indian labor in the same manner that hacendados were supported by their Aymara serfs. This fact gave the Kachitu vecinos greater local control than had rural mestizos in other towns which had far fewer free Indians in their outlying comunidades.

Mestizo Kachituños themselves, however, claim that the principal attraction of Kachitu was love. When asked why their families had moved to town, they invariably answered, "Ah, por amor, por amor!" Indeed, many members of the vecindario were latecomers who married in, and as a result, increased their social and financial position through inheritance of land and prestige. With great dignity young couples with the stature of a residence on the town square or a civil position chose their compadres in a calculated strategy to articulate with more powerful elite in La Paz. By displacing their actual consanguinity with compadrazgo they were able to sanction unequal access to resources on the basis of race. Dependent upon vecinos for anything not produced in Indian comunidades, for anything nonmaterial that involved literacy, for access to judicial or religious services, the Aymara could not deny the vecinos labor and agricultural resources. "Vulnerability," "subordination," "victimization," and "exploitation" were not metaphors but Indian depictions of their own lives under the control of the new vecindario. They laid the cobblestones in elaborate patterns to pave the square. They did all the main entrance work on the church. They built the vecino homes. On holidays and religious festivals—the new year, the town fiesta in honor of La Virgen de la Candelaria, Carnival, and All Saints' Day—long lines of Aymara would dance and play music for the entire distance from their comunidades to Kachitu where they would then perform traditional dances to commemorate the occasion, entertain the vecinos and each other, drink, laugh, quarrel, get drunk, and wear celebratory Indian apparel to symbolize and reaffirm their kinship to each other and their subordinate position to the vecinos of Kachitu. They used these occasions to visit friends, relations, and their vecino compadres and to carry out the activities that required the aid of their vecino compadres in Kachitu, the center of the cantonal universe. The Aymara demonstrated their subordinate status in their comportment. This subservient manner was sanctioned by the mestizo corregidor. They sat on the floor in the back of the Catholic church while the vecinos sat in pews in front. They addressed vecinos in specific terms that symbolized their subordinate status. They would bow and kiss the hand of Colonel Juan Carlos Cordova and his adult sons. They spoke only Aymara. For the vecindario, it was all wonderfully romantic.

The vecinos meanwhile adopted an attitude of paternalism toward the Aymara and of gentility and generosity toward each other, particularly in the form of throwing lavish and spectacular parties. Yet subsisting as they did on Indian labor, their own professions were limited. Those like the Cordovas who had powerful ties in La Paz were appointed to the local political offices, which, prior to 1952, provided no financial compensation, though they brought a good deal of prestige, power to press the local Aymara, and opportunities to meet significant figures in La Paz. Colonel Cordova's grandson Alejandro Cordova kept a small school through which he single-handedly contributed to what literacy obtained in town. Some, who had good compadres in La Paz and who therefore went to school there, were judges. Some worked in the local mines and others ran contraband from Peru. All of them owned tiendas.

Unsuspecting the manipulation of kin categories, I spent my entire eighteen months in Kachitu compiling genealogies from the local population, who adamantly insisted on racial distinctions between metizos and Aymara. Only later did analysis of the data reveal that almost every resident family in contemporary Kachitu, whether mestizo or Aymara, is related either consanguineously or affinally to each other and to many Aymara in the comunidades. These consanguineal and affinal ties demonstrate clearly that ethnic divisions are constructions, and that all Kachituños share confluences of the same culture. The ideology of race and ethnic boundaries, so obviously contrary to actual heritage, took on credibility only because the meaning of *vecino* and *Indian* each depended upon the existence of the other: a vecino was he who controlled and lived on the product of Indian labor, while Indians were the legal dependent subordinates who materially supported vecinos.

In spite of the local prestige the vecindario could acquire, the nature of their power was fragile. They never obtained consanguineal or compadrazgo ties with genuine elite whose lifestyles they tried to emulate. Such elite and the patrons of the haciendas around Kachitu and the mine owners lived in La Paz and rarely passed through Kachitu. Though the vecinos did acquire considerable amounts of land between the late nineteenth century and 1952, they never accumulated sufficient territory to transform it into haciendas. Cultivation of most vecino land was subsistence oriented. Surpluses, large bags of potatoes and quinoa, covered their various obligations to their own compadres and very little was sold on the cash market. Having little financial capital, they survived on the produce of their own lands, on what they could extract from the Indians, and on what they could occasionally obtain from the sale of small surpluses and livestock. By the elite standards to which the Kachituño vecindario aspired, the Kachitu vecino standard of living was marginal at best. More significant, the power of the vecindario proved to be fragile and vulnerable because of the dependency relations upon which it was based. Aymara economic and judicial independence from the vecindario after 1953 would destroy the power of the vecindario.

The extent to which the Kachitu vecindario could not participate in national political and economic affairs and its limited access to political power in La Paz is attested to by the fact that a municipal building was not built in the town until 1951, even though Kachitu had been the center of the canton since 1790. It remains the only government building in town, with the exception of a small jail that was erected in 1977. Kachituños were so offended by the fact that they had to take miscreants all the way to Achacachi that they finally built a small adobe hut in back of the municipal building and installed an iron grill door on one side. Kachitu spent sixty unsuccessful years lobbying the government for permission to tap into electricity lines that bypassed the town; the lines were installed in 1920, serving a mine farther north once owned by a North American corporation. The water piping system, which brings water into the yards of less than half of the town's households, was primarily funded by the Methodist church.

The vecindario was a project in upward mobility and accumulation of power, though its members would have referred to it as a project aimed at bringing "progress" and prestige to Kachitu. The first threat to this project was the arrival in the 1930s of the Methodist missionaries, come to save the Indian from mestizo oppression. Their specific goal was to render the Aymara independent of mestizo control.

THE METHODIST THREAT TO THE VECINDARIO

The Methodist mission threatened the vecindario in Kachitu by waging a religious war against "the evils of Catholicism." To the Methodists, these "evils" were personified by the "unscrupulous corregidor" who tried everything within his means to prevent the mission from establishing itself there. This war, while ostensibly religious, was in fact a class war. It immediately threatened and ultimately, with the help of the revolution, changed labor relations between the Aymara and the vecinos. The high degree of organization within the Methodist mission community generated political power that challenged the monopoly of the vecindario. A materialist perspective inherent in Protestant philosophy adapted to local conditions as the missionaries learned from the Aymara, and it created a new economic class in Kachitu that by the 1970s had accumulated wealth surpassing that of what remained of the vecino class in town. Although the revolution and land reform unleashed the Methodist Aymara from their position in a subservient and agrarian-based class and made their economic transcendence possible, this radical change had its origin in the Chaco War (1932–1935), a war waged specifically to engender a sense of nationalistic solidarity among the non-Indian population of Bolivia.

The Paraguayans had invaded the southeast corner of Bolivia, the Chaco, a desolate and miserable stretch of land. President Salamanca virtually kidnapped Indians from their fields to serve as front-line troops in the ill conceived and disastrous attempt to retain it. Those Aymara taken from Kachitu met other Indians from all parts of Bolivia, as well as disenchanted elites, devotees of Marxist doctrine, political undesirables, and Methodists. The Methodist Aymara they met had studied at the new Methodist school in La Paz which had been established immediately upon passage of legislation in 1906 permitting non-Catholics in Bolivia. These Indians knew how to read and write and had, therefore, access to an entire universe that was closed off to the Kachitu Aymara. Thus while the Kachitu Aymara served as shock troops, they also participated in a banquet of ideological diversity. They were impressed.

Frank Beck served as a physician along the front. He had come to Bolivia with John Herrick,[3] a hell-and-damnation, fire-eyed, strong-willed preacher. Herrick was an educator who helped establish the Indian school in La Paz and another in Huatahata, about fifty miles from Kachitu on the lake. He and Beck intended to spread evangelism in Bolivia by providing education and medicine to the Indians. They believed that education frees the individual from the bonds of superstition and ignorance, making it possible to pull oneself up out of misery by one's bootstraps. Although sociopolitical variables of Aymara poverty were explicitly acknowledged in early Methodist evangelical doctrine to justify the mission's activities, those of the vecindario were not. Aymara poverty was simplified, even personalized, and understood as the single responsibility of the vecindario. Thus, according to Herrick, the Aymara could, with sufficient elbow grease and determination, do anything within the confines of the law. That was so until Bolivian law required employees of all public and private institutions to be paid Christmas bonuses, which the Methodist church could not afford. What they did try to afford, however, was the provision of some medical care. They understood that medicine was the most effective road to conversion. Thus, after the Chaco War, Beck returned to La Paz and completed the establishment of a hospital and Bolivia's first school of nursing. And thus, fifteen years before social relations were inalterably changed in Kachitu, cosmopolitan medicine was a primary resource that affected the access to secondary resources by Indians and mestizos alike. The first secondary resources for which it was primary were converts to Methodist evangelism who specifically sought to undermine the mestizo class, alter relations of exchange, and revise the content of cultural identity.

In La Paz before the war Beck had met Noel Peñaranda, a disenchanted member of the lower echelons of the Kachitu vecindario, and an Aymara named Cleto

Zambrana. They became Beck's and Herrick's disciples and strongest allies, and devoted the rest of their lives to helping them pursue their goal of evangelizing the Aymara, establishing Indian schools, and providing medical care. Peñaranda was expelled from Kachitu vecino society for the effort but with few, if any, regrets on either side.

At the Chaco front these men befriended a number of Kachituños and Chojña Kanatans. During the unbearably hot nights as they sat whispering in Beck's medical tent, these men introduced these Aymara to the Methodist way of looking at things and to the wonders of evangelism. In particular they informed them of Herrick's educational work in La Paz and at Huatahata. Through their story, these Aymara saw visions of a future of self-sufficiency and freedom for themselves and their fellow peons still bound to the yoke of the hacienda or the vecindario. When they returned to Chojña Kanata after the war and shared these visions with their friends and relations, they received an overwhelmingly enthusiastic response. Thus, in 1935 a delegation walked to La Paz to meet Zambrana to request an Indian school for their community. Zambrana told Herrick. Herrick told Beck. Beck told the church back in the United States, and they all gave thanks to the Lord and sent Beck and Herrick out to help Zambrana build a school in Chojña Kanata.

The mission gave Zambrana a small salary and provided a modest house and a school building. In 1936 the mission school opened its doors to sixty students. Immediately Zambrana's house was stoned and his life threatened. Back in Kachitu, Beck and Herrick were imprisoned for opening the school without permission of the corregidor, in spite of the permission they had been given by authorities in La Paz. However, as members of other comunidades saw the school in Chojña Kanata take hold and persist in delivering education, they too requested mission schools, and by 1950 there were elementary schools in thirteen comunidades around Kachitu.

Herrick, Beck, and Zambrana saw evangelism as bringing the power of self-sufficiency into the lives of the superstitious, ignorant, and oppressed. Herrick found the "inferior and exploited status" of Aymara women appalling. Explicitly and publicly he and Zambrana challenged the "eternal" enemy of the Indian and the cause of his wretched position and ignorance—the corregidor and the Catholic church—as easily outwittable through legal means. "Christ has a message for poor folk to help them build lives [here] with new hearts," wrote Herrick. To educate the Indians through Protestantism was the means by which "to make Indian leaders" pilot their "race" out of their "misery." Of those he had taught to read and write he wrote, "Thanks to God that the Aymara now can read and defend themselves with their knowledge of the law." This position did not endear the Methodist missionaries nor their converts to the vecindario of Kachitu.

Herrick's and Zambrana's religious war in Kachitu was revolutionary. According to Copplestone (1973, 1985), the Methodist mission to Bolivia, like the Catholic church before it, initially allied itself with the elite classes in La Paz and Cochabamba under the cautious leadership of William Oldham and the reactionary District Superintendent John E. Washburn, who vociferously opposed any work with Indians whatsoever. Washburn saw the mission's value in providing the children of the elite, the future national leaders, with a liberal education. From 1904 to 1916 the Methodist English schools in La Paz and Cochabamba were enormously popular and made the Methodists staunch allies with the elite. This alliance was critical, as many factions, including a nationwide campaign sponsored by the Catholic church in 1924, mobilized to expel the Methodists from Bolivia. Although the public exercise of religions other than Catholicism was permitted after 1905, Protestant missionaries were prohibited from preaching or evangelizing until 1926. Thus, except for Zambrana's educational work among the poor in Alto La Paz, Peñaranda's work in the Yungas, and a failed attempt to establish a school in Huatahata (named the Penial Hall Farm), the Bolivian elite remained the focus of Methodist missionary interests until 1946.

Herrick's work in Kachitu might have threatened this alliance as Washburn feared had it occurred during the first three decades of the twentieth century. But the defeat in the Chaco destroyed the credibility of the old ruling order. Coupled with liberal intellectual currents informed by Marxist philosophy imported from Europe, defeat in the Chaco created sympathy among Bolivia's young educated elite, many of them educated in the Methodist English schools, for modest efforts to improve the lot of the Indian. This wave of post-Chaco liberalism and the friends the Methodists had among the elite English-school graduates gave Herrick far more access to power than the Kachitu vecindario could mobilize through their compadrazgo ties in La Paz and Achacachi.

Herrick and Zambrana immediately intimidated the vecinos when they bought land in Kachitu by promising that they would not build an Indian school there and then proceeded to build a boarding high school for young male graduates of the schools in the comunidades and making Kachitu the center of the Methodist mission on the altiplano. When construction began, the vecinos actively mobilized themselves to drive the missionaries out through legal means. The dispute explicitly fell along "racial" lines. Herrick claimed the mission bought the land from an Indian whose land it rightfully was and who was willing to sell. The vecinos claimed the land really belonged to one of their own who refused to sell. The missionaries were vastly more sophisticated than the vecinos in legal processes, and even more than the town judge, Don Juan Marquez, and the corregidor, Don Rafael Salazar, who claimed the wall the school would be built against was too old and the street too narrow to support such construction. With their access to the elite in La Paz, the missionaries won the suit hands down, promptly completed the Indian school in 1941, and publicly humiliated Don Rafael Salazar by calling his complaints "absurd," accusing him of "abusing" his office, and publicly exposing him as "incompetent."

On numerous occasions between 1936 and 1943, various vecinos went to El Corregidor Don Rafael demanding that he punish one Aymara Methodist or another for theft or for inciting violence. Again and again Herrick intervened, called the accusations false, and consistently won the case. One means by which he did so was to resort to higher authorities in Achacachi, the capital of the province, or in La Paz, further humiliating the Kachitu vecinos.

When the law failed them, the vecino resorted to inciting their campesino ahijados, or godchildren, against Methodist converts. This strategy was simple and effective because Methodist converts refused to attend fiestas, to dance, or to drink, and therefore no longer participated in the fundamental Bolivian symbols of social solidarity and acceptance. Meanwhile, converts received privileges from Herrick and his growing contingent of helpers which were denied to vecinos and Catholic Aymara alike. Herrick's followers formed an exclusive group. They attended the church and the church school. They formed women's clubs, men's clubs, and youth clubs. They went on joint retreats with other North American–led missionary groups like the Lutherans, Baptists, and Quakers. They became literate. They received personal medical attention from Cleto Zambrana, who determined that medical care was an essential component of evangelism, acquired medical skills from Dr. Beck, and launched the first innoculation campaign in Kachitu in 1938, which benefited more than 1,000 Aymara. When the mission eventually bought a jeep, only Methodists were permitted to ride in it. Under these circumstances, the Catholic Aymara were fertile soil for the growth of antisocial rumors.

As a result of vecino efforts to fight Aymara with Aymara, whole comunidades around Kachitu fought each other from 1938 to 1950 and considerable blood was shed. Frequently Zambrana sought legal protection from authorities in Achacachi for the school-children and for adults enrolled in night literacy classes who were prevented from attending by other Aymara who threatened them with weapons that eventually included firearms. The Methodist schools were repeatedly assaulted by what Herrick referred to as "bellicose Indians" obligated to the vecinos. Nevertheless the Methodist community in and around Kachitu continued to grow. Graduates from these schools became teachers themselves in the increasing number of community schools. Frequently threatened and harassed, Herrick or Zambrana looked to higher authorities to retaliate with all the legal, social, and religious resources they could mobilize. As they did so, they scorned mestizo needs and ridiculed vecino values, until there was effectively no communication between the two groups, and there existed a solid wall of distrust and antagonism.

While some attacks were less serious than others, Herrick did not discriminate. He responded to them all with the moral strength of his convictions. When one vecino youth was caught pulling up some small trees the missionaries had planted, Herrick condemned him as a "terrible criminal," and as a perpetrator of "crime against education." He called for maximum legal sanctions from the authorities in Achacachi, superiors to the vecino officials in Kachitu, to "punish such crime against civilization." The vecinos were more than offended by the North American going over their heads. The Protestant gringo threatened their authority, the legitimacy of their social standing, and their dignity. They were shocked by the turn of phrase: they saw themselves quite specifically as the forefront of civilization in town. In 1944, El Corregidor Don Rafael Salazar wrote to the subprefect in La Paz requesting that the national guard come to restore order in Kachitu. He pleaded that this tragic warfare was caused by a "Bolivian missionary" (Cleto Zambrana) who, being desperately dissatisfied with the limited effect of his preaching, resorted to opening ancient animosities between two comunidades, and thereby had instigated disaster. The subprefect refused to give assistance, saying he had neither the men nor the ammunition to spare.

As the 1940s brought an increase in the expression of radical ideas from Bolivia's intellectual community, the Kachitu vecinos joined the conservative cry throughout the nation and called the Protestants "communists" in order to gain a little momentum. This strategy was effective, and church membership indeed declined. The missionaries persevered. Feeling secure in their by now institutionalized alliance with members of the ruling class in La Paz, the Methodist mission agreed to support Herrick's efforts and by the early 1950s three North American families and two nurses created a small enclave of missionaries in Kachitu. One wrote, "I thank God because during a time of persecution and many misfortunes, there was still a group of loyal members who continued to come to our various activities, even when to do so brought on abuse by the vecinos." By 1950 a girls' boarding school was added to the boys' high school in Kachitu and the thirteen Protestant elementary schools in the comunidades around Kachitu. With the exception of the two boarding schools in Kachitu, every school was built at the request of the comunidades.

The harassment of the mission and persecution of converts began to abate in 1948. Only then was the mission sufficiently established and secure for the missionaries to begin to learn from the Aymara rather than merely teach them the answers to preconceived assumptions about Indian needs. What they learned after the late 1940s determined much of the identity of the Methodist Aymara and of what remained of the old vecindario in Kachitu in 1977 and 1978. The conservative nature of Herrick's earlier mission, however, greatly affected what the Methodist Aymara wanted to teach the missionaries: the necessity of their own autonomy and control over the local church. In twenty years, Indian control of the local church, and thus the high school and the hospital, would challenge the vecindario monopoly of the town. Thus the hard line of Herrick's mission also affected the vecinos' strategies to create a viable position within the same social space with the Methodist Aymara.

The ten years of missionary work under Herrick's direction had been dominated by his strict and somewhat ethnocentric leadership of his religious war. His emphasis on an ethnocentric form of materialism, his lack of attention to the material needs of the young Aymara leaders whom he cultivated, and the vast difference between his material well-being and that of the Aymara in the eyes of the Aymara created a rift between Herrick and the Aymara converts that led to the retreat of the former and takeover of the local church by the Aymara Methodists in the late 1960s, although ultimate authority of Bolivians over their Methodist church had been an intention of the missionaries.

Unlike all those outsiders who had come to exploit the Aymara, raise taxes, exact labor for the mines, and round up soldiers for Bolivia's wars, Herrick came to preach brotherhood and offer a service. Nonetheless, the Aymara detected some hypocrisy in the mission. Herrick and those who followed him lived as North Americans in two-floored stucco houses that boasted indoor plumbing. They ate meat at least once a day and employed Aymara servants, while their Indian brethren, who lived in mud-floored, thatched-roofed, windowless adobe homes, ate soups, dried potatoes, and beans, and worked on the land. Many of the missionaries did not speak Aymara, thereby requiring the Aymara to either learn Spanish, the language of the mestizos and of Aymara's oppressors, or employ a translator. The Aymara who learned from Herrick, however, were bilingual and taught their elementary schoolchildren in their native tongue, which undoubtedly contributed to the success of the mission. Nevertheless, social distance frequently separated the North American and Aymara brethren.

Of much significance in the eyes of many Aymara was the fact that although the Americans always seemed to have access to "vast sums of wealth," they paid the Aymara drivers, schoolteachers, and nurses extremely low wages. Such wages did not cover subsistence when an employee had no land and had a family to support. In 1944, one of the mission teachers wrote to the Reverend Herrick requesting an advance on his salary, explaining that his wife was sick and unable to work and required medical attention. While he only wanted his children to do the Lord's work, he wrote, they were nearly starving to death. "I don't know when the sun of peace will descend upon my house where I am demoralized and depressed with my poverty and my sick wife. So I am asking the big question as our only salvation lies in your buena voluntad [generosity] that you've always had for us." But Herrick did not have access to funds. The mission was supported solely by stateside charity. By their own standards, the North American missionaries lived on a shoestring themselves, and Herrick had to deny the advance as he had to do many times again:

> A small recommendation I wish to give you: perhaps you can manage within your monthly budget with limited salary—we do not give advances. It is necessary that you take into account that none of us are omnipotent and we can't take money out of nothing to advance to you. Our budget is managed month by month by the mission treasurer and we have to direct ourselves to the payment amount at the end of each month. I am sure that you, using a minimum of care and a maximum of prevention, can adjust your budget to these conditions.

In 1948 a U.S. missionary's salary was about $1,500 U.S. a year, while the evangelical schoolteachers' salaries ranged from 5,200 to 9,100 Bolivian pesos a year, which could bring about $120 U.S. to $217 U.S. on the black market, or $80 U.S. to $114 U.S. by official rates of exchange (Pick's *Currency Yearbook 1936–1955*). A teacher named Samuel from one of the community schools wrote to Herrick on December 22, 1941:

> I beg your forgiveness and am repenting to God for what I must do: turn to you for help. You know the fleecing costs of everything: a load of potatoes alone cost 300 pesos. My salary isn't enough to live on. It isn't a quarter of my expenses. I ought to be the first example for the Indians and for this I ought to carry myself well and educate my sons. But to do this I must have some minimum requirements, eat, dress myself, and care for myself following the laws of health. As Proverbs 22 : 6 says, I ought to also continue my studies and buy books. As Proverbs 23 : 12 says, our fathers should give us nothing, not even straw, and so my parents give nothing to help me. I know they can but we don't need their things because we now live in another epoch [that shuns parental dependency]. Therefore I need more money. But I am NOT a mercenary as you call me.

On January 4, 1942, he wrote again:

> The family quarreled with us because this year we have bought nothing, neither a suit nor hat, nothing for my wife, because we eat up all the little salary that we make. A sheep alone costs 80 pesos. The other school-teacher's father was very angry and it is because of that he entered the army [and abandoned his post at the school]. Therefore I tell you that you have to raise the salaries because what you give us is very little.

Herrick's response:

> Read your letter from January 4th in which you tell me of your desire to pull out if we don't raise your salary to 800 pesos a month.[4] Your attitude profoundly surprises me. I did not think that an Evangelical Christian like yourself could think of breaking your contract so easily. Your contract with us is to finish the school year, until the end of March, and sadly we do not have a written contract. But

verbal contracts are good enough for Evangelicals and even more important because they include our word of honor.

Taking into consideration the increase in prices and after I have consulted with others, I have resolved to raise your salary to 500 pesos for the months of January, February, and March,[5] freeing you of any responsibility you had earlier with respect to the mission, and furthermore freeing the mission of any and all responsibility as well. In any case you ought to finish the 3 months wealthy enough to satisfy the Indians of Y—— and furthermore to receive your part in the harvest that they promised you.

I am very distressed that you have returned to being commercial and money-mad, instead of remaining within the true vocation of serving the Indians of our region. Here we are passing years of suffering among the Indians because they lack messages of the truth of Christ. We need more people like yourself, even if your education is quite limited, to free the Indians from exploitation and slavery—worse they are slaves of vice and would be the slaves of the mestizos; and they need those who can preach the good new words of liberty.

Herrick wrote of the incident to an American missionary in La Paz on January 9, 1942:

The times are against us for holding our young men at modest salaries. I enclose a copy of a letter from Samuel. He is also touched by the current craze for money and has been offered 900 pesos a month by the Friends to go to Coracoro—so he says, though I doubt this as I know they are not flush but also living in Coracoro is 100% expense while in Y—— he gets a number of prerequisites such as fuel, foods, etc. and has a share in the harvest coming.

We are sorry about Samuel and he was doing pretty well here, but it is just another case of not knowing when he was well off. He will learn.

While some of the Aymara teachers did not concur with the missionaries' view of the church's operating budget, others felt Herrick did not adequately support their efforts to advance education in the communities and turned his back on them when confronted by higher authorities.

In 1945, the Aymara from the Pojqueata hacienda built themselves a schoolhouse on their own land and invited the mission to come and teach. But once the school was built, some Kachitu vecinos advied their ahijados there that the school would be superior if run by the government and taught by graduates of the government teacher's school near Achacachi, rather than by graduates of the Methodist schools. They advised that the Protestants would prejudice their education. Then they suggested to the administration of the government teachers' school that the Methodists, by establishing a school at Pojqueata, were infringing on the Indians' rights, moving in on their territory. The government educators at the teachers' school agreed that if there were to be a school at the Pojqueata hacienda, it should be under the domain of the government, and sent a government teacher named Jorge Sanjueza to teach there. Herrick moved compromisingly and suggested the school be part government and part Methodist. But on July 13, the Pojqueata hacienda Aymara wrote a letter to Herrick to protest the intrusion of the government into their affairs, their land, and a building that clearly belonged to them:

> Dear Very Respected Pastor Herrick:
> All of us here at the hacienda school have come to an agreement this night, July 13, 1945. We agree that we do not want our community divided into two groups [Protestant and governmental school sections] because it would lead to terrible fighting and would be for you a headache. We now want the Methodist school and we agree that to have it always, we will believe only in one God. We want to quit our vices because they make us no better than donkeys.
> Now all of us Indians here in Pojqueata want you to give us these classrooms that we made with our own hands, and that the government teachers' school not take them away from us, because they didn't help us at all in their construction, and they therefore don't have the right to throw us off, and we don't want government employees, and none has the right to oppose us over the possession of the classroom.
> Señor Sanjueza is procuring to put us in a tangle and in fights. Besides this, he has taken the list of students' names, ages, and parents, and sent it to mestizo officials in La Paz. He made this list in secret without our knowledge.
> We want possession in the name of the entire community, because we are united and want a Methodist school. We want sacred sermons and a separate church to preach the word of God.

The government teachers' school threatened Zambrana:

> This office has been informed that you, through illicit means and against your obligations to your office, have permitted your students to abandon the school [when government teacher, Sanjueza, was sent to teach there]. We hold you responsible as the author of this abuse, and furthermore, the school should be constructed for campesinos who adhere to governmental doctrine. It remains prohibited to use these class rooms which were constructed for the instruction of campesino children of this estate, for a center to inculcate ideas against their own interests and to irresponsible children.

Zambrana immediately wrote to Herrick in Kachitu:

> My dear Pastor,
> It will annoy me greatly to pass the 2 patriotic holidays of July 16 and August 6 here in Pojqueata. Professor Sanjueza is always abusive toward me and says lies about me to the director at the government teachers' school. So I would like to bring my students to Chojña Kanata for July 16th to pass the day together playing games.

Whether due to low finances, concern over possible confrontations with the government, or some other reason, Herrick did not defend the Aymara at the hacienda. To the government teachers' school he wrote:

I have in my hand a letter from the Indians at the Pojqueata hacienda and a letter from the preceptor there, Cleto Zambrana. From these letters it is evident that the Indians at the hacienda think they have right to have a Protestant school in the building for classes. On the contrary, I have told them that we don't have any such rights. They ask me to request of you out of courtesy to cede the use of one of the classrooms for a Methodist school. We have thought a lot about not opening a Protestant school this year at the hacienda but they insist we don't abandon them.

I have agreed with the preceptor Sanjueza that we are not going to take away his students but these students are insistent about this and have made life here unbearable.

Now if you want to speak to the hacienda group and give them your opinion it would perhaps alleviate the situation for me. In all frankness I don't know what to do with them.

The early missionaries were rigid in their authoritarianism. They fired teachers for participating in the traditional annual Kachitu fiesta that celebrates La Virgen de la Candelaria, the patron saint of the town. But keep in mind that, in this new frontier, harassment of the missionaries was constant, persecution frequent, and the work hard.

From the Aymara point of view, this authoritative, paternalistic aspect of the missionaries and the double standard in salaries echoed the patron-client relations demanded by mestizos, though the Aymara did not equate the two styles. The early missionaries seemed to insist upon a dependency relationship with the Aymara, though admittedly of a very different kind than did the vecindario. The missionaries' early attitude seemed to be that the Methodist gringos had everything to give to the Aymara and nothing to learn from them. As the Aymara viewed the superior standard of living, the larger salaries, the occasional "betrayal," and the condescending attitude of the North Americans, many assumed that Herrick's reproaches were empty justifications for continued monopolization of authoritative positions within the church. Some even began to suspect that the missionaries had come, like so many before them, to once again exploit the Indian, establish an organization in which they could monopolize the positions of power within the church for themselves, and cultivate Aymara dependence.

Yet it was precisely the promise of independence that brought the Aymara to the church. Herrick compelled frugality to encourage material gain, education, leadership, and Aymara independence from the vecindario. In spite of the missionaries' authoritarianism, the usual four metaphors—insatiable hunger, subordination, victimization, and exploitation—did not apply to their social, economic, and political relationships with the Methodist Aymara. Indeed, the missionaries explicitly opposed the most visible sector of the economy to which these metaphors did apply from the Aymara point of view: the vecindario. Thus the numbers of Methodist Aymara, attracted by the idea of "liberation," expanded simultaneously with an interest in either usurping gringo monopoly and local control of the church or seeking independence from the vecinos elsewhere. When the revolution began to take force in 1951 and the political possibility of Indian "liberation" took hold in the countryside, Herrick sadly wrote:

> We are very sorry for the absence of many brothers who have left us because of other "movements"; that they say we are not speaking the word of God. They erroneously think that God is a mortal who looks after his material needs. They also say we obey the Bolivian government—which is the pure truth—while they only obey God. They are ignoring the fact that there is always a legal means by which to change the laws if the laws are unjust. We pray that the "lost" return.

Indeed, the education and skills the missionaries gave to their Aymara converts, including much of their materialist doctrine, created the Indian leadership that Herrick strove to provide. This was facilitated by several factors: the expansion of the mission in Kachitu, the reduction in persecution of the Methodists as the vecinos accommodated themselves to the inevitable, the consequent exchange of education between newer missionaries and the Methodist Aymara as the Aymara became more self-assertive, and the eventual transfer of the Kachitu mission to the Methodist Aymara themselves.

By 1944, Herrick and Cleto Zembrana were heavily overworked. The number of their schools and converts had grown, and they asked for help. Three North American missionaries, graduates of post–World War II theological training that provided a progressive interpretation of the "social gospel," arrived in Kachitu with their families and two nurses. By 1952, thirty-seven missionaries and helpers were living in Kachitu.

Coming to a relatively established mission, more confident and open in their thinking because of their greater numbers, and being perhaps younger and fresher than Herrick, this group received from the Aymara as much as they gave and perceived the direct address of material needs as valuable. The new missionaries specifically sought to create an "economic transformation" in Aymara lives. The discourse of the religious war was transformed into explicitly social and economic terms. They determined to increase skills, economic opportunities, and the Aymaras' ability to legally defend themselves. They taught the Aymara how to organize, lobby, and protect themelves from social abuse. Inherent in these goals was the movement toward intrinsic structural change: a change in social relations between the Aymara, the vecindario, and even the urban sectors in La Paz. Quite unlike the fundamentalist evangelical efforts throughout most of Latin America today, which are politically conservative if not reactionary, the Methodist church in the 1940s and 1950s was a progressive organization resembling the Catholic Action movement that was implemented throughout Latin America a decade later under the direction of the new liberation theology. When the Tupac Catari pro-

Indian party was formed after the MNR revolution of 1952 and supported the left-of-center candidate Hernan Siles Zuazo in 1978, 1979, and 1980, a large contingent was Methodist. Without realizing it, these missionaries created Aymara leaders who, when the MNR revolution was declared in 1952, took over the vecino political and economic monopoly and appropriated the vecino social position of power for themselves.

The new missionaries were culturally sensitive. The men made the effort to learn the Aymara language. The women debated the appropriateness of their lifestyle. They shared their habits with the Aymara who came to live at the boarding school. They socialized intimately with their congregation. Their youngsters grew up with Aymara children and became accepted members of the Aymara community. These facts are particularly impressive because only a few years earlier, the anthropologist Harry Tschopik (1947, 1951) wrote his ethnographic account of the Aymara based on interviews with peasants which he carried out on the front porch of the hacienda on which they were serfs, using a translator provided by the patron.

When Anna and I arrived in Kachitu, one of the missionary children named Nathan Robison, by then a young man, surprised us by addressing us in English with a midwestern American accent. He had remained in town long after his parents had left with the rest of the missionaries. He and nine Aymara friends supported themselves by running the only tractor in town, bought with a low-interest loan acquired through the church. At the time of our arrival he was the president of the town council, being the only individual whom both vecinos and Aymara trusted. In 1981 he married a Bolivian woman and presently he works for the Andean Rural Health Project established in 1980 by a Methodist surgeon from North Carolina, Dr. Henry Perry. Dr. Perry tried to initiate the ARHP in Kachitu and failed because of the Aymara Methodists' adamant monopoly of control over the hospital administration, and his refusal to compromise his medical beliefs to accommodate indigenous medical ideology as Dr. Sabas had done in 1978. To survive, however, the Andean Rural Health Project did incorporate Aymara concepts of primary health care and now operates innovatively in a neighboring canton where the absence of a clinic eliminates one resource that medicine can provide and over which factions can compete. Bastien has called it "a thoroughly integrated Christian and Aymara approach to primary health care" (personal communication).

Unlike Herrick, who castigated converts straying from the church, the new missionaries responded to dropouts with self-reflection. They wrote that they were apparently not giving their members what was vital to their lives and would be working harder to do so.

In an attempt to work harder, they expanded educational opportunities at the school in Kachitu by providing scholarships to graduates for study at the university and the medical school in La Paz. One of these graduates, an Aymara named Geronimo Tallacagua, returned to Kachitu in 1978 to practice medicine after completing medical school in La Paz with a scholarship from the church. Inflexible in his medical ideology like the early Dr. Perry, he reversed Dr. Sabas's administrative policies and prohibited the practice of Aymara medicine in the hospital. At the end of two months the patient load drastically diminished, and Dr. Tallacagua left Kachitu.

The new missionaries also established a literacy campaign for adults throughout the Kachitu canton that was structured similarly to the Sandinistas' literacy campaign since 1979: adults who could read were encouraged to transfer that skill to their friends and relations who could not.

They allocated positions of authority in the church hierarchy to Aymara individuals. Francisco Apaza was made Jefe de la Comisión de Evangelization and Mariano Mamani was put in charge of secular activities.

They organized their congregation into Leagues of This and That, each league having its own directive body and decision-making capacity. They formed a men's league, a women's league, and a youth league. Through these leagues they strove to provide medical care, agricultural assistance, and vocational classes to transfer marketable skills.

The women's league encouraged the notion of feminism as understood by the North American missionary women, whose feminist positions appear repeatedly in the league minutes. League activities took the women out of their homes and into an organization of their own, which they directed without overt interference from husbands or vecinos. The women used this opportunity to support church activities that brought them status and to economically and medically benefit themselves and their families. They congregated twice weekly to discuss their encounters with social and medical problems, including alcoholism, wife beating, and pacifism. Through the church they commercialized their traditional weavings, and they spent their profits on medical supplies, on the school, on contributions to the Federation of Bolivian Protestant Women and the Confederation of Latin American Women (to whose conferences they sent delegates), and on a sewing machine for themselves.

The new missionaries also gave materially to the town of Kachitu, which appeased some of the vecindario. They installed a water system that piped water into Kachitu from a natural spring a half mile outside of town. After the revolution, when the vecinos no longer had unlimited access to Indian labor to fetch water, the mission collaborated with the vecinos to install piped water throughout about half of the town.

As Dr. Sabas did twenty-five years later when appealing to Seferino, these missionaries adopted an accommodating attitude toward those whom their predecessors had conceived as antagonists. They took a cautiously sympathetic view toward Catholic priests, thus expanding the extent to which they could effectively participate in the social space of Kachitu. The significance of this accommodation for the politics of medicine is alluded to in a letter written by one of the missionaries to his colleagues:

> The big mistake of the evangelical workers among the Indians has been to alienate the Catholic priests. We have had the habit until today of throwing all the blame for the sad, ignorant and superstitious condition of the Indian on the priests. To a certain point it is not their fault because there has never been enough of them and there is even less today, to give instruction to their congregations. For example, the Kachitu priest tells me that he is so busy with weddings, baptisms and masses that there is no time left for instruction of Christian doctrine. This district of 32,000 people has only one priest. We work in the same district. We have believers whose huts are 45 kilometers from Kachitu, and who do not have the time to walk that whole distance for the Evangelical meetings. This calls our attention to the logistics of the ignorance of religious life among the Indians. They wish to worship God [which they could do apparently in the Catholic Church] but their knowledge of how to do so, and their instruction is so deficient, that they can't tell the difference between the worship of INTI PAXI and the Pachamama from the true worship of God. They have no education of the Holy Ghost, nor do they know much about the teachings of Christ. Their beliefs of San Santiago is heavily mixed with superstition and controls their lives. Evangelicals who have been believers and had education for many years still have visions and experiences with the khan achachi, the malevolent spirit that demands their food, and the Kari Siri, the malevolent spirit who cuts the spinal-back.

The missionaries, of course, assumed that education and "proper medical care" would put an end to the belief in the khan achachi. Twenty-five years later, Seferino, Dr. Sabas, and Pastor Angel came to the realization that this has not been the case.

The missionaries did understand that the politics of medicine affected religious affiliation. In an environment in which tuberculosis and typhus were the major health problems, and in which malaria, brought back to Kachitu from the Chaco in the 1930s, was on the rise, they believed medicine was their most effective resource to convert Aymara to the "good life." Herrick had made specific reference to the importance of medical care reaching "nonbelievers" and Cleto Zambrana had been adamant on this point since 1939, when Dr. Beck vaccinated hundreds of children in Kachitu during a typhoid and smallpox epidemic, saving many lives and gaining many converts. In 1942 Herrick wrote,

> Although the Mission's mission may be to teach and preach, it is time to realize that medical work is more important than education and cannot be further postponed.

In Kachitu 90% of Indian deaths is due to lack of medical attention, and involves the complete ignorance they have of nature and bacterial action. To talk to them about the existence of micro-organisms is like saying to them that the sun is not that which moves in the sky. They take no measures to prevent disease, nor take the appropriate drugs to combat them. When they try to cure someone of malaria, they do the following: first they give a potion of certain things that are unmentionable and by nature undrinkable. The purpose of this is to disgust the disease itself so that it will abandon the body of the patient. If this doesn't work they surprise him by throwing cold water on him when he is already cold. They do this because they think the malaria may be caused by fright, in which case the disease will only go away by being frightened even more. Finally they treat the patient to a good beating when he is experiencing an attack [malarial chills or fever]. The beater responds to the screams and cries of the patient with more blows, swears, threats, and warnings. This is to get the disease to flee from such a hard beating. Truly this creates an interesting comedy. The results are that the patient shortly ceases to exist, due to complications and wounds. There is more but I refrain.

In spite of these bad habits, the Indian is reacting and adapting easily to treatment by drug and aseptic systems. This I tell you with plain evidence and from records we have of use of our tiny scanty medicine chest.

To convince the mother church in New York of the significance of medicine for evangelization, Herrick wrote in 1950 that "Cleto Zambrana has been curing and healing illnesses and offering spiritual healing at the same time. In this way he has gained the sympathy of many, many of which have come into the church."

The strongest advocate for a clinic was Bertha Garcia. She was a strong willed, highly proficient, and independent graduate of Dr. Frank Beck's nursing school in La Paz. She came from the urban elite class which expected her to marry well, to conform to the Latin ideal of her gender, and to devote her life to motherhood. She had no intentions of doing so. Her professionalism and move to Kachitu in the 1940s bordered on scandal in her social circles.

Bertha Garcia's self-confident competence and her fearlessness deeply impressed the missionaries, the campesinos, and the vecinos. She spoke her mind. She saw two needs in Kachitu and voiced her opinion vociferously. Not a missionary herself, she was not vulnerable to the compromising politics of the mission bureaucracy.

First, and with the thorough agreement of the missionaries, she expanded Zambrana's work to include health education. To the women's, men's, and youth groups she introduced various classes and schemes to enable the Methodist Aymara to help themselves with cosmpolitan medical techniques. Her emphasis on self-sufficiency struck a responsive chord in her audience. She persisted in her conviction that a medical clinic should be the priority of the mission.

Second, and in opposition to the missionaries, Garcia also insisted on providing medical care to all Kachituños, Aymara and vecinos alike. This position staunchly conflicted with the earlier missionaries' political position and strategy to gain converts. Excluded from all mission privileges, fingered by the missionaries as the cause of Indian oppression, and humiliated in their failed attempt to rid Kachitu of Methodists, the vecinos could not cross the vast social distance that separated them from the Methodists. They accepted Garcia's medical services, in part because her background was Catholic, rendering her less rigidly allied with the Methodists. Her medical care ameliorated their distrust of the mission. It decreased the political significance of the social gap between the two groups which had rendered cosmopolitan medicine at the clinic unavailable to the vecinos. Thus for the vecinos she served as a bridge between cosmopolitan and traditional medical systems.

Bertha Garcia's strong position on Methodist-vecino relations fortified the new missionaries' desire to change church policy. In 1950 they set up the first Spanish services in Kachitu, making them accessible to the vecinos. Four vecinos began to attend, and as a result, one tried to join the church. His family, however, ostracized him for the move and to resolve the conflict he left Kachitu and joined the army, leaving church and family behind. After his departure, the other three vecinos apparently abandoned their interest in Protestantism. Nevertheless, these gestures altered vecino-Methodist relations to the extent that they could more compatibly inhabit the same social space.

Funds to establish the clinic became available in 1955. Over the following few years the Methodist missionaries installed a dozen beds, a generator, an X-ray machine, a small laboratory, a consultorio where patients are seen, and a humble surgery. They built two houses, North American style, to attract a physician and nurse, and a dormitory for auxiliary medical staff—Methodist Aymara who received clinical training from Dr. Beck. They also bought a van equipped with medical supplies to take medical care to the comunidades. They hired Abelardo Zuidema, a Methodist Aymara, to maintain the clinic compound and drive the van. They built a small house in the compound for him and his family, to which they moved from one of the comunidades. No longer a campesino, and now wielding some authority and considerable responsibility, Abelardo has taken the title "don" to demonstrate that his social status is at least equivalent to that of the Kachitu mestizos.

In contemporary Kachitu, the significance of the clinic and its resources for the politics of medicine and for the role of medicine in cultural identity is threefold. First, because they were so alienated from the mission, few vecinos frequent the clinic, and many do not use it at all. It is perceived as Aymara Methodist territory. The vecinos who believe their future is in La Paz fear that open reliance on Indian resources may be demeaning. Those few vecinos who do use the clinic are among the poorest of mestizos who were never involved in the attempt to evict the Mission, had not been the focus of missionary venom, and are increasingly inclined to associate with the Methodists if they can figure out some socially acceptable way to do so. This use has increased over time as wealthier vecinos moved to La Paz after the revolution. By 1977 and 1978, the greater the downward mobility experienced by a mestizo, the greater was his or her use of the clinic. Antonia de Villazon, who is close to the bottom of the vecino social order, is the clinic's most frequent vecino client.

Second, because these medical resources are obviously valuable and their management requires considerable responsibility, control of them became a subject of conflict between the Bolivian mother Methodist church and the local Aymara Methodists. In need of physicians, the Aymara are dependent upon either the church to send a missionary or the government to send a young medical school graduate on his one year of required service in the countryside, the *año de provincia*. The Kachitu Methodists feel they have fought hard over the years to achieve self-sufficiency, autonomy, and a position of authority. They feel, now that the missionaries are gone, that the clinic should fall under their control. They are extremely protective of what resources and power they have obtained through hard work. Therefore they wish to maintain authority over the attending physician on nonmedical issues, including clinic policy and administration. When physicians such as Tallacagua and Perry insisted on their own authority around the hospital, conflict ensued. Fearful of the conflict and losing its control over the mission in Kachitu, the mother church reduced its financial support to the clinic. As a result, the quality of medical resources has declined since 1955. By the 1970s, finances were so limited that Dr. Sabas sold the medical van that brought care to the comunidades.

Third, regardless of the effects of conflict, the clinical training the Aymara Methodist auxiliaries received from Dr. Beck and the various attending physicians over the years has been acknowledged by visiting physicians and Bolivian authorities as superb. This was in part because such training was provided on a one-to-one basis to Kachituños who were always present in an understaffed facility. The experience they received, therefore, was extensive. By 1978, the principal auxiliary at the clinic, Felipe Apaza, had more than twenty years of experience and knew more medicine than most of the phyicians, particularly the young medical school graduates like Dr. Tallacagua, on their año de provincia. More important, unlike most physicians who come to Kachitu, Felipe Apaza is a Kachitu Aymara. And unlike the missionaries, he understands the political significance of the khan achachi and the *kharisiri*, a phantasm that can inflict disease or illness. He respects yatiris. He supported Sabas's changes in administration policy. He decreases the social distance between cosmopolitan provider and Aymara patient, and serves as a bridge between Aymara and cosmopolitan medicine. As a result, the actual quality of medical care has been maintained, if not improved, at the clinic since 1955. Handicapped by the scarcity of available resources, however, the clinic depends on good social relations between the Aymara Methodists in Kachitu on the one hand, and the mother church, the Bolivian government, and other tappable resources on the other. One potentially tappable resource that is entirely unavailable to them is the Kachitu vecindario. So far, those vecinos who emit veiled evidence of sympathy have neither political nor economic resources to offer.

For the Aymara, membership in the Methodist church before 1952 had meant very explicitly independence from vecinos. When the revolution arrived in Kachitu, Methodist Aymara were ready to step into the commercial and political roles the revolution handed over to them. Coupled with the unequal treatment the missionaries had shown the vecinos, and the gradual deterioration of vecino self-confidence in their dealings with the church, the Methodist Aymara were able to undermine the mestizo monopoly and the established social order in 1952 and 1953 when all administrative positions in town were required by law to be staffed by literate Indians. On the eve of the revolution, the vecinos were completely impotent in the face of armed Indian revolt, in spite of the social, political, and economic position they had fought to obtain for half a century. During the next few years the vecino monopoly of power was completely undermined, and they never regained what they had lost in 1953. The Methodist Aymara, on the other hand, never looked back.

THE REVOLUTION IN KACHITU

The anthropologist William Carter lived in Kachitu throughout the revolution. In those days he was a young seminary student assigned to the Kachitu Mission. When he changed careers, entered the anthropology department at Columbia University (and married Bertha Garcia), and based his master's thesis on the data he had collected as a missionary, he wrote the following about the revolution in Kachitu (1958 : 66–70):

> When the agricultural reform was proclaimed, it struck at the very roots of
> the town's existence. . . . The national government began to form [peasant]
> unions. . . . The union leaders were called into La Paz, given pep talks about the

way that the government was going to return the land that rightfully belonged to them, and were given guns to defend that right. Truckloads of these armed Indians returned to their comunidades, ripe for action. In some, they terrorized their neighbors into joining with them; in one case an Indian who refused was shot down in cold blood. Another was knifed, and his mutilated body was set out on the lake in a balsa boat.

Such goings on terrified the mestizo residents of Kachitu. . . . Rumors ran around the town that the Indians were preparing an attack. Others said that the unions had taken a pact to kill every non-Indian in the area; others told of intricate plans to burn every house of the town to the ground. . . .

The lieutenant visited from house to house, and in order to convince the inhabitants of the seriousness of the affair, told of atrocities committed in the past by Indians who had rebelled against the owners of their estates. Most of the mestizo women and children locked up their houses and went to La Paz. . . . To those who remained, explicit instructions were given. Able-bodied men were to arm themselves with rifles provided by the lieutenant. Women and children were to flee to the top of the escarpment where, presumably, they would be unharmed.

In the first supposed attack on the village, everything went off according to plan. The women and children ran to the escarpment, while the men defended the town below. A number of volleys were shot off, but nothing ever developed that could make it be called a real battle. Because there was no moon, the worst thing that happened was that some of the women and children came near to plunging to their death when they slipped on the escarpment, while others discovered that, on entering a cave, they had sat down in the public latrine. . . .

One afternoon the lieutenant, Don Juan Marquez's brother came running into the town shouting, "Ring the alarm, ring the alarm; we're being attacked." . . . The Indians were said to be encamped on the plain across the river, at the entrance to the town. All was quiet until about ten o'clock, when a shot was fired. Who fired the shot is still in question, but it was enough to send the church bell tolling. The women of the town sought refuge in the church sacristy and, strangely enough, the priest made a special trip to the mission in order to help save the life of the mission nurse [Bertha Garcia]. Two Protestant Indian boarding students and one of the local merchant's families fled to the mission for protection. The hours dragged by slowly and quietly, and to this day no one knows whether the attack was real or merely a tall tale.

There was only one other violent incident. . . . One windy afternoon, all the trucks that had passed through the town on their way to La Paz returned with tales about a tremendous battle that was going on between two different comunidades of Indians. The truck loads of people spent the night in Kachitu, dividing themselves among the church, the mission, and a few of the private houses, and the next morning reports began to come through. It so seems that, following an argument over who should be the union leader for the region, two opposing groups had clashed. In all there were reported to have been up to ten thousand Indians engaged in the battle. Finally, the winning comunidades had sacked the houses of those who had lost, and had proceeded to walk to the plaza of the provincial capital, where they had paraded around with doors, plows, chickens . . . in short, any loose things they had been able to lay their hands on. The local authorities had reacted the same way as had local authorities on the rest of the altiplano. Faced with the overwhelming number of the Indians, and unable to forget the fact that the Indian leaders had modern weapons, they simply watched from their windows. Thus it was that the Bolivian legal code took an enforced holiday for some time. Since 1953 Kachitu has not been the same.

THE DEMISE OF VECINO POWER

The 1952 revolution immediately shattered the Kachitu vecindario, already rendered vulnerable by the rise of the Methodist church. The MNR party, in an attempt to maintain its own shaky control over the government, sought Indian loyalty and support. Conceding the derogatory connotation of the word "Indian" and acknowledging the racism underlying ethnicity to render social class invisible, it banned the use of the term and substituted the term "campesino" in its stead. It expelled mestizos from all rural political and administrative offices and permitted only Indians to occupy them. Being the only literate Indians—now campesinos—around, the Methodist Aymara occupied these positions as well as new positions created by the revolutionary government. Carter, still residing in Kachitu after the land reform, wrote:

> Today both Don Alejandro Cordova and Doña Eva Marquez have had good portions of their land taken over by Indians of the comunidades . . . and real authority in the town has passed into new hands. The most powerful man around is an Indian [Eulogio Añaguaya], a graduate of the evangelista's school. He has been appointed the Director of Statistics, President of the Cooperative, Representative of the Department of Roads, Commander of the Regiment, and Chief of the General Command. Such an accumulation of offices makes him practically the director of the town. The corregidor has very little to do, and what used to be the principal authority in the village has degenerated into an honorary position (1958 : 70–71).

The destruction of the hacienda system, the allocation of land ownership to the campesino population in the form of private property, the acquisition of influential political positions, and the consequential incentive among campesinos to accumulate wealth—the eradication of the very foundation of the vecino economy —created a boom in rural exchange. New market towns sprang up all over the altiplano, established by ambitious Aymara seeking to take advantage of the new, relatively unfettered rural economy and to set themselves up as members of new vecindarios, just as the vecinos in Kachitu had done half a century earlier.

Two new markets were established just north and south of Kachitu that meet on Wednesdays and Saturdays respectively. By selling there, the Aymara avoid paying the Kachitu Sunday market tax to the vecindario. Between the early '50s and late '70s, these two markets grew to major proportions while the Kachitu Sunday market dwindled to nearly nothing.

In the new towns, and even in Kachitu itself, many Aymara set up their own tiendas. Here campesinos prefer to do business and avoid social and economic ties with mestizos. With a more positive impression of prerevolutionary mestizo-Aymara relations than I am depicting in this book, Carter wrote:

> Even the godparentage, introduced by the Spanish brand of Catholicism, seems to become less important every year. Godparents may be appointed . . . [but] it is seldom that mestizo godparents in Kachitu today take their relationship very seriously. . . . In times past, Doña Teresa Cordova, for example, was reported to have over one hundred godchildren. These people would patronize her store, and therefore, for her, it was good business. [However,] the recent upheavals, when these mestizos were nearly driven out of the town, and when some of their leaders lost their land holdings, have put a wall of distrust between them and the Indians that will be hard to break down (1958 : 103).

Contrary to Carter's immediate impressions, compadrazgo relations were in 1978 very much a vibrant institution in Kachitu and throughout Bolivia. They form an essential component of Bolivian social structure and remain the primary facilitator of upward mobility as well as a major form of social security. As a non-corporate structure, the institution allows flexibility in a marginal economy. However, major changes have taken place in the construction of compadrazgo ties to accommodate the social changes initiated by the revolution. As these accommodations were made, the secondary resources for which medicine is primary have also changed. Contemporary compadrazgo relations include the ability of campesinos to pool resources in flush times so that resources can be withdrawn in times of scarcity, much as described by Schneider, Schneider, and Hansen (1972). To do so, egalitarian ties have been valuable, although asymmetrical ties are still used by the upwardly mobile. Compadrazgo relations among Protestants and among many Aymara have taken the form of an alliance rather than of patron-clientage. Medical dialogue is the major mechanism by which such compadrazgo relations are initiated. Because it is both intimate and highly informative about social relations, it is particularly efficacious in initiating egalitarian relations across ethnic lines that would previously have demanded asymmetrical ones. Doña Antonia de Villazon's strategy to do just that with her Aymara friends is a case in point.

The flexibility of these changes in the institution of compadrazgo has rendered impossible the old vecino strategy of accumulating resources through fictive kinship outside a cash economy. Thus all vecinos who had the skill, capital, social ties, and the freedom from responsibilities in town left Kachitu. Many, however, were not so favorably endowed, especially those at the bottom of the mestizo socioeconomic and political hierarchy. For these vecinos, urban migration meant even more dismal prospects of poverty than staying behind in Kachitu. Accustomed to belonging to an elite class in an obscure rural environment, they preferred poverty with a prestigious history in Kachitu to obscurity in the unskilled laboring slums of La Paz. With little or no wealth, these vecinos were unable to take advantage of the entrepreneurial possibilities that emerged after 1953.

In 1976 there are approximately 110 households in Kachitu. Of these 110 households, approximately 25 are vecinos. Only four, including Antonia and Lorenzo Villazon, do not own a tienda. Peluquilla has a tienda but never uses it; she is too emotionally unstable to do so. Several families, including the Cordovas, have two or three tiendas because the family in the household is extended. They still sell the usual inventory of goods with a few additions, including bread, the hottest selling item, baked by Emilio Ordoñez, an enterprising upwardly mobile Methodist Aymara. One of the oldest and most prestigious vecino widows, Victoria Castellano, continues to run the pension that her parents established at the turn of the century. Another widowed vecina who lives on the square serves lunch on Sundays for the peasants who come to town for the Sunday market, as well as coffee and tea every morning to those individuals waiting about for the truck to come through town. Several other mestiza women, like Leonora de Ugalde, wear "chola" dress[6]—the dress of Indian merchant women who articulate with a cash economy—and barter herbs and magical items with campesinos at the Wednesday, Saturday, and Sunday markets in return for grain and eggs[7] that they trade to "chola" women in La Paz for the herbs and magical items. Their profit in grain and eggs is consumed.

The national shift of investment from the highlands to the lowlands also reduced the extent to which vecinos can resort to what few compadrazgo ties they still maintain with the Aymara in order to accumulate resources. Noodles and rice, a postrevolutionary product of the increasing agribusiness in Santa Cruz, is a new addition to the tienda inventory, amenable to the greater cash flow among the Aymara on the altiplano. Because noodles and rice must be brought from commercial establishments in La Paz, they inhibit bartering activity. Alas, because they are commercial, they have greater prestige, particularly among the vecinos, than barley and quinoa, which are considered "campesino food," although they are superior nutritionally, especially in protein. Consequently Kachituños are buying nutritionally less valuable goods as their market expands beyond the limits of its traditional four-zone exchange network, and the vecinos are most vulnerable to the negative consequences. Campesinos, however, tend to stick to their traditional potato, quinoa, and barley diet because they continue to operate principally outside the cash economy.

Teaching school is the only salaried employment available that carries with it the dignity defined by prerevolutionary vecino society. For many vecinos, including the landless and tiendaless families like Antonia and Lorenzo Villazon, teaching is their principal means of support. It is for vecinos, however, highly unsatisfactory. Sadly, its difficulties stem from the vecinos' own attempt to improve education in Kachitu.

In the 1960s the Bolivian government took over the Methodist elementary schools throughout the canton of Kachitu in order to take control over campesino education. Having a small educational budget and assuming that few Indians made it through elementary school, the government ignored the Methodist high school in Kachitu. The national educational system was divided into two sectors, urban and rural, presumably to orient rural education to the needs and interests of the campesinos. The division, however, sanctioned less investment in rural education. All education is provided in Spanish. Materials are nonexistent. Preparation for becoming a rural schoolteacher is only four years, compared to the six-year education required of urban schoolteachers. What is not provided in infrastructure, however, is often compensated for by the rural teachers who are often Aymara themselves, dedicated to the improvement of their comunidades, and willing to invest far more of themselves than upwardly mobile, consumption-oriented urban teachers who have the misfortune to be assigned to the countryside and who tend to be contemptuous of the Aymara.

The vecinos, determined to get their children out of Kachitu, wanted them to receive a classical education equivalent to what they imagined their counterparts were receiving in La Paz. They believed that urban schoolteachers, with their more extensive training, would be more appropriate for their children. Thus they petitioned the government to make Kachitu an urban school, which they hoped would raise the status of Kachitu itself through further differentiating the municipality from the comunidades. They thought it would be an investment in the town.

The Bolivian government obliged. As a result, the vecino schoolteachers were prohibited from teaching there because, being poor, they all had rural teacher training. Urban teachers unhappily arrived to replace them. They were contemptuous of such a backwater hamlet. They pervaded the school with a sense of self-hatred and shame.

Teaching positions are allocated by the Ministry of Education according to the needs of the government, which still operates by the spoils system and is dominated by patron-client relations. In the 1970s teachers were required to pledge allegiance to particular political parties. Desirable teaching posts were given to those who complied, to individuals who had been politically useful, and to people who could pull strings by calling upon compadrazgo relations. To Kachitu they sent first-year graduates to fulfill their loathed required year of service to understaffed areas as repayment for their education, and those teachers least successful in negotiating their way through the urban system. Unfamiliar with the countryside, these teachers were uninterested in it. Their status was dependent upon a non-Indian identity, creating a conflict of interest, since the majority of Kachitu's school-children are Aymara.

Meanwhile, teachers from Kachitu were sent to distant comunidades, rarely if ever in their own canton, because they had no mechanisms to negotiate their way through the bureaucracy in La Paz. Their absence as husbands and fathers for many months at a time created strife and strains on family relations. Two households, rather than one, had to be maintained. Rumors abounded that husbands were cheating on their wives, giving Peluquilla vast resources for her public orations. Neighbors compounded her reports with opinions designed to make themselves look good in light of the disgrace under discussion.

The different interests of the new teachers in Kachitu are yet another affront to what remains of the vecindario, and this inflames the vecinos' desire to leave town, their need to protect their wounded dignity, or their desire to attempt to establish new egalitarian social relations with campesinos. At the beginning of the school year in 1977, a dozen contemptuous, dissatisfied, and thoroughly uninterested teachers from La Paz grumpily arrived in town, most several days late, and vociferously complained about their assignment. To them Kachitu was Bolivia's Siberia. Frequently they left to receive their pay in La Paz several days early and returned several days late, leaving the school unattended. They justified their actions on the basis of the miserably low pay they received, an average of $75.00 U.S. a month, out of which was taken the following deductions: social security, security for children, a required donation to the government to help it build more schools, funeral costs, income tax, health insurance, and mandatory remittance to the teachers' cooperative that permitted individuals to take out loans. If one took out a loan, repayments were also deducted. One teacher brought home less than $44.00 U.S. a month, on which she and her two children subsisted. By the standards of the 1980s, when gross salaries dropped to $20.00 a month, that was a fortune, but in 1977, the teachers complained it was flagrantly inadequate.

On March 3, 1977, the teachers attended a meeting called by the Padres de Familia, the local equivalent of the PTA, to complain of teachers' tardiness and inattendance. The teachers threatened to go on strike. Intimidated, the Padres conceded, and the teachers continued to attend to school in Kachitu as they pleased.

In 1978, beyond maintaining tiendas and teaching school, vecinos do nothing else. Many no longer own land, having sold it long ago for cash. Peluquilla's history is the most extreme but most revealing of the remaining vecinos in Kachitu. When she married in 1950, she and her husband had been highly prestigious, wealthy in land and compadrazgo ties, and respected members of the vecindario. Perceiving himself to have lost everything worthwhile in the revolution, her husband sold what little land they had left and drank himself to death. In the process, he abused his seven children and was probably responsible for the death of two of them. Peluquilla's arm remains twisted and mutilated where he broke it once in a drunken rage. When one of the physicians at the clinic offers to correct it for her, free of cost, she refuses. Perhaps some connection to the good man her husband was before he lost himself is embedded in her broken arm. In 1978 Peluquilla survives on the generosity of the Aymara, the only Kachituños who take pity on her.

In contrast, the Methodists are familiar with the cash economy and proficient in its use as a result of the vocational and organizational skills and opportunities provided by the mission. As many mestizos abandoned Kachitu after 1952, Methodist Aymara moved in from the comunidades and invested their small accumulations of capital in a variety of entrepreneurial activities. In 1978 there are approximately thirty Aymara families in Kachitu who augment their agricultural endeavors with some sort of commercial activity that provides a cash income and has become their primary source of livelihood. All thirty have at one time or another been affiliated with the Methodist church. Perhaps fifteen have tiendas and adults in five of these families also teach school. Several others have accumulated enough capital to buy a truck and transport goods and people from Kachitu and other towns on the altiplano to La Paz.

Emilio Ordoñez was trained as a mechanic by the Methodist church and was employed by the clinic for many years. After the revolution he moved from Chojña Kanata into an abandoned house on the town square. With the income he saved from his salary, he bought a truck and transported goods and people to and from the city, while his wife ran a tienda, out of the front of their house, strategically situated on the town square. With their combined incomes they were able to open the first bakery in Kachitu.

As Emilio's market is guaranteed, he has become the wealthiest man in town. Financially able to sponsor a fiesta by the early 1970s, he has transformed himself into a vecino. Since the missionaries are gone and because his economic position is so substantial, he has not been ostracized from the church for doing so. However, his interest is in having access to the vecino domain, not in abandoning his Methodist identity. Thus, unlike Don Abelardo, who manages the clinic, Emilio has never assumed the title of Don. He and his wife have four children in sound health and have suffered no miscarriages or deaths.

Felipe Apaza, the head nurse at the clinic, came to Kachitu from Qaruru, one of the comunidades in which there had been a mission school. In 1978 he is also the clinic administrator. The Aymara say proudly, "Felipe Apaza is the hospital administrator." As such he wields a lot of power in Kachitu. His authority is substantiated by his having been elected president of the Padres de Familia. As hospital administrator, Felipe Apaza is concerned with constricting funds. It is he who reduces Antonia de Villazon's salary for washing sheets and towels. In her anger she complains to me that Apaza himself receives four salaries: for being administrator, nurse, radiologist, and laboratory technician. Apaza also picks up extra cash by running a private clinic out of his home for people who don't wish to go to the clinic hospital, either because he can treat some cases less expensively, or because he is more tolerant of Aymara medical belief than many of the doctors at the hospital and incorporates indigenous medical resources with his cosmopolitan medical skills. He is very proud of the Aymara medical tradition and wants someday to write a book on it. Felipe Apaza and his wife have five healthy children and have suffered no deaths or miscarriages.

Also in Kachitu in 1978 are Aymara Methodist carpenters, bricklayers and blacksmiths, a butcher, a radio repair man, and a tailor. There are also some shops that are more substantial than the traditional tienda: several bookstores, a hardware store, and a sort of variety store that sells cookware and clothing. The nine friends who run the only tractor with Nathan Robison have become excellent mechanics. While all these activities operate primarily in cash, their initiators continue to cultivate land, providing them with the largest safety net in the postrevolutionary economy. They have all, at one time or another, been affiliated with the Methodist church.

Thus since 1952 the Kachitu mestizos have gradually grown poorer and poorer in wealth and land, have been stripped of the fundamental symbols of cultural dignity, and have been rendered economically, socially, and politically impotent. At the same time the educated Methodist Aymara have become proud, self-confident leaders in their church where they gather to discuss Aymara nationalism and read Freire's *Pedagogy of the Oppressed*. The Aymara campesinos, for whom the revolution was presumably fought, are in many ways only marginally better off than they were before 1952. Although they are now owners of the land they once rented from the hacienda, the amount of such land is so small that it inhibits investment to intensify agriculture. So poor is the national government that few programs have ever been instituted to economically benefit the Aymara, and those who were helped are long since dead. Governing the poorest country in the Western Hemisphere, the Bolivian government, whether it be democratic or a dictatorship, has been unable to develop the altiplano. Though the hacienda system is now history, and the market structure of the altiplano has changed, the Aymara remain the poorest population in Kachitu. Their strategic options are to follow the Methodist Aymara in their quest for the empowerment of their ethnic group or to establish a vecindario in one of the new towns. The political dimensions of these changes in structures of opportunities that have developed in the twentieth century are expressed in medical dialogue. When talking about illnesses Kachituños express all the joy and agony of the past 100 years of the history of the town. Through medical dialogue, they also try to do something about it.

CHAPTER 5

Indigenous Medicine

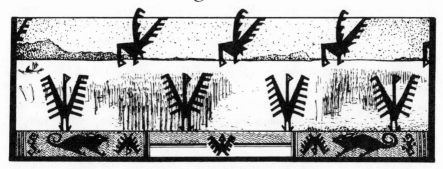

THE CONSTRUCTION OF SOCIAL RELATIONS IN KACHITU THROUGH AYMARA MEDICINE

Aymara medicine, like all other medical systems, consists of nosological categories and etiological beliefs, an inventory of therapeutic resources, and a body of curative theory about their deployment. A compilation of Aymara therapeutic resources and techniques is available in several comprehensive volumes by Enrique Oblitas Poblete (1963, 1969, 1971) and a more recent work by Gregorio Losa Balsa (1977). Joseph Bastien has published symbolic analyses of Kallawaya medicine, from which Aymara medicine derives and which some authors call Aymara medicine (1978a; 1978b). Douglas Sharon's description of a Peruvian *curandero's* therapeutic practices (1978) doesn't differ substantially from descriptions of the practices of yatiris. Comparable data from Kachitu—a list of all diseases and illnesses, their etiologies, and recommended therapeutic procedures—are provided in appendixes 1 and 2. Essential to the use of these resources as primary resources is the transformation of etiologies (and hence therapeutic procedures) over time as a reflection of history and changes in social relations. The history of the etiology of the kharisiri is a case in point.

Throughout the centuries of Spanish colonialism, and indeed until the 1950s, the kharisiri, often called the Kari Kari or other similar name, was widely known throughout the Bolivian altiplano as a phantasm that brought a specific disease, diagnosable by the marks it left on the abdomen.[1] It has traditionally been considered fatal. But in Kachitu in 1977 and 1978, it was not.

Until the 1950s the kharisiri was universally the image of a dead Franciscan monk. It had a broad Franciscan hat and a long beard, and it roamed about the countryside at night where people often sleep to watch over their fields at planting and at harvest. The kharisiri magically removed the fat from its victims' kidneys and gave it to the bishop. Out of the kidney fat of the Aymara Indians, the bishop made holy oil.

Marks remain where the kharisiri makes his incisions. Father Joe Picardi, a Maryknoll priest working in Achacachi in 1978 claimed to have seen three such cases, although he allowed that they were psychosomatic. His work was devoted to changing the Aymara image of the Catholic church embedded in this etiological theory, which he referred to as myth. The evolution of the theory in Kachitu since the 1950s shows that the oppressive nature of social relations between cultural groups hasn't changed on the altiplano; only the identity of the oppressors has changed.

The theory underwent its first paradigmatic shift during the years of the Alliance for Progress, the inter-American program of economic assistance created in 1961. The nature of exploitation expressed in the theory began to reflect capitalist market relations. Many Bolivians interpreted the Alliance as an attempt by the United States to practice genocide for imperialist gain. The popular film *The Blood of the Condor*, or *Yawar Mallku*, portrays Peace Corps volunteers performing involuntary sterilizations on Bolivian peasant women, and in 1978 I was advised not to eat Alliance for Progress food lest it make me sterile. By that time the kharisiri was said to steal kidney fat to sell to the North Americans to run their electricity.

By the time of my arrival in Kachitu in 1977, the kharisiri was believed to be no longer a phantasm but any mestizo who participated in the trade of human kidney fat. The extraction of kidney fat could be learned, and the materials to extract it could be bought clandestinely in pharmacies in La Paz. Such fat was sold to factories in La Paz who used it to make colored, perfumed luxury bath soap for export, for tourists, and for the Bolivian elite. Perhaps because of the presence of the clinic, and perhaps because of a decrease in infant mortality since the land reform, a visitation from the kharisiri was no longer considered fatal, although still considered a serious illness.

The social structure expressed in the etiology of the kharisiri disease and in its evolution is a reflection of Kachitu's and Bolivian history. It expresses how Kachituños understand social relations and their relationship to health. In this etiology, the loss of mestizo power is made explicit. Many mestizos reiterated this medical theory to me. Don Arturo Cruz, said Doña Antonia, died because he *was* a kharisiri. He was in desperate financial shape after the revolution and resorted to this means of making money. She knew this because when Cruz died, his face was black and his body was swollen like that of a toad that is used to ensorcell. In such ways indigenous medical ideology embodies interpretations of social structure and social relations.

Medical ideology is employed, however, not only to locate the subject or patient under discussion within that social structure, but to locate the interpreter— the diagnostician—as well. Through Aymara etiology and medical theory run images of power relations and their consequences: insatiable hunger, the vulnerability of subordination, victimization, and exploitation. Moralism is visibly absent, except as it emerges from the mestizo domain to maintain mestizo dominance over the Aymara. Doña Teresa Cordova's views on miscarriage and abortion are a case in point.

HAIL

Doña Teresa, the town aristocrat, uses the Aymara medical theory of miscarriage and abortion to her own advantage. She herself does not believe in it, she tells me, but everyone else does, and she must concede to the majority. Miscarriage, abortion (both induced and spontaneous), and stillbirth cause hail. Hail is sent by El Tio,[2] not to punish the mother but to satisfy his own hunger. When a child dies before baptism, its soul is unable to enter heaven. It thus may become an agent of El Tio, who uses it as a means to "eat" crops by destroying men. As such, hail is considered a major public health hazard, a community concern, and a community responsibility.

Hail falls frequently on the altiplano. In this environment where the margin of flexibility is very narrow, the destruction of crops by hail may trigger famine for those families whose plots are hit. Some say hail falls on crops within a several-mile radius around the mother of an aborted fetus or unbaptized stillbirth. Others claim it falls over the area where the infant's body is discarded. Following the latter theory, crop destruction from hail can be avoided by burying the fetus or unbaptized child near the mountains, away from the agricultural fields. A woman without child but with milk in her breasts is held responsible for the lost crops. When hail falls, the Aymara campesino authorities, the Jilacatas, go from house to house, examining the breasts of women in search of evidence of an unbaptized dead child.

In my presence, some mestizos and Methodists disclaimed this belief, but it is significant that they have access to a cash income. For Aymara campesinos who have none, crop damage is critical. Holding one person responsible for the livelihood of many efficiently benefits a large number of people at the expense of one. Campesinos do not perpetuate social condemnation of a mother if she fulfills her obligations by financially compensating the victims, and they levy no other social sanction against her. The expense, however, cripples her and her family for years. In 1978, all Kachituños interviewed concurred that a fetus is found after every hailstorm. Vecinos can benefit by extending social condemnation of the mother beyond fulfillment of her obligations, as did Doña Teresa in November of 1977.

Toward the end of that month, a series of hailstorms caused considerable damage in the agricultural fields outside Kachitu. On November 25, a childless campesina named Flor was found to be lactating. Thus she was held responsible for the crop damage. Those campesinos whose fields had been damaged gathered in the corregidor's office in Kachitu to demand that an order be issued to force Flor to financially compensate them for their losses. They fortified their assertion with evidence that she had been seen at the hospital. Flor claimed she had merely gone to the hospital because she had been sick. Her accusers alleged she had gone for prenatal care. To deflect her responsibility from herself, she pleaded that the medicine she had received at the clinic for an illness had caused her to abort. Consensus held that the doctor's role made little difference in her obligation to the community. Flor was found guilty and ordered to compensate her neighbors for their losses, a sum which would place her in debt for many years. A Kachituño remarked:

> The child should be buried away from people and the chacras [cultivated fields]. That is why Flor had to pay a fine to everyone for her abortion. She buried the child near chacras so that the hail destroyed them. Had she taken it to the cordillera, the hail would have fallen in the mountains.

Baptized children are registered in the civil archives and buried in the Kachitu cemetery. These two acts identify the children as legitimate, accepted into the community, and delivered into the hands of God. As such they cannot plague the community with hail and crop destruction. Every Aymara woman carries a responsibility for the entire community within her womb, while the community is responsible for infant legitimacy through baptism and civil registration. Mestizos, however, control the civil archives. In fact, in 1978 they were controlled by Doña Teresa Cordova.

One day that November, I sat taking tea with Doña Teresa in the doorway of her tienda, when a campesino came to register a child. Doña Teresa inquired about the nature of the register. The campesino was at first evasive and finally replied that the child had been born the day before but died within a few hours. He wished to register both the birth and the death. Doña Teresa refused. The man insisted. She was adamant. He pleaded. The two argued in Aymara with obviously harsh words and considerable emotion. In the end, Doña Teresa remained inflexible and the man retreated with a look of anxiety, defeat, and fear. To me she explained:

> When a child is born, it must be baptized immediately. Without being baptized and named, a child cannot be buried in the cemetery, and God only allows children buried in the cemetery into Heaven. If the child cannot be buried in the cemetery, it must be buried somewhere else. Sometimes foolish campesina women bury their children near agricultural fields, where the campesinos believe El Tio can use it to send hail and eat crops. Of course I cannot register a birth if the child is already dead. That is why the man today was in such a hurry to get the child's existence—brief as it was—registered and buried in the town cemetery with the rest of the family and avoid the terror of having to return to an angry community. He will have to pay for all that crop damage. Perhaps the nuns can give an order for the child to be buried in the cemetery, but there is nothing I can do.

Although Doña Teresa responded to my protest by claiming to disapprove of the theory of hail, she most likely was right: it may well have been too late to protect the campesino. Someone else would be found to blame. The theory is a valuable redistributer of resources among those campesinos threatened by hail. But as long as the archives remain in mestizo hands, the proposition takes on further sociological significance. It perpetuates the prerevolutionary arrangement of power allocation. Through control of the civil archives, Teresa is able to maintain her prerevolutionary strategy of cultural identity, at least when it hails. While the metaphor for lack of campesino control is perpetuated in the victimization and exploitation of the dead infant by El Tio, come to eat the crops, the subordinate position of the campesinos to the vecinos is reconstituted in the vecino complaint that hail falls near the fetus, not the mother. The complaint implies that were the mother socially responsible and had she buried the fetus away from the fields, hail would not have destroyed the crops. The campesino mother is, from the vecino point of view, irresponsible rather than victimized by El Tio.

The etiology of kharisiri and of hail are two examples of indigenous medical ideology that is based on an epistemological premise of how the world operates. The world operates the way it does according to "natural laws" that emerged from the manner in which the world was created.

THE KACHITU COSMOLOGICAL UNIVERSE AND HOW IT CAME TO BE

The metaphor for the operative principle behind supernatural human interaction is insatiable hunger. Just as the Bolivian elite exploit the Indian for their sustenance, so too are the supernatural dependent on human beings. They interact with humans principally to satisfy their appetite: they either protect health in exchange for food or impose disease to extract it. Why the supernatural have such appetites is explained in the creation myth that is popular in town in spite of the efforts of the Reverend Angel and Father Christian to impose a version closer to biblical doctrine.

In the early history of the Kachitu universe, according to several Aymara yatiris in and around Kachitu, God filled the original world with all things in abundance and lived there with El Tio in peace and harmony. But El Tio hungered after God's power. In his jealousy he incited the population against God, and thus power took on an evil aspect. God retaliated by destroying this imperfect world with rain, and creating the new one which exists today. Here El Tio's ability to acquire power is limited only by the number of humans—essentially powerless—to collude with El Tio for help. June Nash (1979) and Michael Taussig (1980) discuss in detail the gifts of ore and health El Tio provided the miners at Siglo XX in return for *mesa* offerings and llama sacrifice. El Tio shares the constant experience of hunger with humans. It is El Tio's appetite for power that is evil, and thus his acquisition of it will eventually destroy himself and this world with fire. Out of those who survive Judgment, God will create the third and final and spiritual world. The rumor about town in 1978 was that these survivors would be good Evangelicals and Catholics.

Thus El Tio of Kachitu is a greedy fool who envied the authority to which he was subordinate, and who would play the role of God himself. Unlike the Christian Devil, El Tio himself is not evil, only irreparably self-deceived. The Kachitu God, on the other hand, has little interest in human affairs and remains aloof. In this world, he does not actively rule nor intervene in human affairs. People are left to negotiate their way to Judgment Day through the delicate balance between their own needs and the hunger of El Tio, whose satisfaction often keeps their own hunger and disease at bay.

The complication with El Tio is that, like all God's creatures, he is essentially good. In a maneuver for power, however, he created the evil of insatiable hunger, to which all people—but for luck and circumstance—may fall victim. The contradiction inherent in insatiable hunger is that it must be fed lest it too die. Through insatiable hunger, El Tio's maneuver for power is reproduced.

Limpu is a good example of the reproductive nature of insatiable hunger and how it victimizes and exploits the subordinate (campesino). It is an illness visited upon the campesino witness to a stillbirth. Because the child dies before it can be baptized, it cannot get into heaven. Thus it must spend eternity in nihility unless it can establish itself on earth. But to live on earth it must eat. And so the soul of the dead child enters the body of a witness on the instant it emerges from the womb, and it feeds on that person until that person dies and the soul of the child along with it. Symptoms pertaining to limpu are identical to those pertaining to anemia.

It is not only El Tio who is hungry. Even God must eat. God has three forms. As spirit he is Dios, who will pass judgment upon behavior when this world comes to an end. He will determine the spiritual end of humanity. But God is also life, the giver of life, the Mother Earth, and the protector of the Aymara, the Pachamama. It is the Pachamama who created this world. Although the Pachamama does not actively intervene in human affairs, she does, unlike Dios, prevent evil. She is the essence of preventive medicine. She is the focus of agricultural rites at planting, of the baptism of a new truck or major piece of equipment, and of the ceremonies that initiate building construction and that insure a good harvest, productive labor, and a safe home. To initiate her beneficence, the Kachituño offers food. The Pachamama likes sweet foods, *dulce mesas*,[3] which can be bought in all local tiendas; red wine; and occasionally food such as humans consume: a guinea pig or chicken, potatoes, and llama fat. All Kachituños make offerings to the Pachamama once a year to protect them from evil, bad luck, and poor health. And whenever anyone takes a drink, be it alcohol, soda, or water, one always pours a few drops on the earth to the Pachamama before imbibing.

God is also culture, and as culture he is the Condor Mamani, who lives in the home. Like the Pachamama, the Condor Mamani is protective and does not actively manipulate elements in the real world, and he does not mete out moral retribution, except to withdraw his protective powers if he is not properly and frequently remembered and fed. And like the Pachamama, he prefers the best of what humans eat, although he does prefer cane liquor to wine.

Although El Tio has one form only, he keeps company with a multitude of other supernatural beings willing to actively intervene in human affairs to extract food. They are willing to beguile, convince, contrive, steal, and victimize to be fed, but mostly they are willing to heal. "El Tio is willing to do good so that you will worship him, not God," said a yatiri, "and so he can eat." Indeed his name indicates his beneficial activities, and his kinship with humanity through the need for food (c.f. Taussig 1980; Nash 1979). Many supernatural beings are friendly and helpful in curing illness and disease, like the achachillas who live in the mountains and rivers. Others, like the khan achachi, inflict illness to demand food and will not retract the illness until they have been fed. What the worst of such phantasms demand is often not fit for human consumption: llama fetuses, human placentas, dried toads, and other "delicacies" that are, in fact, expensive to obtain. But the supernatural benign prefer the best of what humans eat, along with dulce mesas and *chiuchi mesas*,[4] the heart of curing rituals.

The relationship between these beings and humankind as expressed through illness and disease is not moral, as is the case, for example, between the Devil and Christians. The Kachitu supernatural victimize and exploit their human hosts. In most cases, however, the host is vulnerable only when he or she is emotionally or socially subordinate: sad, frightened, preoccupied, alone, or Aymara (and more recently, mestizo). The happy, the content, the drunk, and whites are immune except to the most abusive entities.

Achachillas will actively intervene in human affairs in exchange for food. Multitudes of them live in the hills, rivers, and mountains. Indeed, every geographical formation is the home of an achachilla. They are willing to improve both health and material well-being. When Doña Soña Roman brought a yatiri to my house to improve my financial situation, he asked an achachilla to help me.

Unlike the Condor Mamani and the Pachamama, achachillas have very human attributes. The term *"achachi"* is a derogatory term for "old man," but the suffix *"la"* softens it, and renders it wise, familiar, and somewhat affectionate. A yatiri explained to me:

> Many years ago several men gathered together in a room and wondered if God was with them there. They put out their candles and in the darkness they heard the voices of achachillas come to prove to the men their own existence. The men were praying when the achachillas entered making noises and talking like human beings. They drank like humans, making noises, and they chewed coca like humans making noises as they chewed. Each achachilla introduced himself; each had a separate voice and a distinctive name—the names of the mountains and rivers in which they live. But they didn't mingle with the men; they sat apart. Achachillas are like El Tio in that they are yankha: *harmful and noxious to the health. But*

they are not the same as El Tio. They are not dead people who are the property of El Tio. They do not appear in different forms. And they will cure, if you feed them properly.

Nastier phantoms are not located in one place but roam about actively seeking victims upon whom they can place heavy demands for food. *Anchanchus* are teasers and inflict mental illness. They assume two general forms: an image of the victim's lover or of something absurd. An anchanchu appears and confuses the victim who, if the anchanchu takes the former image, mistakes it for the sweetheart, or if the latter, is terrorized by immediate demands. Anchanchus are blamed for many but not all mental disorders.

"There are many anchanchus," said Doña Antonia, peering authoritatively over her cooking pot at me.

They take many different forms, and they live in solitary places like in crevices and abandoned houses. And if you see one, you're in big trouble because you have to do what they say or they'll kill you. My mother saw one. What she saw was a little dwarf with boils on his hands. He could slap you and the boils would kill you. My mother was playing with her sisters by the oven outside and he wanted to play with them. He had little play pots of gold and silver. They were scared. They did not want to play, but they did. If they had not, the dwarf would have become angry and slapped them and killed them with his boils. After he was satisfied they would do what he wanted, he left them alone. But my mother came down with a bad fever afterwards.

Some anchanchus are men and women with huge tits. My mother saw them playing on the bandstand in the park one evening. They were dancing and playing by throwing their huge tits up, first one, then the other. After she saw them, Mother came down with a fever again.

Here in Kachitu there are two anchanchus. One is the old burro who lives in Castelluma, behind the rock outcrop. He killed Jose Ticona a few years back, you know, the husband of the widow Ticona who lives near Genara. He came down with a fever and went crazy until he died.

Then sometimes—at midnight or at dawn—two chariots ride along that sheep path halfway up the rock outcrop behind the town. They ride toward each other as if they are going to crash. I do not know if they crash, because if you look, the sight drives you crazy and kills you.

Unlike any of the more assertive supernaturals, the khan achachi chooses its victims indiscriminately. He demands to be fed, and inflicts illness and death upon those who refuse such payment. While *achachi* is an insulting term for "old man," *khana* is Aymara for net. Hence *khan achachi* is a derogatory term for a personified old net: an old man who is abusive. But *khana* is also Aymara for "substitution for another" or "payment by another," and *achachi kumu* refers to those campesinos in certain parts of Bolivia who disguise themselves as old Spanish men during the fiesta of Corpus Cristi and assert absolute authority over the Aymara dancers. The khan achachi has complete power: there is no security against it.

Its primary form is a ball of fire with a long tail. This fire assaults agricultural fields or family plots, leaving a charred mark where it insists that an altar to it be built. Annual sacrifices of food must then be made on the altar in perpetuity. Lack of obedience is followed by illness, death, and the signature of the khan that appears in the form of a red dog, as in Seferino's case.

Many people in Kachitu claim to have seen the khan achachi. One miner insisted he saw it every night at nine o'clock on the deserted, far side of the valley. Other people have seen several of them as balls of fire dancing on the top of the hill across from town.

But in the Kachitu cosmology, it is El Tio that makes the most extreme demands: human life. In the mines he can crush workers in a landslide or simply make the ore disappear, a signal that he wants a human sacrifice (c.f. Taussig 1980; Nash 1979). Or he can strike in broad daylight in the form of lightning and kill his victim to satisfy his rampant hunger. Such victims must be buried where they are struck and not removed to the cemetery, so that El Tio can eat to his satisfaction and will not—the people hope—seek more victims in the immediate vicinity. El Tio is perceived as the first genuine public health menace. Occasionally he will select an unwitting victim, frighten him with an anchanchu, steal his soul, and let him die a slow death, giving the living the opportunity to give huge offerings to appease his appetite. And like the achachillas, he will actively intervene in human affairs . . . for a price, often the soul of the petitioner.

THE YATIRI

In Kachitu the principle curer is the yatiri. In other areas of the altiplano the yatiri is only one of many indigenous health specialists. *Kolliris, chamakanis,* blind men, Kallawayas, and *jach'a tatas* practice throughout the Bolivian highlands. In Kachitu, however, references to such practitioners are rare. I know of only one case in which any practitioner besides a yatiri was sought. It occurred in a mestizo household when Doña Eva took the advice of a Kallawaya. The terms *kolliri* and *yatiri* were often used interchangeably. Chamakanis, blind men, and jach'a tatas are not resources available in Kachitu, although it was suggested that, as chamakanis talk to living spirits, I should find one and save myself the cost of longdistance telephone calls to my parents. In Kachitu, though, it is the yatiri who monopolizes the indigenous curative practice. What the yatiri monopolizes, however, is not knowledge but power to divine and contact the supernatural. With this power the Aymara yatiri can alter the fate of the entire population of the altiplano, be they Aymara, mestizos, or visiting gringas.

In and around Kachitu there are a large number of yatiris—several per comunidad—although in 1976 through 1978 there were none in Kachitu proper. Kachituños in need had to dispatch messengers to the comunidades and often entice them with higher prices and greater benefits than the going rate of compensation in the yatiris' own comunidades, particularly if the entreator came from a different ethnic group. Some yatiris were born with the skill; others acquired it by miraculously surviving something fatal: a malarial fever or being struck by lightning were the two most common. Because they have the power to learn from and negotiate with the supernatural, they expect to be treated with honor and deference, and perhaps a little fear.

When a yatiri is called in on a case, his first interest is in determining who or what is responsible for it. Thus the first order of business is to divine.

On February 17, 1978, the yatiri who Soña Roman has called on my behalf arrives in town. Soña has determined that, because I did not go to an annual Aymara fair, called *Alacitas*, and buy miniature money that would give me vast wealth in the following year, I am financially irresponsible. She has called a yatiri to insure my financial future. Soña sends one of her children to advise me of his arrival and that I must prepare. She sends me out to buy a long list of things the yatiri will need:

coca[5] leaf	incense
a dulce mesa	a chiuchi mesa
carbon	strips of colored wool
a brazier	llama fat
llama wool	wine
cane alcohol	beer
cigarettes	a *tari* cloth to put the coca in

Then she sends me home to make him dinner. The yatiri will be having dinner at my house and will spend the night, she advises me, and have breakfast, too, she adds after I have done the dinner's shopping. I make a second trip to buy some more things and go home to cook and make a bed.

I am very excited when he arrives at eight o'clock and I have a thousand questions to ask. But he motions for me to be patient and quiet. He cannot talk while he eats. For well over a half hour I sit with my hands folded, silently waiting. I know that the ritual has to end by midnight because it has to be done on Thursday. One can only talk to the achachillas on Mondays and Thursdays. I am anxious while he helps himself to seconds and then thirds. Almost an hour later, the yatiri lifts his eyes, wipes his mouth, and indicates that he is ready. I and Soña, who has come to facilitate my miserable Aymara, have been asked to fulfill a role of reverence and obedience for that hour.

Now he directs us to spread the coca leaves on the tari cloth and sort out the best ones, the unbroken and unblemished. The yatiri, Soña, and I collect several handfuls of leaves which the yatiri wraps up in the tari. He folds the tari over four times and hands it to me, telling me to hold it under my clothes and next to my breast for a few moments so that the leaves can "know" me. He then puts it on the table and sprinkles alcohol over it. He opens the tari and sprinkles alcohol over the leaves. He folds the tari over again and kisses it. He gets up from the table with alcohol in hand and motions to us to go outside where we *challamos*: that is, we sprinkle alcohol all over the yard as an offering to the Pachamama. He drinks a little himself, makes us drink a little bit—I cough as the hard, burning liquor goes down my throat and he chuckles—and leads us back to the table inside. The three of us blow three times on the tari and he says a prayer. Now he is ready to read my fortune. Throughout all this activity, he and Doña Soña have been chatting in Aymara. Soña is so happy to be helping my financial future, and so animated, that she neglects to translate most of what is said.

The yatiri asks me if I have any questions. I ask him four research questions at the same time and he shakes his head. No, no: favors. Do I have any questions or favors I want from the achachillas. I think for a minute and ask that Oldemar, the little boy who lost his fingers when playing with a firecracker get well. This favor is unsuitable. I must ask for something for me, for my *suerte*. All right, I say, remembering that my research is coming to an end. I say I want a job by August.

He strategically places a number of leaves on the tari. One is for the Uchu Machiri, the achachilla that helps him regularly and communicates with this yatiri through the leaves. One is for me, my future, my luck: my suerte. The others stand for my work here, confidence in me among the people here in Kachitu, the job I requested, and a number of different achachillas. Four of the most strategically placed leaves also stand for thunder, my soul (ajayu), my health, and the achachilla responsible for my suerte. These also stand for lightning, the land, my spirit (animu), and my other soul, my *alma*. Each leaf is crossed with another, all face up and pointing in specific directions.

The yatiri now slowly sprinkles the rest of the selected leaves over these strategic leaves, and divines according to the relationship between how they fall and the strategically placed leaves. If leaves fall upside down it goes bad for me; if right side up my future looks good. If they fall on the back side they tell of my poor health; if on the right side they indicate good health. These two negative and positive signs are then interpreted according to their spacial relationship to the strategic leaves.

Generally speaking, things look pretty good for me. However, there is some lack of confidence in me in Kachitu. He asks me about it, and I admit difficulties. "We'll fix that," he says, and he asks the Uchu Machiri who is responsible for my suerte. The Uchu Machiri will respond through the leaves. The yatiri then reads that my husband is going to come and visit. I recall his constant conversation with Soña and wonder what she said to him. I see him looking at Anna and figure he figures I have a husband and knows I have been in Bolivia a year and a half. I tell him that I have been divorced for almost eight years, and that my ex-husband is poverty stricken, and that I do not believe him. I do not think until later that my common sense, not to mention my manners, frequently evade me when I am in the field. He is offended. Soña intervenes, castigates me, and says some conciliatory words to the yatiri. He snorts and agrees to continue.

To get me a job and improve my working relationship with the population of Kachitu, the yatiri removes all the negative leaves except a few, I notice. He is still a tad offended. Then he chooses three that are particularly well situated in relation to the leaves pertaining to confidence and job, and sets them aside.

Then he removes all the coca and begins to make a mesa for the achachilla. By the position of the leaves, he has been able to determine that the achachilla who lives in the rock outcrop behind the village is most significant for me. He takes a piece of paper and spreads the llama wool on top of it in a circle. On top of the llama wool he spreads symmetrically and in pleasing design the colored wool strips, the two mesas, the llama fat, and the coca leaves selected from the divination. He inspects the whole arrangement, makes a few changes, and determines that it is all right. He takes an empty bottle, uses it to grind up the incense, and sprinkles the incense on top. He "challars," or blesses, the mesa with alcohol and some of the wine. He drinks a good deal of the wine himself and asks us to do the same. Then he wraps up the mesa in the paper and ties it with the rest of the colored strips of wool. He puts the charcoal in the brazier and sprinkles it with what is left of the alcohol, and tells us it is time to leave.

In the cold, windy dark of night, the three of us ascend the rock outcrop behind the town. It is nearly midnight, and no one else in Kachitu is awake. There is no light. There is no moon and the stars at 13,000 feet are spectacularly plentiful, but they do not generate enough light to make me feel secure as I try to negotiate my way up the steep and difficult switchback that leads from the town square, up past the fourteen stations of the cross, to the statue of La Virgen de la Candelaria, which Victoria Castellano repaired this year, lest the virgin, distraught by the town's neglect of her, refuse to keep guard over the health and well-being of Kachitu.

We pass the virgin and head north along the sheep path that the anchanchu rides his two chariots on and pass over to the other side. By now I figure it must surely be past midnight, and all of this will have been for nothing. It is cold and I am tired, a little tipsy, and scared.

We arrive at a cave, the same cave the vecinos hid in when the revolution came in 1952. I recall that in his description of the 1952 revolution in town, Carter had mentioned this cave's use as a latrine, and I hesitate to enter. Soña gives me a castigating look that I can perceive without having to see it in the darkness. The two of us follow the yatiri in and kneel beside the brazier. The yatiri sprinkles incense over it and prays while Soña and I hold it and kneel in a supplicating posture. He lights it and holds it over my head while I worry that he is going to burn my hair. He prays. He puts the brazier down on the ground and gets on his own knees and prays a while. He asks for the beer that he had instructed me to bring along, opens it, shakes it, holding his thumb over the top, and "challars" the inside of the cave, first counterclockwise, then in the other direction, and then around the brazier. When he thinks the bottle is empty, he stops, but a great deal of foam remains inside the bottle. This indicates that I will come into a lot of money. With this "challa," the ritual is over and we are free to descend the outcrop and go home.

This ritual costs me approximately fifty dollars U.S. When I complain, I am assured that the ritual will bring me great success in my research, with which I will make a lot of money once I get back to the States. I grumble that the only use of the cigarettes has been the yatiri's enjoyment. On my next trip to La Paz I find two letters in the mail. One is from my ex-husband saying he and his mother are coming to Bolivia in June, and the other requests that I work for the Ministerio de Planificacion y Coordinacion in La Paz during the months of August and September.

THE SOUL

Social structure defines, of course, the indigenous conceptualization of racial constitution. Frequently Doña Teresa told me, as campesinos came to her office to register births, marriages, and deaths, that they were genetically coded to lie, steal, and stab me in the back. Evidence of genetics is in the blood, she said: Aymara blood is red, while white blood is blue, only turning red when it meets the air. This particular theory was quite controversial, and only a few mestizos subscribed to it.

A more general conceptualization that was used in dialogue and cultural identity negotiation during my stay in Kachitu is the conceptualization of souls.

Mestizos have one soul, but Aymara have three—hence my yatiri's use of three references to me: my ajayu, my animu, and my alma.

Some informants argue that Aymara believe everyone, including mestizos, has three souls while mestizos believe everyone has only one. Others argue that the number of souls is a constitutional racial trait. I never heard Aymara and mestizos debate the issue directly. Certain only is that three souls are associated with Aymara identity, and one soul with mestizo identity.

All agree that a child is born with a soul, an animu, which does not become solidly entrenched in the body until adolescence. Consequently, fright, shock, and sorrow debilitate the individual sufficiently to allow the animu to wander off. Any adult is capable of enticing it back. Symptoms of soul loss are general debilitation and loss of appetite, interest, and energy. It does not result in serious illness. This condition is easily distinguished from soul theft or consumption, which cause loss of reason, disease, or death. If the animu does not return it is presumed to be stolen or consumed, and more serious actions must be taken. Adults rarely lose their animus. This conception of soul loss derives from the Hispanic tradition and is common throughout Latin America.

Associated with Aymara cultural identity are two other souls. While the ajayu provides reasoning and consciousness, the animu is strength and courage, and the alma is spirit. The animu follows the Hispanic pattern of growth and development, wandering off during childhood when the child is frightened or sorrowful. The ajayu and alma, however, are more entrenched in the body at birth. The ajayu can be stolen or eaten by evil spirits, causing loss of reasoning, serious illness, and death, and requiring the intervention of a yatiri. Adults are just as susceptible to this type of soul theft as are children. The alma does not leave the body until death, and cannot be stolen. The alma is the spirit that lives on after death.

Renita explained to me when her daughter Maria died of soul theft:

> You can see them [the three souls] in your shadow. If you look at your shadow it has three parts; the fuzzy white top, the yellowish middle edge, and the black, solid part of the shadow. The white fuzz around the edge is the ajayu, the yellow in between is the animu, and the center of the shadow is the alma. When the achachillas eat your ajayu and your animu, your shadow has no edge to it, but just the solid mass part.
>
> This is why I say that there was no hope for my child. Her shadow had lost its fuzzy part. I took her to Rosa, an old woman who knows a lot, and she said it was the child's fate to die. I knew then that there was nothing I could do to save her. It was a waste of time, taking her to the hospital.

When an Aymara or Hispanic child appears ill but lacks the particular symptoms that would identify a disease requiring a specific treatment, soul loss is suspected. The parent puts the child to bed and calls the child's soul. The parent takes items that the child likes to eat—fruit and candy—and wraps them in some piece of the child's clothing. Taking them to the spot where the child was frightened or shocked, or outside in the night air if no specific location is involved, the parent first says the Lord's Prayer and then begins to call out loud to the child's soul, entreating it to return to the child while the adult slowly backs up to the house, showing the soul in this manner where to go. A parent might repeat in a soothing and placating manner, the entire way home: "Ana, Ana, come, come; don't stay where you were frightened," trying to entice the soul to return. Arriving at the house, the parent puts the desirable items next to the child and has the child eat some of the fruit or candy.

The particular details of calling a soul, however, vary greatly as each individual tries to embellish or beseech in a manner he or she hopes will be most effective. Each individual draws upon elements of Kachitu medical beliefs to suit his or her perceived strategic requirements that conform to his or her own view of self in the Kachitu universe: ethnic, religious, or class identity. For example, Doña Antonia said:

> I suspected that calling the soul was useless because my father used to work as an
> auxiliary at the hospital and said it was just superstition. But once my son fell at
> school and came home sick. For three days he lay weak in his bed refusing to eat.
> I took him to the doctor at the clinic and he said my son needed an operation and
> that it would cost a lot of money. We didn't have that kind of money so we decided
> to call his soul and see what happened. That night the nuns at the church had
> made some chocolate pudding, and he loved chocolate pudding so we used it to call
> his soul. When I returned to the house I gave him the chocolate pudding and he
> ate it with gusto and was fine the next day.

When Genara treated Porfirio for his soul loss, she confronted the event with far greater anxiety. She put candy, wine, and bread in his shirt to extract some essence of him and then left it outside in the yard at night for some minutes to attract Porfirio's soul. First she called the soul and then hid. When she saw a shadow without a face near the package, she picked up the package, shielding her eyes from the shadow so as not to frighten it away, and took the package to Porfirio's bed, waving the package over her head and speaking softly, "Come, come," to entice the shadow to follow. At Porfirio's bedside she forced him to drink the wine and eat the bread. She put the candies in a hat, put the hat on his head, and told him to sleep. Then she repeated the same procedure two more times. After each trip she ate some ash from her cooking stove. Finally she left the house a fourth time with alcohol and wine with which she "challared" the yard. She then asked the achachillas to leave Porfirio's soul with him and accept the wine and alcohol instead. After this, she went to bed without saying anything to anyone.

As a campesina, Genara has had a more precarious life than Antonia, and Antonia's life has been anything but easy. Genara assumes that any illness can develop into a crisis and therefore illnesses must be dealt with cautiously and seriously. The items she employs to entice Porfirio's soul are associated with Aymara life and ritual: bread, the symbol for sustenance, and wine to associate Porfirio's soul with the Pachamama. She opened dialogue with the achachillas, requesting their intervention and offering them alcohol and wine in payment. She ingested poison herself on their behalf as an offering of supplication. Like Antonia, Genara relied upon medicinas caseras to cure the same diagnostically and etiologically determined illness, yet the values both women expressed during treatment radically differ.

CREATING SECURITY THROUGH RITUAL INVERSION

The power relationships between the supernatural and the human expressed in these Aymara medical etiologies describe the Aymara political experience over the past five hundred years. Kachituños occasionally reverse these relationships by getting thoroughly drunk on cane liquor. The state of drunkenness provides protection from supernatural evils and is also a good time for the Aymara to tell mestizos exactly what they think of them. The latter inversion is effective because, quite contrary to the notion of the Indian as a slave to vice, the Aymara drink only on ritual occasions, while mestizos drink whenever they have a mind to. Many mestizos suffer from alcoholism. With the temporary power of alcohol, Aymara, mestizo, and Methodists alike confront the natural and the supernatural by simply denying the superior power of these forces. The strategy is effective: by denying the existence of asymmetrical power relations in Kachitu, Kachituños make these relations cease to exist. For the Aymara, drunkenness is ritual inversion.[6]

The significance of liquor to both mestizo and campesino is evident during every fiesta or ritual occasion. Mestizos stretch out the activity all day long to enhance its status-building opportunities. Aymara drink rapidly on a mission to inebriation.

At each fiesta or ritual occasion, one individual from each local community agrees to supply the alcohol, thereby earning for himself the prestige of *preste*, being a sponsor. The greater the occasion, the larger the gathering, the greater the prestige of the preste. The greatest occasion is the town fiesta for La Virgen de la Candelaria, which the population of many of the comunidades attend. There are, therefore, about twenty drunk prestes from the comunidades in Kachitu at this fiesta, the annual ritual expression of ethnic differentiation. The activities of the vecinos and campesinos are distinct and separately maintained, and the subordination of the latter to the former is expressed symbolically in dance, costumes, and music. At periodic intervals the prestes offer a *copa*, or shot glass, of cane liquor three times to each individual gathered about them. Within a few hours the majority of Aymara are drunk, still trying to pour more copas into the mouths of friends and relations who can no longer walk without aid or carry on a coherent conversation. It is consistently at these times that campesinos tell vecinos what they really think of them, and how they feel they were cheated or otherwise mistreated by them.

At these times, the vecinos are drinking too. Vecinos, however, drink beer or pisco, a Bolivian alcoholic beverage, which they might also drink on nonreligious occasions. Alcohol, in the form of beer and pisco, holds a connotation for the vecino that is different from that of cane liquor for the campesino. To the vecino, sharing beer or wine with friends and relations is a form of sociability and gentility. Nevertheless, by the time the campesinos are drunk enough to express their grievances, the vecinos are too drunk to try to sanction the unwritten social law forbidding Indian denunciation of mestizos. By the time everyone has sobered up, mestizos' memories have faded enough to make retribution improbable and not worth the effort. Although mestizo sanction has been radically weakened in recent years, pre-1952 memories are still harsh enough, and contemporary mestizo resources still sufficient, and the symbolism of inversion itself so appealing, that drunkenness has lost none of its charm in postrevolutionary years.

This social reality, which has enormous psychological though little political significance, is transformed into magical-medical power: immunity from the supernatural. The Aymara Methodist Pedro Quispaya, who ran the town tractor in 1977 with Nathan Robison and eight other Methodists, also runs a mill with his father in Kachitu. His wife, Iris Quispe, is also an Aymara Methodist and a nurse at the hospital. His father was an Aymara wage laborer from the valleys, his mother a campesina from an outlying community where the family now works her land. Iris's parents are campesinos from another nearby community. Iris and Pedro Quispaya met in the Methodist church and now live in Pedro's father's old house in Kachitu where Pedro runs the mill, and which is sheltered on one side by eucalyptus trees.

Pedro told me:

> I have seen the khan achachi many times. It is not the same as the achachillas who live each in his own place, in the mountains and rivers. Actually, there are many khan achachis and I have seen them dancing on the top of the hill on the south edge of town. They come to places where lightning has struck and demand that altars be built and sacrifices be given to them. One used to pass over this very house.
>
> When I was a child and we lived for a while in La Paz, we rented this house to some folks who have moved away now. They complained that the khan achachi frequented the eucalyptus trees, and refused to live here after a while. My father later saw the khan achachi here. One night after the revolution he was walking home drunk with a pistol and a machete, when the khan achachi appeared to him. It was close to the ground, right here near the eucalyptus trees. My father tried to kill it with a machete but he could not hit it as it moved too fast. Being drunk he figured he'd walk ahead anyway and if he stepped on it, so much the better. In fact he tried to kick it. It disappeared after he came into the house. Later his pistol, which he had placed on the table, went off by itself. It didn't hurt anybody but it nearly got the dog. The khan achachi never returned here after that.
>
> It is like the waj waj, *a spirit that frequently appears when you go on a trip. It materializes as an enticing woman and kills its victims. When I traveled with my father by foot at night, he would tell me to take charge of our party while he got drunk. When he was drunk he could protect us from the waj waj, and we never had any trouble. As Evangelicals we are not supposed to believe in these things, but they exist.*

Alcohol and drunkenness protected Pedro's father from the khan achachi and the waj waj because the alcohol and the state of inebriation provided his Aymara animu with the "courage" permitting him to invert the relationship of power between himself and the supernatural, just as alcohol and drunkenness permit the campesinos to invert their relationships to the socially superior vecinos during fiestas. Methodists, however, are not supposed to drink at fiesta, specifically because, they say, alcohol is a waste of money that they prefer to invest in material gains. Many do drink, though, upon other, private occasions not associated with religious identity such as marriage and death. Public abstention is a symbol of Protestantism and a practice that unites Methodists by purposefully setting them apart and making them behaviorally superior to the vecinos on those very same moral grounds that mestizos occasionally use to express their superiority over the Aymara. For them, the power of the cane alcohol is its mark of identity that indicates lack of membership in the church. Of drunken mestizos during fiesta, a Methodist might say that their behavior is decadent, wasteful, and indicative of vecino foolishness. Methodists also complained to me in the same breath as they sold beer and alcohol to the participants, that the fiesta is not as grand as it used to be.

Thus Methodists, like everyone else, select and manipulate elements of medical ideology that best serve their economic, social, and political interests, and in the process, redefine the content of their own religious identity. El Tio is good when he cures and empowers, and when he reinforces solidarity. He is even useful when he disseminates disease and thus communicates political struggle against hegemonic forces. For Pedro Quispaya, a very active member of the Methodist community, drinking is good when it supports pride in Aymara ethnicity, but abstention is good when it supports the rise of the Methodist community as a local power. Medical ideology is not a reflection of culture or social class, but rather a dialectical element in the constant restructuring of the meaning of both. Medical ideology consists of cultural resources available to all Kachituños, and these resources are appropriated and used in different ways by members of all classes, ethnicities, and religions as primary resources to get access to secondary ones.

Drawing on medical ideology, Kachituños employ medical dialogue and choose curative strategies primarily to negotiate the content of ethnic and religious identity in order to gain access to material and nonmaterial resources that will provide them with social mobility. They can do so because, in fact, they share confluences of the same culture but mask what is class differentiation with ethnic and religious categories. Dialogue about medical efficacy is dependent upon the content of such identities. Crossing social boundaries may entail upward mobility into higher socioeconomic classes, downward mobility from membership in the mestizo class to mestizo membership in the world of the Aymara, or movement from identity as a Catholic Aymara to that of a Methodist Aymara. Most often, however, it involves gaining access to resources pertaining to another social group by redefining the meaning of one's own social group. In Kachitu, lives are defined by severe and increasing poverty and drastic change. Kachituños are not certain who or what they are, particularly in relation to each other. Through medical dialogue and curative strategies, they make alliances, disassociate themselves from others, exchange resources, and try to forge new identities that will open opportunities and improve their lives under conditions of extreme and seemingly unrelenting national economic contraction, regional peripheralization, and local marginalization. As new identities are negotiated and forged, social life in town is transformed. Within medical pluralism, medical dialogue and resources are a means employed to create social change. In medical ideology political struggle is expressed and, in incremental ways, resolved. As demonstrated in the case of the kharisiri, part of the change that results from negotiation through medical dialogue and resource use is medical ideology itself.

CHAPTER 6

Choices, Strategies, and Changes in Negotiating Identity Through Medicine: Medicine As Metaphor for the Nature of Ethnic Boundaries

In a medically plural environment, medical ideology is not a single logical construct but rather a series of options that permit the negotiation of social relations. Porfirio and Vicente, and everyone who tried to treat, or had an opinion about, their illnesses, found in so doing that medicine served as a primary resource through which the negotiation of social position and social relations was the secondary resource gained.

Porfirio and his father Vicente Callisaya are campesinos. Vicente spent most of his hard life as a peon on a hacienda. He fathered ten children, only five of whom survived. He determined to educate and thus put his greatest investment in Porfirio, his youngest son, born after the revolution. In part because of these efforts, Porfirio became interested in things non-campesino, in cosmopolitan ideals, in getting out of Kachitu, and in becoming an educated man. The politics that confounded his efforts were local, national, and even international and far beyond the anticipation of Vicente, who merely wanted a good life for his youngest son. However, the focus of these politics was the content of cultural identity. These politics became explicit in the illnesses that Porfirio and his father Vicente experienced in 1977 and 1978. The health choices that both men made and that were made on their behalf by others in those years make explicit the sociopolitical complexity behind the conceptualization of health care and its embeddedness in personal history.

In 1977 Vicente Callisaya thought he was ninety-four years old. The auxiliaries and doctor at the clinic figured his age was something between ninety and one hundred. One of the local mestizas said he was only eighty-five. Given that Porfirio was twenty-two years old in 1977, Vicente must have been an energetic man two decades earlier if he was really as old as everyone thought he was. In 1977, however, he said he was a very sick man and claimed he was dying.

Before 1952 the Callisayas, including Vicente's wife's sisters Genara and Julia, had been peons on an Omasuyu hacienda, just outside Kachitu. They recalled the hacendado as being particularly harsh. Genara and Julia fled the hacienda before 1952, and were subsequently landless in 1977, although they shared a housing compound in Kachitu. There they kept livestock, which they took to the hills to graze in order to support themselves. Both are widows. Vicente and his wife, however, remained on the hacienda. Consequently, they acquired several chacras, or plots of hacienda land, through the reform, land that Vicente still cultivated in 1977. Being elderly, he decided when he fell ill that spring to divide his small amount of land among his four eldest, uneducated, and married sons who then had children of their own. He thus excluded Porfirio from an inheritance in land. Divided, each parcel would not be sufficient to feed a small nuclear family. Porfirio was much younger than his brothers, would be the only son to graduate from high school, and would, it was hoped, be employable and not have to rely on land. Unmarried, and with the comportment of an elite schoolgirl, Porfirio shunned hard work and preferred to work at a desk or with gringos whenever he got the chance. His parents expected him to learn a trade. He did not understand his parents' reasoning and had his own, perhaps unrealistic, ambitions. His goal was to learn and teach English and maybe go to the United States.

To insure Porfirio's education, Vicente asked the most prestigious family in contemporary Kachitu to be his godparents: the Cordovas. Consequently agricultural goods and occasionally labor had flowed over the past twenty-two years from the Callisaya household to the Cordova household, while the Cordovas fed and generally watched out for Porfirio and registered him in school. These gifts had diminished in recent years as Vicente's older sons married and had children, reducing Vicente's surplus, and they stopped altogether in July of 1977 when Vicente

fell ill. At that time, the burden fell on Porfirio to do odd jobs for the Cordovas to reciprocate for their generosity and attention. Porfirio lived with his aunts in Kachitu, Genara and Julia, while he went to school, for which his father paid twenty pesos bolivianos a month (one U.S. dollar). He lived the life of a boarding student and was never taught by his father how to work as a campesino.

Genara had one son, Sergio, who went through high school in La Paz where he, like Porfirio, was cared for by godparents. He had since secured a job and was putting himself through the school of engineering. Genara was very proud of her son's achievement, but Sergio was ashamed of his Indian heritage, rejected his family, and rarely came home to Kachitu.

In contrast, Porfirio felt disinherited and excluded from his Aymara family. Because he did not work with his father, aspired to education and urbanity, and was effeminate, he was ridiculed by most people in town. They were contemptuous of what they interpreted as his lack of respect for his Indian heritage, his not knowing his place, and his "grandiose" and "foolish" ideas about learning English. Shunned and rejected, Porfirio sought the company of every occasional North American or European who came through town in the hope that they would get him a "plush" job as a *mozo*, or male servant, in some gringo household in La Paz, and maybe even take him to the United States. Such behavior was met by the Kachituños with contempt, fueling Porfirio's shame. But in fact, Porfirio was not ashamed of his Indian heritage. He determined to associate with North Americans as a response to what he saw as rejection by everyone. He was a dreamer with a soft heart, and, in fact, very attentive to his Aymara aunts. Sergio had been able to avoid campesino work, move to the city, and become an educated man; therefore Porfirio's dream did not seem so improbable to him. And indeed, gringos such as myself did come into his life and eventually he did get a job as a mozo in a North American household in La Paz.

In 1977 Porfirio frequently quarreled with his father who, seeing Porfirio's social difficulties and dissatisfaction, sensed the youth had misunderstood his efforts to secure his future through education and feared he was irresponsible. Porfirio feared that his father rejected him and didn't love him. The town meanwhile abused Porfirio. Only his aunts, humble and poor but very proud and principled, steadfastly supported him. Unlike Sergio, who knew very clearly who he wished to be associated with, Porfirio's loyalties were divided. He desperately wanted to become a respected man, to show up the Kachituños with an envious position that, he thought, would be something associated with gringos. Yet he also felt at home with his aunts, who were campesina women and monolingual Aymara speakers.

On August 30, 1977, Porfirio is preparing to graduate from high school. This will cost money. He needs a suit, a pair of shoes, and a shirt. Doña Teresa Cordova shrewdly suggests he ask me to be madrina for his graduation. I am a gringa and probably have a lot of money. As Doña Teresa is the town registrar for the civil archives that I have permission to copy for my research, I negotiate with Porfirio and Doña Teresa to provide for Porfirio's needs if he can work in the archive office as my assistant. Delighted with the deal and the prestige he imagines is attached to being the gringa's assistant in an "Important Office," Porfirio sets out determined to copy the birth, marriage, and death records.

By September 4 the arrangement has fallen apart. Ten minutes after he begins work he rushes back to my house frightened and in tears. "The books in the archive office are all destroyed," he cries, "and Doña Teresa thinks it is our fault." I realize at this point that the notion of setting oneself apart as an objective observer is ludicrous. I have become very much a part of the town. However, I am not the accepted and intimate participant that my anthropological training has led me to believe "becoming a part of" would entail. Rather I am the local gringa with a particular proscribed status and specific and often conflicting responsibilities as a resident in Kachitu. I am a primary resource. Today I am ombudsman and my job is very delicate. If I play my defense of Porfirio and myself too strongly, Teresa could just as easily condemn me and deny me access to the archives and to information about mestizo culture in Kachitu.

The archive office is very pleasant. It is attached to the Cordova compound, which includes the nicest house in town. An arched doorway opens into a large, cobbled central patio with a garden of overgrown, heavily perfumed plants, a shade tree, and an ivy-covered wall. Along the right-hand border of the patio and behind the house itself is a set of rooms in which Teresa's father, Don Alejandro, the most educated man in town in his day and founder of a small school there, kept a small museum of artifacts handed down in his family over the generations. Alejandro was the grandson of Colonel Juan Carlos Cordova, who first came to Kachitu in the mid-nineteenth century when he secured a substantial amount of land in Chontamarca, a small hacienda outside of town. The Colonel had been the grandson of the Cacique Principal de Urinsaya de Arangayo, who had married the only granddaughter of the Cacique Principal of Carabuco, Ana Maria Choquehuanca Siñani. Seven generations of *capitánes, coroneles,* and caciques, all of Carabuco, separated Ana Maria Choquehuanca Siñani from Wayna Kahpajj (Capac in contemporary literature), the last Inca emperor of Peru to die in Cusco, in 1527, before the conquest (probably he died of European-derived diseases that preceded the conquistadors into the Andes). Thirteen generations away from the Inca Wayna Kahpajj, Doña Teresa Cordova reigns as matriarch of the family homestead in Kachitu, four generations old. Married to a lawyer, Don Ascarunz, she studies law herself in 1977, and she and Ascarunz maintain a home in a new middle-class neighborhood in Alto La Paz, from which they shuttle back and forth to Kachitu, where Doña Teresa has been selected by the government in La Paz to be keeper of the town archives. They and their four children share the Kachitu homestead with two of Teresa's older sisters, the kindly spinster Maria de La Paz and the beautiful but crippled Lourdes. Because of Teresa's superordinate position, which she has appropriated in spite of her younger age and because of her successful career and forceful character, she and her two sisters do not get along.

Doña Teresa is the most prestigious person in town for two reasons. Having studied law and established a house in the city, she has more successfully transformed her life to meet the changes of the postrevolutionary order than any other vecino in town. By maintaining one of the few paid civil jobs in Kachitu, she is the only mestizo from the prerevolutionary period to hold a civil office, to which occupants are nominated by the government rather than elected. Hence she is most able to maintain some of the prerevolutionary mestizo authority over the local Aymara population. One form this authority takes is the reprimanding manner she often assumes when dealing with the Aymara who come to the office to register a birth, marriage, or death. When the Aymara were given control of the archives by the revolutionary government, a number of books were lost, and Doña Teresa, informed by her prerevolutionary mestizo heritage, attributes that loss to a genetic culpability shared by all the Aymara who, apparently, ought to be reminded of it every time they come to the office. When campesinos request services from her that are beyond her powers, she tells them they have to go to the city in a manner that demonstrates how complicated and important the records are, rather than allowing the suggestion that there are some powers of archives that she does not wield. In this manner she maintains her position in a town in which many factions would like to see her power usurped. However, for all her successes, the postrevolutionary Bolivian economy is so constricted that she depends on ahijados like Porfirio and several others she supports in the Cordova household to supply the household with services and basic food items, according to compadrazgo rules. Indeed, her successes, like those of their forefathers, have been somewhat dependent upon access to this resource. As matriarch of the household, her choice of ahijados and her position to monopolize the arrangements with Indian compadres may have formed the basis for disagreements with her sisters.

On September 4 when Porfirio and I come into the office, Porfirio sees Doña Teresa and immediately retreats. He feels stung and is incapable of facing Doña Teresa. The archives are legal-sized books that sit upright on a counter against the wall. Someone has partially pulled out a few and pulled off the back cover of one that contained birth records. No actual records are damaged. Doña Teresa and I look at the book with concern. I point out that Porfirio and I have been working with the death records and that when she left the night before, everything was in order. She exclaims that she never meant to suggest that I had anything to do with it, overtly accusing Porfirio of committing the crime. I reiterate my confidence in Porfirio, and thank her for suggesting that Porfirio work for me. I intimate that a little Aymara boy, another ahijado whom she cares for in return for agricultural resources and labor from his parents or her compadres, may have done it. He hangs around the office when I am in it, occasionally stands in the doorway strangling cats, and often throws chickens in the window to get my attention.

Doña Teresa thinks that is reasonable. She nevertheless remains angry with Porfirio for telling me about the incident (and implying that I had anything to do with it), and for running away and not responding to her. Porfirio had not stuck up for himself but had stood immobilized with head hung as Doña Teresa yelled at him. His behavior conforms to her stereotype of an Indian and her behavior conforms to his stereotype of a mestizo oppressor, stereotypes that held the pre-1952 town culture together. As they do here, these stereotypes still get reproduced, in spite of postrevolutionary changes, whenever it is in someone's interest to do so and they are able to pull it off. The power differential between Teresa and Porfirio is such that she can easily pull it off. Only the night before Porfirio had told me, in his gratitude for the job, how wonderful Doña Teresa is. That was the last time I ever heard him say a good word about her. He refuses, now, to work on the archives whenever Teresa is in town, which outrages Teresa. He refuses to take meals at the Cordova household, and he stops doing odd jobs for Doña Maria de La Paz and Doña Lourdes. Doña Maria de La Paz explains: she says the problem is that Porfirio is poorly educated. I reflect that Porfirio is just about to graduate from high school. She also says that Porfirio has not gone recently to see his ailing father Vicente, that his mother has come begging him to return home, but that Porfirio has refused to go ever since his father fell ill. There is much truth to this.

In the subsequent months, Porfirio remains in town attending school and working for me for cash to pay his aunts for his upkeep, and he does not return home to see his parents. As word about Porfirio's timidity in facing the Cordovas gets around town, the children begin to call him Porfiria. His childish and effeminate response fuels the children's taunts. Often he asks me to tell the children's mothers to get them to stop. Porfirio's deteriorating reputation is exacerbated by the absence of Doña Teresa's protection, and what little support he had had among the mestizo adults is eroding. In response, Porfirio makes up stories that he thinks will impress his persecutors. Antonia tells me that the tailor told her that Porfirio had told him that I am going to take Porfirio back to the United States with me and will leave all my possessions here to his mother and father. Doña Ana tells me that Genara's son Sergio told her that Porfirio had told him that I am going to give Porfirio my typewriter when I leave. Don Antonio, director of the Protestant high school, told Porfirio that if he went to the United States he would spend the rest of his life picking up after gringos' shit.

As Porfirio spends more time around our house, Anna and I observe the remarkable extent to which he is incapable of doing (or unwilling to do) any manual labor. He does not know how to do simple tasks that all campesino children know, and that we are trying to learn: how to make adobes or mix grain for the chickens. This does not mean he refuses to work. He often comes to the house at 8:00 A.M. and transcribes records until 8:00 P.M. He talks about getting a job in La Paz after graduation, as a mozo for gringos. His concept of how much money he will make far surpasses reality.

In early November of 1977 Porfirio graduates from the Methodist high school in Kachitu, but his parents do not attend to witness his achievement. Their home in the comunidad of Sallcapampa is a walk of several hours from Kachitu, and Porfirio's father, Vicente, is still ill—dying, Porfirio tells me when I ask him—and cannot make the trip. When his parents don't attend graduation, many people in town say it is because Porfirio did not invite them, and that he is ashamed of them. Doña Ana and Doña Lourdes, who have always sympathized with Porfirio, in part because they do not approve of Teresa's authoritative manner, see this incident as a turning point in their own support of him. They do not believe that Vicente is too ill to attend but that Porfirio has not asked him to come. They say the one unforgivable sin is shame of one's parents, even if they are campesinos. In this way, they transform a problem of adolescence, created in part by a misfired strategy in child rearing, into a crime of ethnicity and conflict of cultural identity.

Just after graduation, Porfirio fell ill. He lay in Genara's and Julia's house and they fussed over and cared for him. He felt extremely weak and had diarrhea. Out of concern I went unasked to the clinic and spoke to Dr. Sabas. Dr. Sabas prescribed Lomotil, which had the immediate effect of clearing up the symptoms. But two days later Porfirio was ill again.

This time he suffered from constipation and there was blood in his stool. Doña Lourdes did nothing but advised me to mix manioc flour in cold water, then dissolve it in boiling water with chocolate. Doña Leonora, who sells magical and herbal medicines, advised me to give him a *mate*, or tea, of two popular herbs, andres hualla and heriondilla. These are cold herbs and are good for hot illnesses. I gave all these to Porfirio and the next day he felt better.

Two days later he relapsed again. At this point, Genara and Julia determined to wage all-out war and apply a comprehensive approach. Their strategy was to provide a wide spectrum of specific therapies and diagnose the disease by seeing which therapy Porfirio responded to. Over three days Genara administered cures for the khan achachi and a lost ajayu. At the same time, Julia administered a cure for the kharisiri while also giving him a variety of herbal teas. I complicated Porfirio's treatment by delivering another prescription from the clinic. At this point, Porfirio got better.

After all was done, the two aunts decided that Porfirio really had had kharisiri, because it was after that treatment that Porfirio most clearly took a turn for the better. Therefore they said Porfirio ought to drink wine but no cold water every day for several weeks. What he suffered from was cold, so he ought to consume hot foods and drink, and the wine would seal the holes the kharisiri made when he stole the fat and prevent the cold from entering. To increase his strength they gave him a regular diet of egg whites beaten with a small bottle of dark beer, potatoes, and lamb.

Porfirio agreed with his aunts' diagnosis and gratefully accepted their treatment. At no time did he request treatment by the physician at the clinic. After he recovered from kharisiri he left Kachitu and took a job as a mozo in an elite American-Bolivian household in La Paz. They found him to be naive, effeminate, and grateful for the job: the perfect mozo. It took about a year for Porfirio to discover that being a mozo in an English-speaking household was not the solution to his life and that Don Antonio had been right.

In 1986 I learned that Porfirio had become a rural school-teacher for Aymara children, and today he acts as a culture broker between Aymara and mestizo (and gringo) worlds. Thus for him the kharisiri diagnosis made sense: it gave him an opportunity to situate himself within a complex cultural environment in which he did not reject his ethnic heritage but could not comply with mestizo expectations that he subordinate himself to them. It facilitated the formation of his own identity, and empowered him to pursue his own ambition: an Aymara teaching English to Indians to empower them to confront mestizos.

Shortly after Porfirio's illness, Vicente finally came to town to be seen at the clinic in a last and desperate attempt to regain his health. Vicente was a comically blatant manipulator of medical dialogue and resources to get what he wanted. Alas, like many, he rarely succeeded. He had initially fallen ill in July of 1977. At that time he went to a yatiri who gave him a potion that, he said, made him feel better temporarily but did not cure the illness. He went then to another yatiri who spoke to the khan achachi and claimed that the khan achachi was the source of Vicente's illness, made a sacrifice, but did not make Vicente feel any better. Vicente then went to a third yatiri who also supplicated the supernatural. He too gave Vicente a potion to drink and burned offerings and mesas to the achachillas, the Condor Mamani, a chullpa spirit that inhabits pre-conquest graves, El Tio, the serpent of the Devil, and the khan achachi, hitting all bases at once. Vicente still did not feel any better. At last he went to a fourth yatiri who diagnosed limpu (identical to anemia) and told him there was no hope of cure.

In August of 1977 I had visited Vicente at his home in Sallcapampa with Porfirio. He cried with desperation as he related his misfortune. He professed to feel pain in the central chest area and in his stomach. He was vomiting blood and had no appetite. He was growing thinner and his ankles were swollen. He said he was ninety-four years old, and was, at that time, taking the potion prescribed by the first yatiri, claiming it relieved the pain but wasn't curing him. He was about to initiate his quest for the other yatiris to see if they could be more successful. None were. (My own opinion is that he was suffering from heart failure and simple old age.)

On that trip I noted that he had four piglets and a half dozen scruffy but egg-bearing chickens. The little farm looked bright and well cared for. He and his wife's extreme generosity, however, made me suspicious of these appearances. Thinking they needed cash, I offered to buy some livestock or an aguayu, a hand-woven shawl that women wear on their backs in which they carry babies and produce; I bought the latter for 200 pesos bolivianos, or $10 U.S.

On December 6, 1977, only weeks after Porfirio's high school graduation, Vicente walks into town. He seeks shelter at Genara's and Julia's and then goes directly to his compadres, the Cordovas, to request aid for his ailing health. He is unaware of the gossip about Porfirio's disloyalty to him, and too sick to reflect on his diminishing fulfillment of obligations to the Cordovas that form the context he now enters. Doña Teresa reflects that she has done quite a lot for Porfirio that has, in the past few months, gone unappreciated and unreciprocated. In her medical opinion Vicente suffers from moral decrepitude.

He next stops at my home to get my llama that Porfirio has told him he can have. I explain, as I did to his wife two days earlier, that I have long ago given the llama to Genara in return for medical information. She charges me a full llama because, she says, I will take her information to the United States and make a lot of money with it. Porfirio now informs me in Spanish that Genara no longer wants it. She finds it a bother, he says, and calls it "una mal criada." He says that, as she doesn't like the llama, what was intended as a gift from me is actually care for an animal I no longer maintain myself, and Genara wants 100 pesos from me, 70 for taking care of the llama and 30 to cover what it has destroyed, he says.

An hour later Genara comes to my door and talks to me in the street. She is upset with me and talks so fast that Porfirio has to translate. My eye catches Doña Ana motioning to me from the street corner. Genara is complaining, says Ana, that she cannot understand why I am trying to take back the llama and give it to Vicente instead. I bring Ana over to translate. Porfirio sullenly disappears into the house. I ask Ana to tell Genara that I gave her the llama last spring with no obligation. Genara retreats apparently appeased. Vicente is upset because he doesn't get the llama Porfirio promised him.

Porfirio is angry for two days. He says Genara changed her mind on him right there in the street. In a huff he goes to La Paz with the money I gave him. Vicente, however, comes to my house again upset about the llama and talking fast. I get Ana to translate. Vicente says he is very sick. He hurts all over and cannot eat. Could he stay for supper? I ask about his inability to eat. He explains it is campesino food he cannot eat. He says he has had nothing to eat at his house except potatoes for many months. He is in great pain, particularly in his stomach, and in need of good food. He suggests I cook him the six sausages I have hanging from the rafters. I ask about the pain he had in his chest when I visited him in Sallcapampa. "Yes," he says, "there is a pain in my lower chest, right where my stomach is."

"And how is the swelling in your legs?"

"My legs aren't swollen. The pain is in my stomach."

"Were they ever swollen?"

"No."

"Well, then, what are you taking now for the limpu?"

"Nothing," he replied. "I don't have limpu."

"But you went to a yatiri and he said you had limpu."

"Yes, I have limpu, but I have something else too: my stomach hurts, and it needs decent food. We campesinos have nothing to eat except potatoes."

"What did the yatiri say?"

"I saw three yatiris and they said nothing."

"Then what happened to the six hundred pesos [thirty U.S. dollars] that Porfirio gave you?" (I had given Porfirio this money to send to his father for medical care.)

"Porfirio never gave me any money. In fact, my other son gave him money to give me and I never got it."

"I saw good things to eat at your house besides potatoes. Why don't you eat eggs?"

"I don't have any eggs."

"But you have chickens."

"They don't lay eggs."

"Then why don't you eat the chickens?"

"I can't because they lay eggs. Once in a while they lay eggs. Sometimes I can eat eggs."

"Why have you come to Kachitu?"

"To wait for Porfirio. I want him to take me to the hospital."

"Porfirio is in La Paz, so I will take you to the hospital now if you like, but I will not pay your bill."

"All right. I will let you take me to the hospital but what will it cost? Can you talk the doctor down in price?"

Dr. Sabas examines Vicente and says the old buzzard is as sound as a bell, with absolutely nothing wrong with him except anemia from not eating. He takes down some vitamin and iron supplements from the shelf in the examining room and gives them to Vicente, along with the bill. Vicente nods at the bill and hands it to me, explaining that I will pay it. As so many people in town have handed me bills to the point of exasperation over the previous year, the medical staff in the room find Vicente's gesture pretty funny. I remind Vicente of our agreement. Foiled, he digs into his pocket and pulls out a fat wad of fifty-peso bills! The bill is forty-one pesos bolivianos ($2.05 U.S.).

The next morning as I make my daily visit to the hospital, one of the patients mistakes me for a nurse and asks me to give my attention to a man doubled up in pain on the ground outside the back door. I look and find Vicente. I run for the doctor. Sabas says he has already seen Vicente this morning and that Vicente had been drinking, which upset his stomach. He had asked the auxiliary Iris Quispe to give him something. I have the day book in my hand and note that Vicente's name is not there. Sabas queries Iris. She says that Vicente had no money. Often when a patient has no money, the auxiliaries do not record what care they give them lest they get into trouble for providing health care free. Sabas brushes that off and asks her again if she gave Vicente anything. She says yes, an Alka-Seltzer for his stomach. Vicente insists he did not have anything to drink that morning except a bottle of soda at Genara's house and complains that all Iris gave him was a little pill. I explain that Sabas says it is all he needs, but I feel angry that he hoodwinked Iris into giving him the five-peso (twenty-five-cent) item for free when he has a fist full of pesos. I walk him home to Genara's and tell her in an exasperated tone of voice what has happened, and that the doctor said if he doesn't drink and eats reasonable food, he'll be fine. Twenty-four hours later, Vicente Callisaya is dead. Before he died, he told Genara that he was dying of limpu and that nothing could be done about it.

Porfirio and his father were not a couple of con artists, but rather disoriented explorers on a quest for a satisfactory identity that would provide them with some security. Caught between conflicting images of their own heritage, contradictory faces of mestizo and elite domains, a rapidly changing world, and social pressures, they appropriated etiologies, diagnoses, and therapies to negotiate their own identities. Both Porfirio and Vicente found it in their best interests to adopt, in the final analysis, Aymara illnesses, not for medical, but for social reasons.

Contrary to the desires of all medical institutions, etiology and diagnosis are determined primarily by nonmedical practitioners. Etiology and diagnosis are proposed by the patients themselves, by their families, and by anyone else who is interested—and in a small town, everybody is interested. Illness is a favored topic inspiring the opinion of everyone, in part because it gives them an opportunity to say something about themselves and about somebody else. Therefore nosological, etiological, and diagnostic concepts are significant not only as they are translated into actual cures but also as instruments to initiate changes in social status. Doña Teresa and Porfirio's aunts both contributed to Porfirio's social standing in town and his ultimate image of himself.

If a main determinant in health-care decisions is identity negotiation, then individual choices of nosology, etiology, and diagnosis are determined by a wide variety of factors: social standing; economic, political, and religious parameters; and historical processes, as well as medical concerns. Since these factors differ for most individuals, any two individuals of the same social group but of different economic standing, or of the same economic standing but different religious orientation, may not make the same etiological and diagnostic decisions. Decisions may well differ when individuals are concerned about themselves rather than others. As class, social, economic, political and religious elements and relations in an individual's life change over time, and as the content of cultural identity also changes, the type of health-care decisions that an individual makes changes.

Thus the determinants of etiological and diagnostic choices are a complex set of elements that form an open and flexible system. The relationship between these elements and their significance within the system change over time as they change in the lives of the individuals concerned.

The Aymara, the Methodist Aymara, and the mestizos in Kachitu each perceive the significance of their group's identity in distinctive ways and differ from each other in degree of social solidarity and of economic and political power to which they have access. However, because the actual boundaries between these groups are vague and undefined, a given individual may pledge allegiance to a group different from that to which he claims membership under advantageous circumstances. Such change of allegiance stems from the current lack of consensus about what it means to be a campesino, a Methodist, or a mestizo since 1952. Definition of what it means to be a member of one group depends a great deal on the definition of what it means not to be a member of the other two. Doña Teresa taught us that.

Although groups differ in political, economic, and social world views, all three agree upon the general medical nature of the universe and the general nature of the medical universe. Through the medium of this consensus, medical pluralism provides a social idiom in which to express values, evaluate social relationships, and explore potential options. Members of different groups rely on this social idiom as a primary resource to get access to secondary resources: to change social relations and access social mobility. Though segments of medicine are identified as cosmopolitan or as Aymara, they constitute a shared culture. Campesinos, Methodists, and mestizos distinguish themselves from each other not by expressing different medical beliefs, but rather by perceiving themselves as holding different positions within the same medical universe. In this context, ideology is not a specific body of beliefs, but rather options employed as much according to social context as to symptomatology. Porfirio and Vicente taught me this.

CHAPTER 7

Choices, Strategies, and Changes in Negotiating Identity Through Medicine

THE POLITICAL DANGERS OF ETHNIC BOUNDARIES

Doña Antonia, Felipe, Dr. Geronimo Tallacagua, and Eugenio all use medicine and medical dialogue as a primary resource to get access to secondary ones. Doña Antonia, who is in a process of downward social mobility, wants egalitarian relations with Aymara to get access to agricultural resources. Felipe and Dr. Tallacagua, both Aymara, are both actively using medicine as a means of upward mobility. But Tallacagua understands that to mean a denial of his Aymara heritage, while Felipe sees it as a prideful reassertion of Aymara heritage, given the perspective of entrepreneurialism he learned from the Methodists which he now attaches to medical practice. The Aymara Eugenio uses medicine primarily to get health, and medical dialogue to assert the dignity of his ethnicity in contrast to the exploitative nature of mestizos and Methodists. With different interests, these three make alliances and forsake others. Close attention to their medical dialogue exposes the fact that the use of medicine as a primary resource and as negotiation over the meaning of identity has multiple consequences: what is negotiated is not always in the best interest of everyone. One evening in 1978 the political dangers of the ethnic boundaries that have caused so much conflict in Kachitu revealed the dimension they hold within medical dialogue.

That evening a number of people including myself, Doña Antonia, and Eugenio, a campesino from Chojña Kanata, gathered at Felipe Apaza's house to celebrate his son's rutucha, the first haircut. Long after the hair was cut, the ceremony over, and the pisco and alcohol consumed, the four of us sat in the warm glow of companionship and talked of other things. The conversation landed, as it inevitably does, on illness and social relations, and through it, the mestiza Antonia, the Methodist Felipe, and the Aymara Eugenio, made an alliance as they agreed among themselves that curers exploit medicine for their own ends. A context for their own opinions reveals yet another dimension in which medical dialogue was used this night for nonmedical ends.

Tonight the pros and cons of Dr. Tallacagua become the focus of discussion. Tallacagua is the new physician replacing Dr. Sabas, who left for La Paz where he thinks he can do more for the oppressed by being a journalist. Dr. Tallacagua is originally from one of the communities around Kachitu, a graduate of the Methodist school, a beneficiary of a church scholarship to attend medical school, and the pride of the Methodist missionaries in Bolivia. Up from the peasantry, it has been expected that he would return to serve his own people and give his people a physician who talks their own language.

Tonight, the problem with Tallacagua as Antonia sees it is that he refuses to speak Aymara at the clinic except with monolingual Aymara speakers. Felipe, my host, feels ambiguous. On the one hand he, as the nurse trained at the clinic by Frank Beck, strongly supports the hospital and the medicine he helps dispense there, in spite of Tallacagua's apparent arrogance. On the other hand he also supports Aymara medicine, identity, heritage, and pride. As a Methodist, his investment in medicine has been to equalize social relations across ethnic and religious boundaries. Thus he does not bestow upon Dr. Tallacagua the great prestige that usually attends a physician. Given his many years of practice and Tallacagua's youth, Felipe probably knows a lot more medicine than Tallacagua.

Furthermore, these two medical men both began their lives as Aymara campesinos but employed very different strategies to define their own cultural identities. Felipe is an Aymara Methodist who respects his heritage. Dr. Tallacagua believes in science and progress, and that the road to progress necessitates abandoning the Aymara heritage.

Doña Antonia feels angry, not only at Dr. Tallacagua, but at Felipe as well, because the two have reduced her salary as hospital launderer from one peso per item to one peso per six items. Antonia is the only vecina employed at the hospital—Aymara Methodist territory—and she is the only vecina who washes clothes for a living. Landless and tiendaless, she and her four children depend on the money Lorenzo sends home from his rural teaching post. He earns 1,200 pesos bolivianos a month and sends her 600, which is $30 U.S. Because she cannot cover expenses with 600 pesos, and because he is ashamed that he cannot send her more, he calls her a spendthrift. He threatens to leave her for another woman who is more financially responsible. When she takes him seriously she fears she and the children will be thrown out of the house with nothing and will starve. She frequently has "attacks." At such times, Dr. Sabas would come to her home and inject her with a tranquilizer, but now she is afraid of Dr. Tallacagua. Her poverty and emotional outbursts are a source of shame for the other vecinos, in spite of the fact that most of them are just as poor. They feel she reflects badly on them, particularly by being employed as a launderer at the Aymara Methodist hospital. She behaves like an Indian. Worse, her present employer, Dr. Tallacagua, is an Indian, a disgrace that could only happen at the Kachitu clinic. However, Antonia receives more from her association with the Aymara, Methodist or otherwise, than she does from her association with mestizos. The Methodist Aymara at least gave her a job. Given Felipe's presence, she would appreciate Eugenio's moral support. But she is not so mad at Felipe that she would not attend the rutucha.

Eugenio does not like Dr. Tallacagua at all. Given that he and Tallacagua are both Aymara, I ask him to explain. He relates that in recent months his five-year-old daughter suffered severe pains in her lower abdomen. Medicinas caseras had no effect on her. After five days she was profoundly ill. On the fifth day, Nathan Robison and Pedro Quispaya brought their tractor to Chojña Kanata to plow some fields. The little girl was so sick that Eugenio asked them to drive him and the child in the tractor to the Methodist clinic in Kachitu. But after Dr. Tallacagua examined the little girl and met with Eugenio to discuss her case, Eugenio refused treatment on her behalf and took her home. Tallacagua had said she had appendicitis and needed surgery immediately. As Eugenio explains his interpretation of Tallacagua's diagnostic interview, I gradually realize with horror how the political context of the dialogue almost cost a little girl her life.

Earlier this year Eugenio had gone to the clinic and met Dr. Sabas. He liked Sabas. Though a mestizo, Sabas spoke a few words of Aymara, said something about it being the first human language, understood at least to some extent Kachitu medical beliefs, and respected yatiris and their medical tradition. Furthermore, Sabas socialized with the Methodist Aymara, accepted payment in kind, and explained diagnoses to patients and their families. He earned enormous respect and increased the patient load at the clinic, said Eugenio.

Dr. Tallacagua is apparently of the opinion that everyone should learn to speak Spanish as soon as possible and that he should facilitate that by being a role model. He also refuses to accept payment in kind. He tells his patients bluntly not to come to the clinic unless they are prepared to pay for services in cash. I realize that, with little cash to stock the pharmacy, Dr. Tallacagua actually had a legitimate reason for implementing an unfortunate set of policies at the hospital, but it is clear tonight that Eugenio perceives these policies as condescending and interprets them as signals of intended social and ethnic (class) superiority because Tallacagua has access to Bolivian elite society. He is trying to negotiate his identity. Eugenio sees him as one of his own turned oppressor, someone else intent on taking advantage of Eugenio because Eugenio is "still an Aymara 'Indio' in Tallacagua's eyes," he says. When Eugenio rejected Tallacagua's diagnosis, he did not think Tallacagua was ignorant or mistaken. He thought Tallacagua was intentionally wrong, lying in fact, in order to exploit Eugenio.

It is not clear to me that Eugenio understands what appendicitis is or the serious implications of its inflammation beyond the fact that its diagnostic term situates it within the realm of physician care. Eugenio perceived Tallacagua's manner and explanation as being condescending and abusive. Not trusting Tallacagua, Eugenio decided to postpone his permission for surgery until he had discussed the issue further with relatives at home.

Anxious for the child's health, Dr. Tallacagua protested loudly. He must have been angry that his medical authority carried so little weight when the problem at hand was so urgent. He angrily warned that the child could only count hours to live, that the operation was so serious that it would cost 500 pesos ($25 U.S., an enormous sum), that the child was so sick now, because Eugenio had waited so long to bring the child in, that surgery would be risky, and that he, the doctor, could not even guarantee its success at that time, let alone later if the father hesitated to change his mind!

Eugenio interpreted these words as further confirmation of Tallacagua's exploitative intents. He told Tallacagua that he did not know what his daughter had but doubted she had what Tallacagua said and had decided to take her to a yatiri. For some miraculous reason the child survived. Maybe Tallacagua's diagnosis was wrong.

Explaining his reasoning to Antonia, Felipe, and me, Eugenio points out that Tallacagua had demanded cash. Eugenio has virtually no cash. The ethnic (class) group to which he belongs has virtually no cash. Tallacagua knew this. Cash belongs to the more powerful world of mestizos and markets which flourish by exploiting Eugenio's "ethnic group" and denies Eugenio entry. Now Tallacagua asked him to contribute an outrageous sum to that ethnic group, and to a man who had betrayed his own Aymara identity and community to join it! Given Eugenio's earlier experience with Sabas, Eugenio saw the demand for cash as unnecessary. Con-

sequently the demand had to be malintended to serve Tallacagua's personal interest at Eugenio's expense. As Eugenio saw it, that interest was to join the oppressors
and exploit his fellow Aymara.

Eugenio's analysis that Tallacagua was abandoning his Aymara identity to become not just a mestizo, but a member of the elite, appears to be correct. Tallacagua's implication that Eugenio could not or should not understand cosmopolitan
medical information is the first evidence to that effect. Having switched class
membership through the medical profession, Tallacagua could now assert cultural
superiority and use the medical encounter to mine Eugenio's meager wealth.

Then Tallacagua accused Eugenio of irresponsibility and ignorance by crit-
icizing him for bringing the child in at such a late state in the illness. Actually the
timing felt quite reasonable to Eugenio, who like everyone else in and around Kachitu, could not easily afford to see cosmopolitan (or yatiri) medicine as a medical
resource of first recourse.

Finally, Tallacagua threatened Eugenio with the child's death if he did not accept Tallacagua's demands. To Eugenio, Tallacagua behaved in exactly the same
way as the khan achachi. Unlike a yatiri who reads positive or negative outcome
before treatment in the coca leaves, Tallacagua told Eugenio that the treatment
might not even be successful. Not only did Tallacagua insist on differential cultural identities between himself and his fellow Aymara, he also insisted that Eugenio openly acquiesce and reaffirm Dr. Tallacagua's newfound ethnic affiliation by
agreeing to accept nothing in return should the treatment fail and the child die.
The words the doctor probably intended as sincere warnings were interpreted by
Eugenio as threats because of Eugenio's definition of Tallacagua's chosen cultural
identity, which Tallacagua substantiates by maintaining a social distance from the
campesinos, by living apart from them, and by making no compromising gestures
to reform that identity.

Antonia understands immediately that the topic of this conversation is not
Tallacagua's medical skills nor the little girl's illness, but social relations. Social relations and social movement across ethnic boundaries are exploitative by nature.

She agrees with Eugenio's suspicions and relates the following story to support the idea that any curer is capable of exploitation and victimization, if the curer
does not claim to be of the same ethnic group as the patient. She explains:

> A good many years ago my father became ill with some kind of pain in his side.
> A yatiri from one of the valleys came to look at him. This yatiri asked what things
> of extraordinary value my father had with him in the house. My mother took out
> her pair of gold earrings with her manta (shawl) that were worth more than a cow.
> When the yatiri saw what items of value my mother had, he claimed that these
> things were what were causing my father's illness and that he would have to take
> them with him.

Years ago George Foster said that indigenous populations avoid physician care because of the social gap between them and the physician (Foster 1958). Eugenio and Antonia disagree. They concur that it is not the social gap but what it means.

It can be any social gap. It may exist between mestizo and yatiri as much as between campesino and the elite physician that Tallacagua was trying to emulate. The gap may be created as Tallacagua did, following the vecinos before him. What is essential to exploitation is the ethnic boundary that justifies the action. Healing is particularly amenable to this use. Physicians, yatiris, and the supernatural have access to curative powers that vecinos and campesinos do not. With this power they can extract resources for value, things to "eat," as long as curer and patient do not share or acknowledge the same ethnic identity. To share or acknowledge the same identity, or even elements of it, is to form an alliance, make an agreement of mutual trust, create a friendship.

This is exactly what Eugenio and Antonia do tonight. Their conversation itself is an idiom through which they negotiate the content of their own ethnic identities with each other, by agreeing to the moral of Eugenio's tale, to the immorality of Tallacagua, and the nature of social relations across ethnic lines. They agree that ethnic differentiation is a tool by which other people exploit them, and they mutually acknowledge how people do that. Like Tallacagua, they negotiate their cultural identity. And in this dialogue, Eugenio and Antonia negotiate theirs in relation to each other.

From another perspective Tallacagua was not the evil character Eugenio and Antonia made him out to be. They had their own reason for doing so: to negotiate a friendship with each other. An attempt to understand Tallacagua's own strategy, however, reveals a very different picture.

Tallacagua saw himself as an ambitious Aymara with a medical degree: as forging a new frontier and thus as being an anomaly in Bolivia. The only one of his kind in medical school, he finished six years in five and graduated near the top of his class, yet friends of mine who attended medical school at that time assured me that Tallacagua had not done well and was a fool. No one knew what to do with a professional Indian, least of all Tallacagua. Upward mobility, while it takes place all the time, is covert, just as Indians arranged their entry into the Kachitu vecindario at the turn of the century. Tallacagua, however, came directly from the campo, offending everyone by breaking the rules.

As a professional in La Paz, everything that revealed the immediacy of his Aymara Indianness worked against him. At the same time, scientific medicine itself had been good to him. He did well in school. One of his teachers referred to him as brilliant. He felt that were he not discriminated against, he could enjoy a successful life and help lift his own family out of poverty. They were expecting him to do so and he honored his familial obligations. Hence, Tallacagua wanted out, to go to Brazil, where he believed his Indianness would have no negative significance and his talents would be appreciated.

In order to do so, however, he had to play by Bolivian elite rules. He had to show those people with power in La Paz what he thought they wanted to see before they would help him secure a job elsewhere. So he perfected his Spanish. He socially distanced himself from the Aymara whose association he thought would jeopardize him. He changed hospital policy to approximate as much as possible the policy of the teaching hospital in La Paz, and in ways that emphasized efficiency and the Importance of Scientific Medicine. Aymara medicine was not tolerated. Neither was payment in kind. Given that most of the drugs in the dispensary had surpassed their stipulated shelf life, cash was desperately needed. Any step toward financial self-sufficiency would reduce dependency on the U.S. Methodist church and make the hospital stronger. Tallacagua felt he was contributing to the "modernization" of the Kachitu clinic. He also hoped to capitalize on those efforts. An article appeared in the La Paz newspaper referring to his work at "Tallacagua's clinic" in Kachitu. That reference offended many Kachituños, and after two months, Tallacagua left town, much to the relief of all parties, particularly himself.

As Aymara, Felipe Apaza was far luckier than Tallacagua, and medicine served him differently. As a nurse trained in the Kachitu hospital by Dr. Beck, medicine provided him with multiple incomes at the clinic and a private practice out of his home. With his long and successful career he had become covertly the primary authority at the hospital, although he carefully allowed the doctors who came and went to take credit for decisions that Felipe supervised. He was also the president of the Padres de Familia. Everyone in town, Aymara and mestizo alike, looked up to Felipe. He was also, perhaps, the only person in town to actively pursue the negotiation of a settlement between ethnic and religious groups, and the development of a single, united community. When Father Christian called a meeting to castigate his Catholic flock for not attending church, not fulfilling their obligations to the church, and letting the building fall into disrepair, it was the Methodist Felipe Apaza who was the first to donate money to repair the padre's roof. He saw the meeting, and the repair of the church, as a community issue, not a Catholic one. And in pursuit of community unity, Felipe was very respectful of Aymara medical beliefs. "Perhaps you can help me write them down," he said to me once; "I want to preserve them before they disappear." Because Felipe Apaza's strategies at the hospital were successful and Dr. Tallacagua's were not, there was no need for him to worry about the disappearance of Aymara medicine.

CHAPTER 8

The Use and Abuse of Ethnic Boundaries: In Which the Doctor Begins His Medical Education and the Legal Values of Medical Etiology Are Exposed

When Dr. Tallacagua left Kachitu, Dr. Alejo Acietuno arrived to serve his required year of rural service, his año de provincia. Dr. Acietuno saw himself as "too educated" to be aligned with any religious group, but like Tallacagua, he arrived in Kachitu fresh out of medical school and was devoted to the wonders of modern medical science. When he first arrived he told me in confidence that the advantage of a position in such an out-of-the-way place is that there is no supervision, no one looking over the physician's shoulders in Kachitu, and so he could practice and finely tune his art. He made a public display of scoffing at Aymara medicine and snorted at the suggestion that it might have some value. And as he practiced medicine in Kachitu he made mistakes both medical and social. Over the year of his residency there he learned less about the art of modern science than he did about the art of deploying it. He learned that to practice medicine in Kachitu, a physician must abandon much "modern science" and accommodate himself to the local belief systems and the sociopolitical context in which they exist. The sociopolitical context in which they exist defined his own ability to practice what medical science he knew, forcing him to either maintain the notion of "scientific purity" and serve no one or accommodate himself to the sociopolitical realities of which he was indeed a part, not an objective observer of, as Dr. Sabas had done before him and as Felipe encouraged

159

him to do. He learned a lot from Felipe Apaza, the nurse and hence subordinate he thought he would instruct. His education was long and hard and costly, and his first mistake was Bartolo.

I found out that Bartolo had blown off two fingers and the thumb on his right hand as I emerged from a mass for Doña Soña Roman's husband's father—dead three years then—with nearly two dozen dogs yelping at my feet.

Doña Soña Roman's husband belonged to that contingent of disgruntled mestizos who believe that all the best of Kachitu disappeared with the revolution, even though he was desperately poor himself. Thus my presence at mass as a foreigner—and as he tried to make it, resident diplomat—held much importance for him. My failure to attend would be evidence of my lack of propriety, education, and value as a worthwhile human being.

It was an embarrassing moment, the type one wishes to forget, particularly when faced with an accident like Bartolo's at its culmination. My dog Metze was in heat. There were no veterinarians in Kachitu to spay a dog. Bimbo, Doña Elsa's dog, fell in love. For days he howled outside my door. I threatened to beat him to get him to go away. He merely cringed, ready to accept a beating rather than move. I begged Doña Elsa to keep him locked up but she resisted. I poured water on him but he persisted! My neighbors and I could not sleep. I grew worried that someone might ask me to get rid of my dog. Early one morning while I was still not ready to wake up and vaguely aware that it was, for a change, quiet, Doña Elsa came pounding on my door, yelling that Bimbo was missing and that I certainly must be responsible. That was the only morning in a week that Bimbo was *not* at my door and I indeed hoped someone had poisoned him.

Grumpily I stumbled out of bed and let her in. She looked around and when satisfied that I was not detaining her dog, smugly left. I went back to bed exhausted. I had not slept in a week! Five minutes later Bimbo started his vigil of howling outside my door. Elsa was long gone.

I knew I would not be able to get back to sleep, and it was time to go to Soña's husband's mass for his father. I got dressed and left for the church. At the door I vainly threatened Bimbo and moved to leave, when Metze got out! Bimbo chased Metze to the center of the town square and began to satisfy his desires. The racket and the smell of Metze's presence attracted the entire local canine population. Suddenly there seemed to be thousands of dogs in the town square. I suppose Metze became frightened, or perhaps she intended on remaining the center of attention. Whatever her opinions, she became attached to Bimbo. Now they were stuck together, and Metze began to get mauled by the other dogs. By now a large crowd had formed. Kids began throwing rocks at Metze. Behind me I could hear the mass begin (Oh God, I'm late!), and a terrorizing image flashed through my mind of Doña Soña's husband, outraged at my tardiness and the disruptive chaos I had created. Midst cries and whoops of laughter I rushed for a bucket of water to throw on the two dogs. With belabored success, I took Metze home and humbly returned to the church. Meekly I padded softly down to my designated seat in the second pew. I did not realize that the smell of Metze remained all over my clothes.

I took a moment to orient myself. Father Christian was delivering a long, flowery speech for the benefit of Doña Soña's husband. Just as he arrived at the most reverent part of the sermon for the dear departed—Don Julio Trujillo, head of the vecindario and Big Man in town in his day, may his soul rest in peace—just as everyone bowed their head in dramatic concurrence, the sound of scuffling emerged from under my pew. The noise increased. Beads of sweat formed on my forehead and dripped down my nose and into my eyes. My heart began to pound. The sound of scuffling was so loud I could hear it reverberate off the church walls and mix with the growing cries of dogs as they began to fight under my pew. All eyes were on me, the reverent foreigner who came to show her respects. The pew began to move, and under it some two dozen crazed dogs competed for my skirts and tried to find the Metze dog in their folds. I looked at Soña. Her face was a petrified image of horror. Her husband was appalled. His face was red with anger. The priest's bore a pleading expression. In the midst of his prayer, I fled from the church leading two dozen dogs out from the second row.

The recollection of a Mark Twain tale of similar effect flashed through my mind, but that tale was told from the point of view of two mischievous boys who let some pigs loose under the chapel. His story was funny. Being the victim of the present scenario, this story did not seem funny from *my* point of view. My face glowed red as I gathered the chaos about me, tripped over my feet, and scrambled for the front door.

Oldemar stood at the front door waiting for me, oblivious to the chaos, and not laughing as I thought he might, not being very fond of Doña Soña's husband, and being rather mischievous himself. He appeared almost as if he had sent the dogs in to get my attention. His face was white and serious. Bartolo had blown off several of his fingers and was afraid to go to the hospital. Would I please come. Confused between comedy, embarrassment, and the sudden sense of fear and urgency, I ran home to change my clothes before going to the hospital.

Bartolo and Oldemar, two bright, enterprising young boys who found themselves frequently in rather innocent trouble, lived with their landless mother Bonifacia in a single, windowless room with nothing but a bed in it, off the main square. At mealtime Bonifacia would bring her small stove and her one pot into the street to cook. Her children's father had died. Her own family was too large to help her. Hence she moved out of her family's household in one of the comunidades to Kachitu to serve as a middleman between Kachitu and La Paz in the exchange of agricultural produce for magical items and spices. Often left to their own devices, the boys had learned that I love trucha and utilized that information to promote enterprise in Kachitu.

They also took up occasional residence in our house, where they pored over everything Anna and I owned, tumbled off our few sticks of furniture, raided the pantry, and borrowed toys. They always returned the toys. We grew fond of them and usually delighted in the trouble they managed to get themselves into as a testament of their unbounded energy and enthusiasm.

Like most people in town, they did not care for Doña Soña's husband. He was always abusing and castigating them, calling them nothing but "Indios." Today, with several other boys including Enrique Ordoñez, son of the Methodist baker Emilio Ordoñez, the wealthiest man in town, they decided to play a joke on the old curmudgeon. They decided to let off a few firecrackers outside the Catholic church and disrupt the mass. I seemed to have saved them the trouble. Enrique, the only one of the boys wealthy enough to obtain a firecracker, lit it and threw it on the church steps. The firecracker, however, did not go off until Bartolo bent down and picked it up. It blew off most of his index and second finger, and his thumb. In shock and whimpering, Bartolo knew that the place to go was the hospital, but he had never been there before and was afraid of Dr. Acietuno. He asked me to go with him and stay with him throughout the ordeal.

Dr. Acietuno was not there. Oldemar, Bartolo, two little cousins, and I waited. By the time Acietuno showed up it was dark. The electrical generator would not work. Silently the doctor lit a kerosene lamp which was also running low on fuel. Throughout the ordeal Acietuno said nothing as he cleaned and stitched the grisly wound. I did not see him use any anesthetic but assumed I must have been mistaken. Before he began, Bartolo asked Oldemar to wrap a rag around his eyes so that he would not see the wound or the doctor working on it. He was afraid that the sight of it would give him fright, and that he would lose the most important of his three souls and die.

It took close to three hours to sew up what was left of his index and middle fingers and thumb. His thumb was a mere stump, and his fingers were torn off to the last knuckle. Bartolo was in such pain he vomited. Oldemar was scared and crying. The two little boys sat on the floor by the door, covered their faces, and kept silent, barely breathing, waiting for Bartolo.

Other than Bartolo's pleas that I take him home, and my continual promises to do so, the only words spoken were those of the young European volunteer who softly told him not to scream, not to move, because "it didn't hurt." Horrified by the pain that Bartolo seemed to be experiencing, she asked the doctor if he did not need more anesthetic, but Acietuno said nothing. I thought perhaps he did not hear the question, for he was concentrating intensely on his work.

Dr. Acietuno finished just as the last flicker of the kerosene lamp died. Bartolo was so cold I bundled him up in a blanket I stole from the clinic and took him home after what seemed to be all night of promising him I would do so. Dr. Acietuno still said nothing.

On the following day I approached Dr. Acietuno and humbly asked if I could give Bartolo some Darvon. I did not wish to harm Bartolo by giving a drug that would complicate whatever he was already taking, or by offending the doctor. Dr. Acietuno said "sure" so definitively that I was taken aback by the briskness of his response. Somewhat confused, I asked him what he was giving Bartolo and he said, "nothing."

For two weeks Bartolo and I went to the hospital every other day while Dr. Acietuno cleaned the wounds. Every time, Bartolo would cover his eyes with a rag so as not to see his hand and lose his soul. His pain was difficult to witness. Acietuno suggested I not attend. We began to fight about the anesthetic. Dr. Acietuno claimed authoritatively that an anesthetic would increase the chance of infection by decreasing the flow of blood to the fingers. I protested, but having no medical education, I was on risky ground. He said Bartolo's cries were only his nerves, a comment with which I had to agree. He added, "Indians do not feel pain the same way we do."

Caught between the acknowledgment that I did not know enough to be medically responsible, the suspicion that Dr. Acietuno was wrong, the risk of offending Dr. Acietuno and thus hurting Bartolo's chances at the clinic, and the knowledge that Bartolo's pain was unbearable, I gave Bartolo massive doses of Darvon. Acietuno did not prohibit me from doing so, but let it be known that if anything went wrong, it would be my fault for meddling. I worried that he was right.

Our fight began to become the topic of town gossip. This visibly worried Acietuno and made me uncomfortable. One afternoon I mentioned in passing that I had heard that Bartolo said he had only lost the tips of his fingers, and that I was worried about his ignorance and the shock he would experience once he learned the truth. He had after all, kept that rag over his eyes whenever his hand was exposed, and the hand heftily wrapped up at all other times. That afternoon, Dr. Acietuno sat down with Bartolo for the first time and had a long talk with him.

Iris Quispe was an Aymara Methodist and a nurse at the hospital for several years until she had children. She still provided occasional services to the clinic and kept up with what went on there. When asked if she understood why Acietuno had not used any anesthetic, she said she thought that Acietuno was scared after events of the previous week. An Aymara campesina came in from one of the comunidades with a hernia that Acietuno could easily repair. He told her to eat nothing the evening before the operation, but she, not understanding the significance of his request, did not follow his instructions. Under the anesthetic, she vomited, choked, and died. Rumors that Acietuno had murdered her had rippled through the Aymara campesino community. Acietuno was startled.

After two weeks of cleaning and stitching Bartolo's hand, it became clear that there would not be enough skin to cover the exposed bone. Acietuno amputated the fingers down beyond the first knuckle so that nothing but stumps remained. For the operation, he gave Bartolo a local anesthetic and a tranquilizer.

Meanwhile, Bartolo's misfortune became the center of town gossip, and the inevitable question of why it happened was answered on all sides. Doña Soña's husband pronounced that the little brat deserved what he got and many others agreed: they maintained that Bartolo was trying to hit one of the nuns with the firecracker when it went off in his hand. No one was willing to reveal the truth. No one mentioned Bartolo's companion, Enrique Ordoñez, except Doña Margarita Garcia viuda de Bilis. Doña Margarita owned the house on the square in which Bonifacia rented her room, but she lived most of the time in La Paz. In La Paz she rented a small room herself, and lived off the income she got from Bonifacia, several chacras of land she rented out, and small business deals she mustered in the city. She was not living the way she did in 1952 nor in the way she had expected to spend her old age. In 1952 her husband had been alive, their land holdings extensive, and their larder full of potatoes, quinoa, beans, eggs, and pork given them by their Aymara ahijados.

Doña Margarita Garcia viuda de Bilis kept her own council, except to advise Bonifacia that the incident was Enrique Ordoñez's fault. Doña Margarita maintained that Enrique ensorcelled Bartolo. She held as evidence the considerable wealth the Ordoñez family had obtained over the past twenty years and the extraordinary pain the doctor was putting Bartolo through. She maintained that if Bonifacia filed a complaint with the corregidor, she could force Emilio Ordoñez to cover Bartolo's hospital bills. To facilitate this and look out for Bonifacia's interests, Doña Margarita Garcia viuda de Bilis obtained the necessary papers and helped her fill them out and file them.

Terrified of the impending bills, disoriented by the accident, and understanding ensorcellment to be a logical possibility, Bonifacia filed. Everyone saw ensorcellment as a possibility for anything, and many participated in it. Only the week before, a *mesa negra*, a llama fetus, and some other unmentionables were dug up in the far side of the soccer field, and as it turned out, our team won!

The corregidor found no evidence of guilt on Ordoñez's part, although he did not rule out the possibility of ensorcellment. Doña Margarita's efforts fueled the feud between herself and the Ordoñez family and destroyed Bonifacia's reputation in Ordoñez's mind. However, they also influenced Dr. Acietuno. Alarmed that the details of his treatment so easily and thoroughly became public knowledge, appalled that they were used to substantiate a justification for witchcraft, and relieved that he was not made the target of the accusation, Acietuno determined to protect his own interests in the future by reinstating the hospital policy that Sabas had implemented, and he embarked on a campaign to encourage yatiris to practice there.

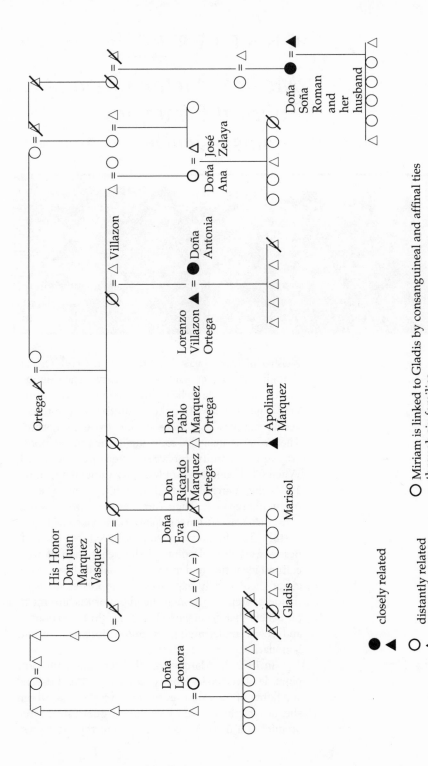

His Honor
Don Juan
Marquez
Vasquez

Ortega

Don Ricardo
Marquez
Ortega

Don Pablo
Marquez
Ortega

Doña Eva

Apolinar
Marquez

Gladis   Marisol

Lorenzo
Villazon
Ortega

Doña
Antonia

= △ Villazon

José
Zelaya

Doña
Ana

Doña
Leonora

Doña
Soña
Roman
and
her
husband

● closely related

▲ distantly related

○

△

○ Miriam is linked to Gladis by consanguineal and affinal ties through six families.

CHAPTER 9

Medical Metaphors and Political Strategies: Gladis's Death

Neither of Doña Eva's daughters wanted children, although they never said so explicitly. They simply made it impossible to have any. They were two of the first children born after the revolution to prestigious vecino families that were unable to leave Kachitu. Their parents struggled to maintain the prerevolutionary vecino identity for years afterward and failed. When Gladis and Marisol Marquez came of age in the 1970s they entered a world for which they were entirely unprepared. They came armed with a world view that was no longer appropriate, viable, or even useful. They found no reason to reproduce. Their illnesses were critical points in the negotiation of their cultural identities, and in the 1970s, all the lurid gossip about them vividly expressed the processes of negotiation of identity through the idiom of Kachitu medical beliefs that developed in response to the economic and social undermining of prerevolutionary ethnic boundaries.

In 1952 the Marquez family represented the very pinnacle of vecino sociability. Doña Eva's first husband and father of the eldest seven of nine children to whom she gave birth was Don Ricardo Marquez Ortega, the product of a marriage between two of the most prestigious old vecino families in Kachitu. In the 1940s, Ricardo Marquez's father, Judge Don Juan Marquez Vasquez, insured Marquez's respectability by marrying first one, and upon her death a second girl of the Ortega family, and thereby claimed more than respectable amounts of land and pride. His Honor Don Juan ultimately had three wives and seven children, but Pablo and Ricardo were the only two children born to his last two wives and were his favorites. To them he left his legacy in Kachitu: most of his land to Pablo, and his tienda and house with some land to Don Ricardo. The others settled in the city of La Paz. To further insure the land and social standing of Pablo and Ricardo, His Honor Don Juan fought vehemently against the intrusion of the Methodist church in 1941; indeed, he led the vecino battle against the church, which he felt sought to incite the Aymara to revolution and undermine the social order in town.

Don Juan, however, lost his battle with the Methodist church. The revolution in 1952 and the land reform of 1953 almost eliminated the Marquez land holdings and left only enough for subsistence for one household, and the tienda was looted. Juan died of old age just after his eightieth birthday, and Ricardo followed shortly thereafter when he fell off a roof he was rethatching, not being able to get Indians to do the work anymore.

Doña Eva was left a widow at the age of twenty-six, with six living children to support on a tienda and a subsistence plot, all that was left of the Marquez estate. She was left to confront what all the Kachitu vecinos faced: economic, cultural, and political impotence, an unpredictable universe, and a distrustful social environment.

Pablo courted Eva but she shunned him, though she lent him the tienda to subsist on. When he married and decided to move to La Paz he refused to return the tienda, showing papers that claimed he inherited it from Don Juan. Knowing the tienda was one of the few hedges Eva had against the cost of rearing six children and sending them all to school, he insisted she buy it back, which she did, digging into her already nearly empty pockets.

By the 1970s, Eva, like the other vecinos who remained in Kachitu after the revolution, had the glory of history but little of substance to pass on to her children. The help the Marquez and Ortega families could give her, which Juan had thought he had insured for his daughter-in-law, was nil. With the death of the only Ortega male, that family ceased to exist. Because Don Juan's other children had a different mother than Ricardo, there was no Marquez upon whom Eva had any claim. Individuals with whom she had had compadrazgo ties and who had fled to La Paz abandoned their responsibilities to her. Kachituño vecinos who successfully migrated to the city after the revolution joined the commercial urban sector in which compadrazgo ties took on new significance and required new strategies. For them no benefits accrued to such ties with poor rural subsistence-oriented villagers. Consequently Eva, who had married well and securely according to the mores of the prerevolutionary social order, now found herself completely alone in a village in which her social equals, the other remaining Kachitu vecinos, also found themselves alone and armed with impotent cultural resources.

Eva's greatest prospect of security now lay in remarriage. While she looked, she encouraged her four daughters to secure their own futures and also marry as soon as they came of age. There were, after all, two boys who would have to have good educations, preferably in La Paz if money were available, and then if she remarried there would be more children. A second strategy, then, was to educate the girls as well: a career would increase the girls' social status in their quests for husbands and provide them with incomes, leaving Eva's income from the tienda to invest in her sons' educations. Thus Gladis and Marisol became rural school-teachers, the only career available.

At the end of the 1960s a Kallawaya medical practitioner passed through Kachitu and stopped at Eva's house because, he said, he sensed trouble there. He divined in the coca that illness would plague the Marquez household until Eva married. An anxious attempt to secure a husband and rescue her children from sickness left Eva abandoned and pregnant, and publicly humiliated. Before Eva finally married Luis Meza, an enterprising man of some wealth who owned a mine and some land outside Kachitu, and had one more child, her eldest daughters expressed in two protracted illnesses the anxiety of life in the social limbo in which they all found themselves.

The actual historical events surrounding the illnesses are impossible to reconstruct in their entirety. There were no historical records, and there were as many witnesses with a slightly different twist to their recollections as there were Kachituños willing to be interviewed on the subject. Of significance is not my reconstruction but rather the variations of recollections. These variations are further attempts by Kachituños to negotiate their cultural identity through the illness episodes of these two young women.

MARISOL'S VERSION OF GLADIS'S DEATH

Marisol was in her late twenties when I first met her in 1977. She had beautiful, thick, curly, long dark hair, sweet eyes, and a sad smile, and she always seemed to be sighing. For a reason I could not possibly fathom and never would have guessed until she told me a year later, she spoke English! I immediately hired her as a research assistant. Over the year and a half we became intimate friends. We would work, eat, drink, and laugh together several times a week. Yet it was long after she knew what I was up to that she was willing to discuss with me the illnesses in her own family, and how her own illness was related to her learning English and to her sister's death.

Marisol's illness and her sister's death are examples of two processes by which people use medicine as a primary resource. Through their illnesses, which they first defined in cosmopolitan medical terms and later as Aymara diseases, both young women and their family renegotiated the significance of their ethnic identity and their ethnic affiliation: they became mestizo subordinates to the demands of a yatiri and socially marginalized by the other Kachitu mestizos, but in the process, financially secure. By offering their own medical opinions, everyone else in town shifted their own social positions by defining their relationships to the young women. The yatiri who ultimately cured Marisol gained through his therapeutic administrations both wealth and power.

Secondly, their illness episodes were two of seven similar cases that befell the young adult children of the mestizo class between 1970 and 1978. Until Marisol's sister's death, consensus among mestizos held this virtual epidemic to be of psychiatric origin, or perhaps epilepsy, and that it was appropriately treated by a physician. Not until the cases were defined in Aymara terms did victims, including Marisol, survive.

Marisol gave the following explanation of her sister's illness. She explained that Gladis died at the age of twenty-six in 1975 (at the same age as her mother was widowed), from an illness she had been suffering from for four years and which began while she was studying for her rural teacher's license. In 1971, Gladis unwittingly precipitated the illness herself by trying to prevent her menstrual cycles with cold baths. She abhorred her monthly cycle and while living at school, submitted herself to cold baths during her period until she stopped menstruating.[1] Her periods became irregular. Headaches developed. After a year they went away entirely and she never menstruated again. Marisol regretted that Gladis was never willing to discuss her feelings related to these events with her mother Eva.

Marisol explained that Gladis graduated from the rural teacher's school in 1972 and was assigned to a post in the lowlands. During this year she became ill, spent many days in bed, complained of feeling tired, and did not want to work. At one point, she left the school and disappeared. The school notified her mother, who traveled to the lowlands to search for Gladis. By the time she arrived there, Gladis had returned. She cried. She was depressed, yet she decided to finish out the school year. After several months, however, her stamina dissolved and she returned to Kachitu. Upon her arrival she broke open the family's front door, shed her clothes, and danced about the room, apparently unconscious of what she was doing. Marisol and Eva struggled to put her to bed. Later she did not remember what she had done, but she repeated the behavior for several weeks. Marisol said she was never violent.

As Gladis had teachers' health insurance, Eva took her to a psychiatric hospital in La Paz. Marisol said the doctor recommended surgery but she did not remember on what or why. Gradually Eva became suspicious of the hospital care.

She believed the doctor rarely appeared and the nurses were not kind. Gladis was never operated on and after three months in the psychiatric facility she remained the same. At that time, the doctor claimed she was not improving at the hospital and recommended she return home.

At first, back in her own home, Gladis seemed to be her normal self. However, at that time her brothers and sisters were away at school and her mother was busy trying to court Luis Meza in hopes of ridding the house of illness. Eva married and promptly gave birth to a ninth child, which demanded much of her time. Gladis, therefore, spent much of her time alone. "I feel bad now," reflected Marisol, "because I didn't spend more time with her. Perhaps she needed more company. She would ask me to take her for a walk or to the movies in La Paz or to some place where she could have a good time."

At this time Eva and Marisol learned that Gladis had been romantically involved with a man who taught at the same school. His father was the school director. Contrary to the mestizo code of propriety, Gladis had moved in with him. Occasionally he beat her, probably, explained Marisol, in an effort to control her during her lapses of consciousness and odd behavior. The man claimed to love Gladis, however, and both Eva and the director approved of a marriage.

The director, Marisol said, arrived in Kachitu to express his concern shortly after Gladis's discharge from the hospital. Gladis greeted him by calling him the devil. She slapped him and threw a glass of water in his face. Thus began her relapse, said Marisol.

Nevertheless, except for this incident, Gladis seemed well for some months. When the next academic year began, Eva and Marisol encouraged her to return to school. She reluctantly agreed, but was back in Kachitu and very ill within three months. She hated her fiancé. He had betrayed her, and it was apparently significant that the other woman was black,[2] making it clear that Gladis was quite conscious of the social significance of ethnicity. Gladis was not satisfied when, upon her return to school, he deserted the other lover. On the contrary, said Marisol, her illness grew worse.

She avoided light and would lie or sit in dark corners of the house. She refused to see people. Though Catholic, Eva turned to the Reverend Angel and begged him to perform an exorcism in the house. When the Methodist minister's administrations brought no change in Gladis's behavior Angel explained that she suffered from a disease common in the United States. Marisol could not remember the name of this disease.[3]

Eventually Gladis refused to eat. She removed herself to her bed and would not get up. She grew anorexic, afflicted with bedsores, and unable to walk. Finally, Eva consulted a yatiri. He divined in the coca and prophesied that Gladis would die, that any attempt to cure her would be futile.

Marisol explained:

Toward the end, Gladis wasn't crazy any more. She acted normal. She said that as soon as she got better she would change; she wouldn't go away from home any more and would stay here and help the family. She dreamed of living in La Paz with me and would ask about our other brothers and sisters.

The day before she died she told Mother she was going to go on a long trip and asked what she could wear. Mother got out her best clothes and then went for the priest who came and gave Gladis her last rites. In the night she called out three times to our brother who was sleeping in the same room, but he did not get up. In the morning she was dead. She had been sick for four years.

SOCIAL INFORMATION AND POLITICAL STRATEGIES CONTAINED IN DIAGNOSTIC OPINION: Eva's Version of Gladis's Death

Eva was both the warmest and most distant friend I made in Kachitu. On the one hand, she was the first person in town to talk to me. That meant a lot because no one would talk to me at all during our first month in Kachitu, except to briskly answer yes-or-no questions, or to gesticulate an apology and disclaim they spoke Spanish—which of course they did speak. Eva broke the ice, invited me to sit on her front stoop, and divulged confidences about local political goings-on, faked genealogies, the bogus nature of the town social structure, and other intoxicating tidbits of gossip. But she would rarely discuss her own family, particularly the illness they had suffered. She seemed wary and reserved whenever I asked her about Gladis, and I was perhaps unkind to persist. Four times during the research period of 1977 and 1978, Eva agreed to discuss Gladis's death. Each time she described different social events surrounding the illness that grabbed her attention. In this way, through medical dialogue, Eva negotiated her relationship to me. As is usually the case, though the overt topic was Gladis's illness, the real topic of Eva's monologue was us.

The first time Eva discussed Gladis's death, she said she thought maybe Gladis had died of *amartillo*, the Hispanic folk disease caused by the loss of a beloved, in Gladis's case her father. Through this diagnostic interpretation, Eva told me her family had once been prestigious and wealthy, despite present appearances, and had suffered more than enough to warrant my respect. Gladis, said Eva, had been very close to her father. He had been a great judge, president of the vecindario, and intoxicatingly enchanting to his Victorianly frail but elegant daughter. Her heart suffered greatly from his death. Attacks to her heart increased when she returned to school because, besides missing her father, Gladis studied too much. Her heart condition was exacerbated by headaches from overextending her attention to her studies. Eva added that she herself suffered greatly from Gladis's death.

The second time Eva discussed Gladis's death, she used a diagnostic interpretation to tell me that Gladis's death was not her fault. Her medical discussion also told me she trusted me enough to reveal she had confidence in yatiris. She thought maybe Gladis had died from an illness in the house because she had consulted a yatiri who said so. He predicted that Gladis would die in three days which, in fact, she did. This particular yatiri was so capable that he now conducted his practice in La Paz, she said. He was particularly capable, in this case, of relieving Eva of guilt.

The third time Eva discussed Gladis's death, she impressed upon me her wisdom. It was her wisdom to trust in yatiris that brought her financial security. Other mestizos, such as Doña Teresa Cordova, were not so wise. She explained that she had sought the help of many yatiris to cure Gladis but they all told her the case was hopeless. One, however, read in the coca that Eva must marry Luis Meza to rid her house of an illness that killed Gladis and would attack her other children. This marriage, he predicted, would bring health to Eva's family and wealth and happiness to her. She protested that she had never spoken to Luis, who had recently moved to town and bought the tienda next to hers. The yatiri, however, claimed his prediction was accurate, and that she must accept this offer to insure the well-being of her family after Gladis's death. As it happened, related Eva, she sat next to Señor Meza on a bus shortly afterward, and they struck up a conversation. Later he did ask her to marry him and she accepted. "And now I am rich, healthy, and happy," she said, ignoring the frequent discussions she had had with me over her lack of finances. The marriage, however, did provide her with a financial security she had not possessed since the death of His Honor Don Ricardo.

Toward the end of the research period, Eva discussed Gladis's death one last time. She and I had not seen much of each other for some time as I was busy collecting data. I sensed she felt offended and resented having revealed so much to me, worried about what I might do with intimate details that might incriminate her. She explained that Gladis had effectively stopped her menstruation with cold baths. The condition of not menstruating attacked her brain and killed her.

OTHER DIAGNOSTIC OPINIONS: Other Social Strategies

The only people willing to discuss Gladis's illness were other mestizos. Those Aymara I asked simply stated they didn't know, and Methodists demurred. The vecinos, however, had a great deal to say about it. What they said revealed much more about themselves and the strategies of cultural identity they had chosen than it did about what actually happened to Gladis. From their varying responses emerged a grammar for the use of medical dialogue as a mechanism for the negotiation of the content of an ethnic identity that was gradually dissolving into social class.

Seven parties proposed different explanations. The responses fell within three categories: that the death was ultimately Eva's fault; that it was Gladis's fault; and that it was blameless. The type of response cleanly corresponded to the degree of kin relationship between the Marquez household and the respondent, the economic standing of the respondent, and the rigidity or flexibility of contemporary use of the prerevolutionary ethnic boundary-maintenance strategies of the respondent.

THREE CLOSE RELATIONS

Three respondents closely related to the Marquez family claimed that Gladis's death was Eva's fault. Apolinar Marquez, the most closely related, being Gladis's father's brother's son, gave the most fictitious account. He claimed that Eva had had an affair with the local policeman and that this fellow had had sexual relations with Gladis on the side, instigating Eva's jealousy, and shaming Gladis with incest. Gladis, he said, died from attacks caused by this "horrible" and "tragic" situation.

The youngest respondent, and a rural schoolteacher himself, Apolinar longed to live in the city where his father, Pablo Marquez Ortega, now lives. Although

Apolinar was presently economically unable to do so, he had his youth to encourage him. He had tried living in the city with his new wife and infant son, but was unable to secure a job. Out of economic necessity he returned to Kachitu but aspired to a cosmopolitan identity. He saw himself as belonging to a new generation that aspired to Bolivian development and entry into the world market as a major power. He divorced himself from the prerevolutionary social order and the remnants of the old vecindario which still attempted to hang on to it. He was only superficially and minimally sociable with the Kachitu vecinos.

Most significant in his diagnostic opinion was the policeman, not mentioned in any other analysis offered. The first cousin and most closely related respondent evidently knew less about the incident than anyone else. Yet he blamed Eva and in part Gladis (he did not suggest that she was raped) and thereby set himself apart from the one element in Kachitu that would hinder his establishment of a new cultural identity and ethnic affiliation: close and visible poor mestizo relations. He knew few details of what happened, in spite of his close family relationship to Gladis and Eva, because he no longer had any social ties with them.

Antonia and Lorenzo Villazon were also closely related to the Marquezes. Lorenzo's mother was an Ortega. Lorenzo claimed that Gladis had been very normal and pleasant until her mother forced a wedding upon her, a new detail not mentioned by previous informants. Eva was a widow at the time of the wedding, he said, and did not want people to gossip about her unmarried girls, assuming that men might not marry the unprotected daughters of widows. The new husband, however, disappeared shortly after the wedding and never returned. Gladis moved away to teach in the lowlands when it became clear to her that her new husband would not return, and there she fell in love with another man, presumably the fellow mentioned by Marisol. Eva went to visit Gladis, discovered her daughter's lover, and flew into a rage. She accused Gladis of being "dirty" because she did not attend to her lover appropriately. She told Gladis that the lover was really in love with Eva herself. Gladis in the meantime was upset over the illegitimacy of her mother's affair with Luis Meza, as Eva had not yet married. Gladis grew exceedingly thin. Her mother locked her up at home and refused her permission to leave the house. Gladis became timid, refused to talk to anyone, and died.

Unlike Apolinar, Lorenzo was Eva's age. He had suffered the same postrevolutionary losses she had. Also a rural schoolteacher, without land or tienda to augment his income, and with four children and a wife to feed and clothe, Lorenzo had tried to maintain the dignity of a prerevolutionary member of the vecino class while his wife, Doña Antonia, had made equilateral compadrazgo ties with campesinos in his absence, taken the disgraceful job of washing at the Aymara Methodist clinic, begged and borrowed from other vecinos in order to feed her children, and thereby humiliated him. Their social status among vecinos had consequently dropped in spite of Lorenzo's efforts to present himself as a dignified member of the old order. This in turn had led to public arguments between him and Antonia over their differing survival strategies, and consequently to greater losses in prestige.

Lorenzo's diagnostic analysis, which was given in Antonia's presence, was bitter. His monologue about Gladis seemed really to be a love song to his wife. A week earlier, he had gotten drunk, fought with Antonia, called her a spendthrift and threatened to file a denunciation against her with the corregidor. Later she had one of her attacks. As his own attempts to maintain and negotiate his pre-1952 ethnic identity failed even in his own house, he pointed out this night that at least Antonia was faithful and decent and a good mother by pointing out in his rendition of Gladis's death that Eva lacked these qualities. The picture he drew of Eva was particularly condemnable by the chivalrous pre-1952 vecino standards that he implied Antonia upheld.

By accepting his compliments and agreeing with his analysis of Gladis's death, Antonia inadvertently legitimized the values he had been insisting upon and which she did not follow because they were economically unfeasible. Furthermore, Eva was a close relative who underwent losses, disorientation, and humiliation. By denying that Gladis's death had any relationship whatsoever to his own life, Lorenzo denied that the vecino class as an ethnic group was impotent. By denying any association with Gladis's death Lorenzo justified his prerevolutionary values and ethnic identity. As a landless schoolteacher and as a male, however, he had no alternative. There were no other economic and social strategies for him except that which Antonia had so prudently developed. To follow these particular strategies, however, would cost Lorenzo his social standing among the other vecinos in town, as well as the justification of his heritage.

Soña Roman was also closely related to the Marquez family. Soña epitomized the poor but hardworking wife of a status climber. She had no friends except her children and disapproved of most everyone in town. Tyrannized by her usually absent husband and perpetually empty money jar, she devoted her life wholeheartedly to her four loyal, obedient, and helpful daughters; a jolly infant; and her overly proud, thoroughly spoiled, domineering, and relatively useless teenage son, to whom the entire family except the father deferred and who was called Papicho, or little father.

Soña claimed that Gladis died from lack of care; her death was Eva's fault. Soña, echoing Lorenzo, related that one year an older, mature man came to Kachitu for the fiesta and made strong advances to Gladis. He and Gladis had sexual relations in public in the river that runs by the west side of the village. Horrified, Eva made them get married. The man, however, left for La Paz right after the wedding and was never heard from again. It was this trauma that caused Gladis's illness.

When Gladis began to behave oddly, Eva locked her in a room for six months and did not try to cure her because she didn't have any money. For some months she did put Gladis in the psychiatric ward at the worker's hospital in the city. But when she was discharged, Eva was occupied with her project to lure Luis Meza and paid little attention to Gladis. Gladis died from lack of care, and the fault lay upon her mother Eva.

Doña Soña Roman's husband was an outsider in Kachitu and encouraged that status. He migrated to Kachitu when he married Soña because he owned no property, while Soña's mother lived in one of the nearby communities. The mothers of both Doña Soña Roman and her husband wore polleras: they wore the prerevolutionary female mestizo outfit which, by the postrevolutionary period, became Indian dress. His mother bartered spices at the Sunday market in exchange for eggs and grain which she sold in the city. In spite of this poverty and close affiliation with the Aymara, Doña Soña Roman's husband perceived of himself as socially superior and better informed than everyone else in town. He felt no loyalty to the town and scoffed at the idea of wasting his time and money to sponsor the annual town fiesta. He neither attended any social activities nor permitted Doña Soña to do so, and Doña Soña, though warm and loving, socially exiled herself. He had invested his money in a television set which sits packed in its box in the corner of their two-story, two-room house, waiting for electricity. Continually trying to improve the house and the little yard behind it, he had imprinted upon his family his own special dream for which his entire family worked: that Papicho become a more prestigious gentleman in the new Bolivian world than himself, just as he was more educated and sophisticated than his own parents. Such improvement would mean eventually abandoning Kachitu for the city.

The social world of Doña Soña Roman's husband's perception was the prerevolutionary rigidly stratified hierarchy in which the Aymara, many of whom were much better off financially than he was in 1978, were his own social, intellectual, and cultural inferiors by virtue of their genetic makeup. On this point he agreed with Doña Teresa, who thought he was a boor. While Doña Soña shared her husband's sociological view, probably because it was his view, she was a woman, she told me, an inferior being within this sociological imagery, and conscious of the limitations of her own social worth. There were people who, even though they might be abominable, were her social superiors, and she not only knew her place but the place and behavior appropriate to everyone in town.

Somewhat like Apolinar, Doña Soña and her husband recognized that the old order was dead and that new cultural identities must be developed. Socially, Doña Soña and her husband made it clear to the villagers that, from their point of view, the good old days were gone, the town was going downhill, and they did not want to be associated with it. Doña Eva was not only a Kachituño of whom Doña Soña and her husband disapproved, but a vecina who had been negatively affected by the events of the past twenty-five years rather than enlightened, like them, that the future is in the city. Gladis, in their view of history, was abused by a man from the city, an older, "mature" man who took advantage of the woman's rural simplicity and then returned to the city to disappear in the bowels of its vast and complex urbanity.

Relying on prerevolutionary values to support their new, postrevolutionary view of the world, distinctions in social hierarchy for Doña Soña Roman and her husband had not changed so much as they had multiplied. A rural-cosmopolitan distinction overlaid the old Indian-vecino distinction, justifying Doña Soña's husband's antisocial strategy in the village. Gladis's death was a further justification for making that distinction.

Though Soña claimed Gladis died from lack of care, Eva's culpability did not lie in disinterest. Indeed, Eva had taken her daughter to the hospital in the city. Her culpability lay in the fact that she had no money. The fact that she paid little attention to Gladis while she concentrated instead on her fiancé was not condemnable but necessary, particularly given her six children. Eva was guilty for remaining in Kachitu where, these days, there is no hope of amassing wealth.

Although Doña Soña Roman and her husband aspired to the modernization of the city and condemned the provincial poverty of Kachitu, they could not move to the city themselves. In fact, as much as they desired such a move, the city was also frightening and unknown. From it emerged the "older, mature" stranger who precipitated Gladis's illness and destroyed her life, only to disappear back into it. The city hospital did nothing to help Gladis. In the city, Doña Soña Roman's husband would be a lower-class mestizo and a far cry from the image of himself he tried to negotiate in Kachitu. His image of the city was not the poor section high up in La Paz where his mother sold eggs and grain and bought spices but rather the lower, richer, modern district where people spend their evening watching television and where he could not go because he had no business nor social ties there. The association between Gladis's death, poverty, and the rural-urban distinction was an easy one for him and Soña to make, as it enveloped their hopes and fears.

DISTANT RELATIONS

Jose Zelaya and Doña Ana are both distant relatives of the Marquezes, less by kinship than by social class, their involvement in commercial activity, and their cultural identity. Neither viewed Eva as culpable in Gladis's illness and death. When asked about it, Don Jose recalled two other recent deaths in town, both close relations to Gladis. Based on that history, Don Jose determined that Gladis died of epilepsy, which is genetically inheritable and runs in Gladis's family, he said. Ana, though, explained that "Gladis was crazy. She used to scratch her mother's face.

They had to lock her up in a room and pass food in to her quickly through the door. She was naked mostly."

In 1978 Ana and Jose Zelaya shared the distinction of being one of the two wealthiest vecino families in Kachitu. Being wealthy relative to the other Kachitu vecinos, however, meant that they still watched carefully where every peso went and never indulged. They were the only mestizos who made a commercial adaptation to the changes that occurred after 1952. They responded to an increase in demand for goods and opened a hardware store. They turned their tienda into a bicycle repair shop. They also fixed kerosene lamps and sold bicycle and lamp parts, notebanks, pencils, paper, school supplies, plates, pots and pans, batteries for transistor radios, and contraband margarine from Peru. They sold anything they could get which they figured would sell. Don Jose was also a judge and heard complaints and cases in his house, while Doña Ana and the children minded the store. The Zelayas enjoyed the reputation of being unquestionably the most industrious vecinos in Kachitu. Furthermore, the vast majority of their customers were Aymara campesinos whom they defended against vecino complaints. Because they were industrious and economically secure, because Don Jose was a judge, and because they did not socialize with the other vecinos in town, they had earned the respect of campesinos and vecinos alike. They had changed their definition of their own ethnic identity.

Ana, however, was a Cordova. Thus, in contrast to Jose, her family was the most successful in maintaining the prerevolutionary ethnic strategies. The Cordovas' large property on the town square was not affected by the land reform as it was not agricultural. Thus it presently allowed the family to maintain an extended household instead of establishing nuclear households like everyone else since 1952. Taking advantage of this, the Cordovas steadily increased the family income as brothers and sisters pooled their resources earned from several tiendas, practicing law, teaching school, and running the civil registry. Their interests, therefore, included supporting the vecino class of which they were prestigious members and from which they could claim social superiority over the Aymara. Therefore Ana chose not to focus the blame for Gladis's illness upon some culpability of her mother's, but rather to support Eva, who had to face, as did Ana's family, unfortunate setbacks in life. Gladis's death did not represent to either Jose or Ana a failure in their ethnic identity.

Two other vecinos remarked upon Gladis's illness, and both saw Eva as at least partially culpable. Doña Miriam thought that Gladis had died of a broken heart. During one of the town's fiestas, she said, Gladis had a publicly sordid affair with some gentleman who had come from the city to participate in the festivities. The two made love in the open by the river that runs along the east side of the village. Eva forced them to marry, but on the day after the wedding, the husband disappeared.

Bereft, Gladis took to her room and refused to come out, to sleep in her bed, or to wear clothes, and she died of a broken heart. Miriam saw Eva as partially culpable. Miriam was closely related to the Marquezes and relatively speaking, economically secure.

Miriam was economically secure because she was elderly and lived by herself in the house on the square that her family abandoned after 1952 when they moved to the city. In her house she had a small tienda that sold the same goods that did the other mestizo-owned tiendas except Jose Zelaya's. She also had a small parcel of land which she rented out. Though she was seventy or older, she visited her family in La Paz several times a year, and they came to Kachitu for the fiesta. Some of her nieces and nephews were well educated and affiliated with the national university or the military. Miriam remained in Kachitu because she was elderly, never married, and had no immediate family.

Miriam perceived the Kachitu prestigious society to have entirely removed itself from the town, leaving only herself as a lonely and elderly citadel to witness silently and uncritically the inevitable social changes that had made the village "not what it used to be." She rarely ventured from her tienda to pass about the village, having the store to tend and her arthritis to inhibit her movements. As clientele of all ethnic and religious groups patronized her tienda and lingered to share their gossip with her, she was well informed of the ongoing activities of the town.

In Miriam's opinion, Gladis's illness was a tragedy, brought on by the exuberance of youth, which had gotten out of hand since the old social order fell apart. The illness and death were part of the inevitable changes that followed the revolution and the end of vecino dominance: losses of morality, respect, and proper values. Though Eva forced Gladis's marriage, which probably precipitated the illness, propriety gave her no alternative.

In contrast to Miriam, Leonora was beset with poverty. Her sick and alcoholic husband could not work except for the little help he gave the corregidor. Don Valentino had been a rural schoolteacher before he took ill. In 1977, he had no land and four young children. Leonora earned an extremely modest income from the sale of herbs, magical items, and spices that she would buy "wholesale" in La Paz, paying with eggs and grain, or gather in the hillsides. On the other hand, she was not closely related to the Marquez family. Her strategies, like those of Antonia, consisted of establishing equilateral compadazgo and trading relationships with campesinos. Like Doña Soña Roman's husband's mother, she continued to wear a pollera even though the campesina women now wore them too. She wanted her childen to find a better life in the city, but did not have the economic means to prepare them for it. Resigned to her fate, she worked at least as hard as the Zelayas, hunting and trading for food, caring for her children and husband, selling her goods at the three weekly markets in and around Kachitu, and traveling to La Paz to replenish her supplies. But she was not considered industrious because, unlike the Zelayas, her work did not produce any symbols of commercialism: she did not have a repair shop; she did not even have a tienda. Leonora consequently had no dreams of leaving Kachitu like Doña Soña Roman and her husband, nor nostalgia for a dead social order in which she would have been a lower-class member.

Doña Leonora determined that Gladis died of attacks of the head (*ataques de cabeza*). Before she became ill she had been well liked. She was fifteen and studying for her rural teacher's license when Eva forced her marriage to legitimize an illicit affair. The husband turned out to have a wife and two children in La Paz. The marriage lasted two days and her husband disappeared. Upon graduation from teachers' college, Gladis got a teaching post in the lowlands but fell sick during her first year there and returned home, where she refused to see anyone. She said her head hurt. Slowly she became crazy. Both doctors and yatiris tried to cure her to no avail. Finally Eva locked her in her room. After two years she died. Leonora noted that two of Gladis's close relatives also had died recently of similar illnesses. Gladis's illness and death did not represent to her a way of life that was either lost or degenerating, but rather one which was unpredictable and oppressive.

In these ways, the nuances of the various responses reflected the changes in cultural identity each respondent had chosen, changes which in turn were related closely to their economic and social situations. Those who were relatively more secure economically, and successful in negotiating their cultural identity, were able to maintain sufficient distance from the post-1952 losses suffered by the vecino class, and they were able to look upon Eva's trials without criticism. But those who were not suffered some insult to their own cultural identity from the tragedies and failures of their fellow vecinos. Furthermore, the more closely related vecinos were to others who suffered from changes brought on by the revolution, the greater the impact upon their own cultural identity, and the more difficult it was to renegotiate a new one. When respondents were closely related to the Marquez family (specifically, Apolinar, Antonia and Lorenzo, and Soña) they tended to see Gladis's death as being her mother's fault. When respondents were distantly related, they saw the death as being either Gladis's own fault or as due to a family disease (Jose and Ana de Zelaya). The particular respondents who were distantly related to the family were also the most financially secure vecinos in town. Only one relatively economically secure vecino, Miriam, saw the death as the mother's fault, and Miriam stood in a close kin relationship to the Marquez family. The one respondent who claimed the death to be Gladis's own fault, Doña Ana, was still close to her brothers and sisters, the Cordovas, who maintained the prerevolutionary ethnic identity more openly, explicitly, and successfully than all other vecino families in Kachitu, in part because the family controlled the one resource in town which permitted them to do so: the town registry. Only one respondent who was distantly related to the Marquez's, Doña Leonora, claimed the death to be Eva's fault, and this respondent was among the poorest of Kachitu vecinos; she also claimed, however, that the illness ran in the family. "How can we succeed," they seemed to be saying, "if our own family is unable to do so?"

I never found out what really happened to Gladis—but that is not the point. The point is that whatever really happened is secondary to people's perceptions of what happened. And people's perceptions are defined by their social, economic, and political positions and situations in town.

Doña Teresa's town archives lists Gladis's death as caused by "congestion cerebral."

CHAPTER 10

Ideological Shifts and Acquisition of Power

Two years after Gladis's death, Marisol fell ill. As in Gladis's case, Marisol's history and romantic involvements may have contributed to the nature of her illness. Because her illness occurred outside Kachitu, only Marisol and her mother witnessed it, and they kept quiet about it. Hence, there was no variation of opinion among the Kachituños. Significant, however, is the symptomatology and curative strategy that Marisol remembered and described to me on at least four separate occasions. Her descriptions were consistent and confirmed by Eva in two interviews. To manage this illness in the wake of Gladis's death Eva revised her curative strategies. Because of the manner in which Eva and Marisol interpreted her illness as differing from Gladis's experience, their diagnostic opinion and Eva's choice of therapy expressed a considerable change in their definition of their own ethnic identity. Through Marisol's illness medicine as a primary resource facilitated social shifts not only for Marisol and Eva but for Marisol's healer as well, with significant political implications.

My interpretation of Gladis's death is that she had been a victim of historical change and the development of a new social, economic, and political order for which Eva had been unarmed to prepare her. When Marisol fell ill, Eva did not resort to cosmopolitan medicine but turned the responsibility of her daughter's health care over to her daughter's fiancé, who in turn appealed to a yatiri. Perhaps no cosmopolitan medicine was available or she felt she couldn't afford it. She claimed that Aymara strategies were most appropriate because the illness was beyond the physician's control: Marisol had been in the hands of El Tio. The odyssey to an Aymara disease for Marisol the mestizo was striking in its convolution.

At the tender age of sixteen Marisol spent a year with a Peace Corps volunteer in Plattsville, New York. She and Eva assumed that a romantic relationship was involved. He had worked in her village, recognized her bleak future there, and took her to the States to teach her English and thereby enable her to work in La Paz, "perhaps in a travel agency," he said when I called him in 1978. After a year, she returned to Kachitu and waited another ten years for mail and romance from the North American. In her own mind, she left New York as a strategy to manipulate a reluctant lover with the loneliness of her absence, hoping he would follow. He understood that she had returned when her visa expired and the educational purpose of the trip was completed.

During Marisol's absence Eva married Luis Meza. Meza was interested in settling in Kachitu because it lay on the road from La Paz to a mine he owned. Under the reform regulations of COMIBOL, which nationalized all major mining operations in Bolivia in 1952, his mine qualified as a "small mine," thus permitting him private ownership of it. It was located near an Aymara community three day's travel from Kachitu. Its operation was dependent upon less than two dozen Aymara miners and one young trusted mestizo manager whose father had been Aymara. The ethnic difference between ownership and labor and the lack of managerial staff placed the burden of supervision of the operation on Meza himself who, once married, frequently transferred that responsibility to his new wife, Eva. Upon Marisol's return from the States, he further transferred that responsibility to her. As a result, Marisol frequented the mine and met the young assistant. Somewhat reluctantly, and with her mother's and stepfather's strong encouragement, she accepted his proposal for marriage.

Marisol and Doña Eva concurred on the unfolding of events. A week before the wedding Marisol fell ill. The onset of her weakness was relatively rapid, and she claimed she was barely able to sit up. Eva's and Marisol's dramatic description of her symptoms and their chosen course of treatment reveal how they perceived the illness as related to social relations defined in this place and time by Aymara rather than mestizo values, and how, through her illness, social relations changed in the mine.

The first relationship to change was Marisol's. Eva encouraged her fiancé to take responsibility for Marisol's health care in prospect of his upcoming marital role. Perhaps she thought such care would solidify the marriage. In doing so she pushed Marisol into her fiancé's household in the Aymara manner of prenuptial relations and contrary to mestizo values.

The second relationship to change was Eva's. Marisol moved to her fiancé's house on a Friday, the day before the wedding, and her fiancé immediately called upon a yatiri. The yatiri attended Marisol for four days. During that time an Aymara woman intimated to Doña Eva that the yatiri was in fact killing her daughter. When Eva confronted the yatiri with this accusation, the yatiri admitted it. He argued that Eva had falsely accused his son of stealing from the mine. Indeed, on her visits to the mine Marisol had noted that materials were missing. On this advice, Eva had concluded that they were stolen and accused a certain employee. She did not realize that he was the yatiri's son. The yatiri now sought revenge through his supernatural powers. Only after repeated obsequious displays by the entire mining community of Aymara and mestizos alike acknowledging the yatiri's superiority, and a public and humiliating display of Doña Eva's desperate pleading, did the yatiri agree to stop his curse and effect a cure.

On Friday, Marisol explained, her gums were bleeding and there was a little spot on the end of her tongue. When I asked she told me she had had no fever. Marisol explained:

> I was too sick to see the yatiri's face. He brought a washtub in which he put hot water and a very hot stone—it was almost red it was so hot. He said three prayers and, coming to my bed three times, he touched my forehead, and my wrist, telling me not to worry, that I would be better after my bath. He made me get up from bed and take off my pants and straddle the tub with the hot water and stone in it. He put a blanket over me and my husband helped me stand there for maybe fifteen minutes until I sweated profusely. He did something else but I did not see what it was because my face was covered with the blanket. I wanted to vomit, but I couldn't because I had nothing in my stomach. The yatiri said that this was a bad sign, my wanting to vomit, and that I must be treated immediately, but that it was too late that evening. He said he would come back in the morning, which was my wedding day. He and my fiancé put me to bed and I felt very weak.

On Saturday morning, the notary married the couple at the husband's house. Food and drink were served to guests who arrived for a day's feasting and dancing and which, following custom, would be followed by yet a second day of festivities. Marisol said:

> By Saturday my tongue was swollen and completely white. My teeth were bigger than usual and began to protrude from my mouth. My head hurt so badly that I couldn't touch it. I was too tired to sit up or eat. The guests wanted me to dance but I stayed in my room, which everyone saw as a bad sign because a bride and groom must be constantly together on their wedding day; so they told my husband to go to sit by me and not leave me. He was just a little drunk. In the afternoon I asked him to send everyone away because the noise hurt me. He was very worried for me.

The yatiri did not return until Sunday morning to complete his cure. He advised Marisol to rest alone and permitted only the husband and himself to attend her. Nevertheless, the wedding guests returned to the house to continue the wedding celebration, unaware of the seriousness of Marisol's condition:

By Sunday I couldn't talk and there was a lot of saliva in my mouth. One of the guests was the wife of another yatiri. When she saw me she told my mother her husband could cure the illness that I had. Mother waylaid my yatiri with wedding food while this woman's husband came to examine me. He read in the coca that I was caught by El Tio because of a deal my yatiri had arranged. He had already buried something of mine which was a sure sign that I would die.

When the second yatiri told my mother this, she confronted the first yatiri. He acknowledged that my death would revenge our accusation of his son. He demanded not only our respect and obeisance but those of the whole community. The second yatiri advised us that my life was in his hands, so we agreed to accede to all his demands. After Mother returned the stones that she had confiscated from him the first yatiri agreed to pray. But after a brief beginning, he refused to continue until the whole community acknowledged that his power made him superior to Meza's.

When he finished praying, he asked for a plate, a big wooden spoon, a chicken, two guinea pigs, two pig fetuses—one male and one female—a dulce mesa, alcohol, and a bottle of wine. It was too late by this time to get all these things, so he agreed to come back Monday night. He also asked for two women and four men of different names to be present for the curing on Monday night when he would make an exchange of these items with El Tio for my life.

On Monday night he asked each of these two women and four men to come to me and ask me if I had seen anything strange or if I had fallen. But I couldn't talk. I could only move my head to indicate no. He asked them to leave my bedside. He took the two guinea pigs, cut them open, and put them against the bottom of my feet. He made the chicken drink the wine and then made me hold the chicken against my chest. As he did these things he read and reread the coca to clarify that El Tio would accept these offerings. He concluded he would have to wait because El Tio kept saying through the coca that he did not wish to accept any offering for me. The yatiri said out loud to El Tio "Why don't you leave Marisol alone when we give you all these things; she already has a husband!" Mother asked the second yatiri if the first was really curing. He told her not to worry, and that El Tio was obliged to accept these gifts, and that we merely had to wait until he did so.

Long after midnight El Tio finally agreed to accept the offerings if they were delivered in the mine within a half hour. Many people were waiting outside the house to hear what would happen. The yatiri asked for two men among them to take the mesas with the animals to the mine; but they were afraid to go because they feared something would happen to them if they did not arrive there within so short a time. My husband could not go because no relative can make such an offering. Another man offered to go but he was a jilacata (Aymara official) and had therefore promised never to have any dealings with El Tio. My stepfather offered money to anyone who would go and one man then agreed to make the trip if accompanied by his friend. The yatiri agreed to this arrangement.

These two men left with the offerings, but took too long. An hour passed and the yatiri worried. He told my mother that something terrible would happen. Months later we found that one of these men did not believe. He had said to his friend that the yatiri was merely trying to make them feel ashamed and that the illness I had was only a natural illness. When he saw where the sacrifice was to

be given, he said this was some stupid and wasteful thing to do, that the chicken was fat and should be good food. So they stole the chicken for themselves. Within a year the first man's wife left him for another man, and his two children died. One of the children of the second man also died. I was cured, however, though it took fifteen days before I felt well again.

Marisol's and Doña Eva's interpretation of these events was that El Tio had exchanged her for the high quality ore in Meza's mine, probably because the mine was exhausted shortly after this incident. Marisol's own travels, Eva's and her unfamiliarity with mines, and their status as mestizos had inclined them to ignore such beliefs. Particularly after having been in New York, Marisol had distastefully viewed as suspicious the annual practice of giving fetuses, male and female, and dulce mesas to the Condor Mamani and the Pachamama at the mine, an action that the miners carry out for their own protection every August (Taussig 1980; Nash 1979). Sometimes, she explained, they bury a live llama, and occasionally, when there has been a rash of accidents, a human.

Meza fruitlessly dug another shaft to relocate the vein or find another. Within a few months he closed the mine and turned his attention to coffee in the lowlands. Marisol's marriage ended in divorce a year later, having never been consummated.

Three issues of significance emerge from Marisol's and Eva's story. First, the yatiri's ability to extract immediate compliance on the part of the gathered community and the longer term reinforcement of faith in and respect for the yatiri's office occurred at a time when the spread of cosmopolitan medicine and commercial activities and resources were no longer eroding the yatiri's authority. Until the

1970s the Bolivian government had condemned indigenous medicine. Following the mandate of the World Health Organization declared at Alma Ata in 1978 to support indigenous medical system's the government shifted its policy. Through this and similar incidents the yatiri was able to reinforce that shift and gain some advantage, particularly over, as he saw it, the abusive relationship between his accused son and his employer.

Second, the yatiri's revenge demonstrated to at least two mestizo women that an Aymara can demand justice on his own terms and through his own arts without resorting to mestizo officials.

Third, the curative strategies Eva employed to cure Marisol were very different from those she used with Gladis. Though she did not abandon Marisol, she feared that, having been unsuccessful before, she might be unsuccessful again, particularly in an ethnic environment in which she was an outsider. In fact, there was no longer a cultural environment to which she could comfortably belong.

A comparison between Marisol's and Gladis's illnesses, and between the experiences that led up to them, further accents the use of medicine as a primary resource to implement a shift in Eva's and Marisol's "ethnic" identity. On the one hand, Marisol's travels and experience before her illness contrasted sharply with those of Gladis. Gladis fell sick away from home, particularly in the lowlands, a medical otherworld beyond the Andean passes where *apachitas*, or protective offerings left along the trail, give testimony to the evil and hungry supernatural beings that haunt the bridge between the security of the altiplano and the magical dangers of the unknown. She sought relief in several domains—in the magical optimism of an imagined world, in the promise of cosmopolitan medicine, and in the security of her own backyard—and found nothing.

Marisol, in contrast, traveled much farther away, the effect of which was to vividly impress upon her the poverty and powerlessness of her home village and its mestizos. Denied access to U.S. society, she had to return to a powerless rural mestizo status. She receded into the Aymara world of the mine, not because she sought it but because she was obliged to her mother's husband in order to save the family from financial ruin and to try to maintain their mestizo status.

Upon her illness, Marisol and her mother accepted a yatiri as curer more immediately than they had during Gladis's illness, at least in part because the yatiri's abilities to unleash her from the claws of El Tio had become that much more evident. Here she succumbed to those metaphors that she and other mestizos in Kachitu are appropriating from the Aymara in the postrevolutionary era as descriptive of their own social relations. In Marisol's and Eva's minds, her strategy essentially reversed the relationship between Aymara and mestizo. Eva pointed out that her strategy was highly successful because, unlike Gladis, Marisol was cured.

Juxtaposed with this contrast between the two illness events is a striking similarity: neither Gladis nor Marisol wanted to take their mother's advice and marry. At school, when she effectively prevented her menstruation, Gladis stopped her ability to procreate. It appears as well that she went to school only reluctantly. Gladis was in a position in which the values her mother and her social class taught her were no longer positive, adaptive, or viable. As a member of an impotent group in a new social order that made no room for that group, Gladis had to make decisions that no one had made before. Had she married and had children, she would have had no way of knowing who or what her children would be or what opportunities they would have. As a possible strategy, she lived with a man in the lowlands, a custom prohibited by the prerevolutionary values of the mestizo class, but practiced commonly by the Aymara (e.g., Bolton and Mayer 1977; Carter 1965; Carter and Mamani 1982). This strategy failed. Gladis's response to her fiancé's relationship with another woman who was black shows that Gladis was acutely conscious of class, ethnicity, and social relations. That is, the social order to which Gladis belonged was impotent in a universe that had become, for her cultural group, chaotic and uncontrollable, and for which one could not prepare. Her illness and death may be interpreted as having resulted from the strain of her inability to make order of and control events in that universe as they pertained to herself and her future.

Marisol was faced with the same set of values, the heritage of a dead social order, and a chaotic universe in which there was no niche for her. Her trip to the United States, however, might have solved the problem of Marisol's social position and ethnic identity had the volunteer invited her there with the intentions she and her mother so mistakenly imputed to him. Though Marisol was active upon her return and willing to marry ten years later, a marriage to a first-generation mestizo with a limited future would have been a social step down from the dreams she had harbored for ten years. Her wedding was marked by her near death at the hands of a symbol for Indian exploitation and oppression. However, through trying its suggested solution, she recovered from her illness.

The process by which other mestizos in Marisol's and Gladis's village are also increasingly shifting their position in Aymara medical cosmology, the extent to which this shift is related to the economic and political effects of the past thirty years on the altiplano, and the extent to which medicine is a primary resource by which to do so was further evident in the tragic illness of Peluquilla's son only a year after Marisol's recovery.

CHAPTER 11

In Which The Medical Anthropologist Demonstrates the Limits of Her Education and the Doctor Demonstrates He Has Learned a Lot

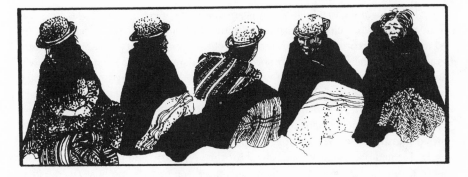

Peluquilla was crazy and everybody was afraid of her. Drunk by early morning, with the smell of red wine and coca on her breath, her eyes were still crystal clear and her voice strong, assertive, usually accusatory, and occasionally cacophonous. She survived entirely on the generosity of the Aymara, but their generosity was double-edged. They gave her as much alcohol as food, and enjoyed if not benefitted from what she did with it. What she did with it was talk. Far more powerful than the town seer, she somehow knew everything that went on in town and made it public. The mestizos abhorred her.

Like Doña Eva, Doña Antonia, and everyone else, Peluquilla had been a different person in 1952. Both she and her husband, Don Magno, had come from the most prestigious vecino families. Their wedding was the largest social event on that part of the altiplano in

189

the 1940s. Their union brought together an enormous amount of land. They had two houses in town, one on the town square that rivaled and mirrored the Cordovas house, situated directly opposite on the square. Don Magno had been a blacksmith, president of the town council, corregidor, judge, and general enthusiast. Because both families were prestigious and old, Peluquilla was, after the wedding, related either consanguineously or affinally to every mestizo in town (and to a lot of Indians as well, as was, of course, everyone else). As kin to every mestizo, she was rightfully everyone's obligation, yet few helped her. Vecinos shunned her because she embodied so dramatically what had befallen all of them.

By 1955 the land reform had taken most of Magno's and Peluquilla's land. Many Aymara ahijados refused to fulfill their compadrazgo obligations or frequent their tienda. Within a few years their economic status, political power, and prestige had eroded away.

Their inability to adjust to the postrevolutionary environment was the most dramatic in town. Peluquilla had never gone to school. Her parents were intent on educating her according to their notions of elitism and gentility: young ladies were graced with social skills, not burdened with mundane hardships that included literacy. For women and many men on the altiplano there was little need for literacy before 1952. For young ladies of noble ambitions, literacy could be perceived as a handicap. Servants and a strong family were supposed to leave her free to entertain, raise children, and create a scene of domesticity that would make the family proud and increase their prestige. Only Don Alejandro Cordova had felt differently. He had opened the small school for the vecindario and preached the importance of literacy for progress, but his daughter Teresa was one of very few girls who attended. Thus Peluquilla was completely unprepared for the turn of events after 1952.

Don Magno was literate and proud. When he lost his civil positions, he lost his pride as well. He took up drinking. To pay for the liquor and to support his growing family, he sold the little land the reform had left them. Shortly he was left with nothing. His greatest loss was his dignity. Perpetually drunk, he often took out his disappointments and rage on his family.

Magno's drunken child abuse was probably responsible for the death of three of his eight children. A fourth child died under circumstances similar to Gladis's, although many vecinos claim the cause of death was epilepsy. Attacks of either nerves, the head, or epilepsy are popular causes of illness and death of young mestizos in the contemporary Kachituño medical memory. Don Magno's daughter died of "attacks" in her early twenties.

When Peluquilla defied Magno, he would fly into a rage and beat her. He often tied her to a bed and beat her. Consensus had it that his prime complaint was that she refused to drink with him and share his sorrows like the loving wife he had married. Her sobriety humiliated him. Thus after he broke and displaced her arm so that the upper arm met the lower arm some three inches below the elbow, she began to drink too.

Before he died of a "ruptured liver from drinking too much," concurred most everyone, Magno terrorized the four remaining children. Peluquilla spared her daughter by sending her to live as a servant in a compadre's home in La Paz. When Daneri, the eldest surviving child, grew old enough to defend his mother, his father determined to teach him authority and respect. Once he tied Daneri's wrists and ankles together and hanged him from the rafters. When he awoke from an alcoholic sleep and saw what he had done, Magno released Daneri, and overcome with guilt and shame, started drinking again. When he tried to bury Daneri alive, other vecinos were able to intervene. By 1977 Daneri was in his late twenties and lived at home taking care of Peluquilla. He did the cooking, the cleaning, the laundry. He put her to bed when she was drunk. And he did not talk much, although he smiled a lot. By 1978, Daneri was *tonto*, feeble-minded.

The youngest son, Mario, escaped the brunt of his father's abuse in part because of his age, in part because he ran away from home. As a result Mario was not traumatized by either his father or the rigid elementary educational methods that, because there are no materials, are based on rote memorization and discourage independent thinking. By 1978 Mario had returned home, was the brightest youth in town, and was putting himself through high school with financial aid from Nathan Robison and me. Robison at the time was president of the town council because he was the only person in whom mestizos and Aymara alike could place their trust, he being neither. His support legitimized Mario in the public's eye, and gave him self-respect and a future.

The middle surviving son, Gonzalo, had been too old to be immune from his father's abuses, but young enough to escape. Horrified at Daneri's "punishments," he ran away from home. Afraid to go to La Paz lest he be found there and dragged home, he fled to the lowland city of Santa Cruz, center of *Camba*, or lowland, territory. Being a *Kolla*, or highlander, in Camba territory, he fell victim to centuries-old rivalry and was virtually rejected by Camba society, which distinguishes itself from highland Indian populations by calling itself "white." The political and economic shift from La Paz to Santa Cruz since 1952 has fueled the Camba-Kolla distinction. With no education, he found it difficult to get a job. He finally found employment as a cook in a pizza parlor where he worked for several years and saved his money. When he was certain that his father was dead, and satisfied that he had something to show for running away, and armed with his savings, he returned to Kachitu full of promise and excitement, planning to share all his adventures with the Kachituños, his family, his hometown. He had come home.

The year 1978 was a special one for coming home to Kachitu, and a lot of people did, including many old vecinos long since moved to La Paz. In 1978 *Car-*

naval followed immediately after the fiesta for La Virgen de la Candelaria and a preceding week of preparations, and Carnaval was followed by the beginning of the school year and thus a week of *despedidas,* or good-bye parties, for the town's rural schoolteachers. Thus a full four weeks of festivities distinguished 1978. It was a great year for Paceños, folks from La Paz, to take their families back to the "old neighborhood," display their successes, and enjoy being big fish in a small pond.

The fiesta for La Virgen de la Candelaria requires a week of preparations. It is always the grandest event of the year in Kachitu. For weeks before the event, youths climb past the fourteen stations of the cross on the escarpment to the statue of the virgin that Doña Victoria Castellano repaired and remodeled that year, and they play Andean music on their *sampoñas, churangos,* and guitars, so that the town may fall asleep dreaming of the fiesta. As the fiesta of 1978 neared, Paceños arrived daily until Kachitu was crowded with people. Old homesteads that were closed and boarded up were suddenly alive with activity. Windows were opened, dust was cleared away, and from these usually silent citadels emerged laughter, the sounds of children, the noise of glasses clinking, and the tones of sociability.

On the first day of the fiesta, long lines of Aymara slowly danced their way from their comunidades to Kachitu. These strings of dancers followed a flute player whose music grew more and more audible as they got closer to town.

By early morning the square was already crowded. Midst jolly fellows pouring liquor down one anothers' throats, and the groups of dancing Aymara, strings of mestizos would emerge from various households at different intevals, dance around the square, and retreat.

At the climax of the festivities, Father Christian emerged from the church with cross held high in front of him. Behind him four exquisitely attired footmen carried a platform on which was displayed the newly dressed virgin in all her splendor. Behind them the whole town gathered to march around the square, return the virgin to her proper place in the church, and then retreat to Doña Victoria Castellano's pension for the grand feast, she being the *preste,* or fiesta sponsor, that year.

People jammed Doña Victoria's doorway, a sure sign of the fiesta's success. As each guest entered, he or she pinned paper bills to Doña Victoria's chest until Doña Victoria was covered with money, a symbol of her prestige as preste, her wealth, and her respectability. Family members mingled with the growing crowd offering glasses of pisco and beer. Alcohol was served outside for the Indians. Chattering away about this one's achievements and that one's advancements, and anticipating the coming display of food, the crowd was gay, tipsy, and exuberant. At the very height of jubilance, midst exultations of pride among the old vecinos who were now Paceños returned to their unforgotten homeland, and among this celebration of the old social order and temporary amnesia concerning the past twenty-five years, in walked Gonzalo, Peluquilla's son.

Gonzalo turned out to be the most pleasant, sociable, and generous of all the homecomers. Nobody liked him at all. He bought everyone beers and launched into outlandish stories about his adventurous life in Santa Cruz—stories that bore no credibility whatsoever. He was a great cook. He had beaten five Cambas in a single fight. He had so many girlfriends he could not count them, but they all treated him like a king. Gonzalo's stories were intended as much to entertain as to impress. They were exaggerated and flamboyant. No one believed him, but I was not sure he meant anyone to. He was never offended and merely laughed when his audience expressed their doubts. His stories were no more flamboyant than many others' stories, although his enthusiasm made them a lot funnier.

In four weeks Gonzalo spent all the money he had saved buying other people beer. Although none refused his offers, few reciprocated. For four weeks running, Gonzalo tried to act like a Big Man, like the other returnees. This meant that for four weeks Gonzalo drank heavily and ate little. In a gesture of gallantry, he offered to stay on even after the festivities to walk his uncle, Don Lorenzo Villazon, over the mountains to his rural teaching post in Llojñapata. On Sunday, February 19, 1978, the morning after the last despedida, or good-bye party, Gonzalo and Don Lorenzo left for Llojñapata, accompanied by Daneri who, because he was tonto, would keep them safe from supernatural intervention on the long trip over the narrow Andean passes and into the valleys.

In the early morning hours of Tuesday, February 21, after the night of Gonzalo's and Daneri's return, Gonzalo tried to burn his house down. Then he ran to Iris and Pedro Quispaya's house and banged on their door. When they did not answer he threw rocks at their windows—precious items in Kachitu! He ran to Doña Soña and her husband's house and broke their windows, enraging Doña Soña's husband. He went to Ana's house, banged on her door, and yelled obscenities. Finally he went to Doña Victoria's pension, raised a ruckus, and broke her pig fence.

By the time the sun rose, half the town was knocking on the corregidor's front door demanding he do something about Gonzalo. No one saw the issue as criminal. The town universally agreed that Gonzalo was sick. Because Peluquilla was crazy, the corregidor was given the responsibility of guardian. At that very moment Gonzalo was in Eva's tienda accusing her of saying bad things about him. She was very upset and frightened. Gonzalo asked Mario who his enemies were. Mario said that while he may have made people angry, he had no enemies. After that performance, Gonzalo returned to his home and went to bed.

That morning I went immediately to Gonzalo's home and found him in bed. I asked him what had happened, what was he thinking. He did not know and he did not remember. As I turned to leave, he grabbed my arm and told me that on the road home from Llojñapata, in a lonely place where no one lives, he had seen the disembodied form of an old lady. Daneri confirmed that Gonzalo had been frightened by a vision on the way home. When Gonzalo had cried out, Daneri had refused to look and made, instead, a cross in the dirt, and ate some of the dirt, to protect himself from whatever Gonzalo had seen. Initially the whole town concurred with that story: Gonzalo had seen an anchanchu that stole his third and, hence, Aymara soul, and he, a mestizo, was dying of an Aymara disease. My own impression at the time was that he was an angry adolescent acting out.

Over the next four months hypotheses about Gonzalo's illness changed. After two weeks of treatment in Kachitu which included the services of five yatiris and over a week of hospitalization at the clinic, the majority of the town came to the conclusion that Gonzalo suffered from a disease defined by cosmopolitan medicine—"inflammation of the brain" was the most popular diagnosis—and should be treated by a physician in La Paz. A few people, such as Antonia, shifted their opinion back and forth between Aymara and cosmopolitan etiologies as news surfaced of the progression of Gonzalo's illness and of other people's diagnoses. Dr. Acietuno never felt certain about his diagnosis, and so he collaborated with several yatiris. Only Peluquilla, Felipe Apaza, Doña Soña's husband, Doña Eva, and Gonzalo himself remained consistent in their diagnosis: that Gonzalo suffered from an Aymara disease. The reasons they did so, however, differed.

The message behind Peluquilla's, Gonzalo's, and Eva's diagnosis was the shift in their own cultural identities from prestigious vecinos to that subordinate image that they, when they had been prestigious vecinos, had maintained of the Aymara. The message behind Doña Soña's husband's diagnosis was the urgent and desperate persistence of his ethnic identity as an important member of the mestizo race and its dictates of appropriate behavior in the face of evidence to the contrary. The message behind Felipe Apaza's diagnosis was his pride in Aymara heritage in light of the limitations of cosmopolitan medicine.

In the end, however, in July of 1978 when treatment ceased, the vast majority of the inhabitants of Kachitu shifted their opinions once again, to concur with Peluquilla, Gonzalo, Eva, Doña Soña's husband, and Felipe Apaza. Only by assuming the Aymara etiology of supernatural intervention could they be free of further responsibility to Gonzalo. For Gonzalo, like Gladis and Marisol before him, there was no place in contemporary Kachitu society.

Tuesday, February 21: As the most responsible member of the family, Mario assumes responsibility for Gonzalo's treatment. On Tuesday night, with money collected by the corregidor from members of town, he pays a yatiri to cleanse the house, particularly the garden. He requests a particularly powerful cleansing, using a mesa negra and a great deal of alcohol to "challar," explaining:

We will use a mesa negra because Gonzalo's illness is grave. If the Pachamama is angry she [*permits the anchanchu to*] *send a serious illness. Thus if you are sick and nothing else works, you use a mesa negra to talk to her and get her to stop the illness.* I think this is what happened to Gonzalo. *We have not challared our house in many years and for this the Pachamama may be angry. This is a particularly dangerous house. Listen, Libbet: before he got sick, Gonzalo had dreams about the garden next to the house. When we were children our father used to frighten us and beat us in that garden. He would get drunk and go out there in the middle of the night to talk to the devil. Now we have to challar.*

That night Peluquilla, Mario, Daneri, and a yatiri challar their house, but Gonzalo does not get any better.

Wednesday morning, February 22: Gonzalo goes to the Methodist high school and throws a few students' bicycles around the yard. He runs about town in a directionless state of agitation. When he begins to break windows again, Daneri takes him home and acquires another yatiri.

The yatiri enters the house praying to God. He puts a rosary around Gonzalo's neck, ties colored thread around his wrists, and waves a cord from a stick of dynamite around in his hand while he prays. He steps into the little garden where he burns charcoal and incense. He brings the smoking brazier inside and waves it around Gonzalo's body to "smoke" it. As he leaves he refuses payment, saying Mario does not have to pay until Gonzalo is cured. And he warns that for the spell to work, the dogs must not bark. But they did bark, says Mario later, and Mario fears this caused Gonzalo harm. As it turns out, Gonzalo does not get any better and the yatiri never gets paid.

Thursday, February 23: In the morning Gonzalo announces that he is better. Hoping it is true, Mario accompanies him to the town square to meet friends. But shortly Gonzalo begins to fall apart. He begins to run disconcertedly from place to place and talk in disconnected sentences. He insists he has to get to La Paz and work. His friends try to calm him down. He asks them what day it is, and when they answer, he yells, "They're trying to kill me! Tomorrow I'll be in my coffin!"

Eventually the corregidor, along with seven other concerned mestizos and a yatiri, corner him in his office. Gonzalo resists, but the assembly hold him tight. Mario asks the yatiri what Gonzalo suffers from. "From El Tio," the yatiri replies. "Tonight we must make an exchange in an abandoned mine near where Gonzalo was frightened. We'll kill a large red dog. Gonzalo must eat the head and drink the blood. Then we'll give the body to El Tio by throwing it in the mine. Then El Tio will release your brother." The yatiri had arrived armed with a preparatory fusion for Gonzalo to drink immediately to help release him from the grip of El Tio. As

Gonzalo drinks it down, the yatiri explains that the ingredients include a lizard and sewage from the river. I recall John Herrick's letter of 1942 to the Methodist Mission which related similar treatments, and try to remember that, as a medical anthropologist, I am not supposed to be experiencing what my head and stomach are presently undergoing.

At that point, a messenger from the hospital arrives with a request from Dr. Acietuno that Gonzalo be brought to the hospital. All including the yatiri agree to the idea, and accompany Gonzalo to the clinic. Dr. Acietuno injects Gonzalo with a tranquilizer and requests that Daneri stay with him.

In the afternoon Gonzalo determines to get out of bed, saying he has to get to La Paz to work. Felipe Apaza calmly tells him to have patience, and assures him they at the hospital will take care of him. Gonzalo says no, he is all right, and he does a few gymnastic dance steps to demonstrate how well he is. Hearing the noise, Dr. Acietuno strides into the room, and says that if Gonzalo is fine, he should take a bath to prepare to leave. Gonzalo agrees. But before the water is warmed, he jumps into the bath. The doctor yells. He, Felipe, and Daneri struggle to pull him out. Gonzalo struggles to dance and sing. Acietuno gives him another tranquilizer.

When the water is finally ready, Gonzalo changes his mind. The three men have to lift him into the tub. His body goes limp like a rag doll, and Daneri has to wash him. He is put back to bed where he sleeps until evening.

That evening, the yatiri does not appear. After waiting many hours and realizing he will not show, a delegation disappears into the night and finds a dog. Peluquilla kills it and prepares it. Gonzalo eats it. I notice it was neither large nor red.

Friday, February 24: Yet another yatiri arrives, located at the last moment as a replacement. The delegation, led by the corregidor, approaches Dr. Acietuno and informs him of their proposal that the yatiri treat Gonzalo in the clinic. Dr. Acietuno agrees, with the following reservations: that Gonzalo be given no alcohol, that the doctor be informed of any items of consumption to control for interference with the medication he himself is giving the patient, and that any burning be done in a rarely used room. The yatiri agrees, saying, "El doctor tiene razón," and gives Gonzalo a "tea" made of river sewage, the dog's blood, a lizard, and several herbs. The doctor does not interfere. In the evening Daneri accompanies the yatiri to the mine, while Mario stands vigil by Gonzalo's bed.

Saturday, February 25: Gonzalo awakes in the hospital and asks where he is. He gets up, begins to cry, and goes looking for the doctor, who sends him back to bed. As soon as he is left alone, he flees the hospital and heads for home. But at home, he finds the yatiri, so he heads toward the plaza. Angry, the doctor demands that

Mario bring him back to the hospital, but Gonzalo refuses to go. He does, however, take another dose of the yatiri's preparation.

Sunday, February 26: Gonzalo arises in good condition, strolls the plaza, calmly talks to friends, and returns home for lunch, and word spreads that he is better. But by afternoon his condition again deteriorates. He runs to the park and yells at Doña Teresa Cordova. He runs everywhere and nowhere, until he finally runs home to bed. After a few moments of silence he jumps out of bed and yells, "Where are the pigs, where are the pigs?" and goes running off, presumably to find them.

Mario runs to the hospital. Dr. Acietuno gives him two tablets of valium and some advice. Gonzalo accepts the tablets from Mario, but they have no effect. He continues to drink the yatiri's potion and run aimlessly about town. Mario returns to the clinic. Gonzalo takes two more tablets before he falls asleep.

Monday, February 27: Gonzalo is out of bed and running about by early morning shoeless. Mario, Daneri, and the corregidor coax him up to the hospital, where he insists he is well and wants to go to La Paz and work. Felipe approves the idea, and suggests he take a few pills to insure a safe trip. These pills are tranquilizers Acietuno had ordered. Gonzalo refuses to take them and throws them on the ground, saying he is well. Dr. Acietuno retorts angrily that he is not well and orders him to sit down. With more resignation and despair than anger, Gonzalo sits down. The doctor gives him a heavy dose of a tranquilizer by injection. Gonzalo sleeps for three days. Daneri never leaves his bedside. When Gonzalo awakes on Thursday, March 1, he appears catatonic, though movement in the eyelids when one addresses him directly suggests otherwise.

Thursday, March 1: I leave the house as early as possible to visit Gonzalo at the hospital but get a late start because Primitiva Mamani viuda de Yanique, the blind lady who lives across the street, wobbles through my front door, proceeds to my table, sits down, and rests expectantly and with great dignity. I try to explain to her (in English) that today I am in a hurry and cannot feed her. She responds in Aymara so I have no idea what she is saying. But she says it with such force and conviction that I return to my stove and begin to cook her breakfast.

The road to the hospital is paved with opinions. The first person I run into is Doña Antonia. At first Antonia had thought Gonzalo suffered from malnutrition because, unlike Peluquilla and Mario, she said, Gonzalo never invited himself to dinner. When Dr. Acietuno ran a blood test and found no evidence of anemia, Antonia decided he suffered from masturbation. "Masturbation will make you crazy," she told me, and I had to agree that Gonzalo probably did not have any girlfriends in Santa Cruz. She approved of Peluquilla's *sinapismo* application of ground barley and fermented urine to the bottom of Gonzalo's feet to extract pain. She added that this treatment is also good for headaches, eyeaches, and toothaches. She was adamant, however, that Gonzalo did not suffer from a supernatural disorder. The diagnosis angered her because it rendered Don Lorenzo responsible for Gonzalo's travel across the dangerous road to Llojñapata and his passage by the old mine, and hence rendered him partly responsible for Gonzalo's illness. Today she had learned that Felipe Apaza had run another blood test and discovered an elevated white blood cell count. Thus she has decided Gonzalo suffers from an inflammation of the brain.

The doctor remarks that her diagnosis is silly, that the elevated white blood cell count has nothing to do with Gonzalo's mental condition. He states authoritatively that Gonzalo has Bleuler's disease, and that the white blood cell count accounts for an accompanying bronchitis. No one, of course, knows what Bleuler's disease is, particularly me, the focus of this declaration. The diagnosis hides the fact that Dr. Acietuno does not know what Gonzalo suffers from. He secretly suspects schizophrenia, for which Bleuler's disease, I discover later, is an obscure term. As Bleuler's disease sounds cosmopolitan, Antonia points out that Gonzalo should see a physician in La Paz where the public hospital has more sophisticated technology than the clinic in Kachitu.

Antonia, however, has an easy time convincing the corregidor of her diagnosis—inflammation of the brain—given that he has orchestrated four unsuccessful yatiri treatments. He also agrees that Acietuno has been unsuccessful. Thus the corregidor offers to send an *oficio* to Radio Nueva America and Radio Illimani soliciting financial aid over the air to pay for hospital bills if Gonzalo is sent to La Paz. Once the corregidor arrives at this decision, other people in town are inclined to follow his opinion.

Felipe Apaza, however, disagrees, although not openly in front of Acietuno. He softly recalls that a very similar case had occurred in Chojña Kanata several years before. The fellow had been brought into the hospital at Kachitu where they could do nothing for him. Finally the community took him home where he was cured by a yatiri. Felipe's words disconcert Acietuno who, in his own uncertainty, looks to Felipe for support. When Acietuno leaves the hospital room, Felipe says, "The doctor is not going to be able to cure Gonzalo." He suggests the Methodists come to pray.

Doña Eva tends to agree with Felipe. If Gonzalo suffers from a fate similar to Gladis and Marisol, then her own switch in Kachituño medical cosmology from a person who was not vulnerable to the supernatural because of her social standing, to a victim of such disorders, will be confirmed. It justifies Gladis's death and her own treatment of Marisol which was successful. "El Tio is killing all our youth," she tells me.

Doña Soña's husband is adamant that Gonzalo has been attacked by a *maligno*, a supernatural being. "Gonzalo is nothing but an Indian," he says. "He does not amount to anything. His mother is crazy. The whole family would be better off dead. We ought to clean up this town." Doña Victoria compassionately agrees. "Gonzalo has no future and would suffer less if he died," she says.

On Thursday afternoon Dr. Acietuno examines Gonzalo and in the process, applies pressure to his abdomen. Felipe explains that he left two marks on Gonzalo's abdomen with the pressure of his fingers. Thus he does not agree with Peluquilla when she sees the marks and exclaims, "Kharisiri! That's what he has! Kharisiri!" and calls in the fifth yatiri.

In the evening the yatiri arrives with a potion he tells Daneri to administer to Gonzalo every hour for two days, after which time the yatiri will perform a healing ceremony. The potion consists of an odd mixture of indigenous and cosmopolitan ingredients: incense, bicarbonate of soda, wine, aspirin, lemon, alcohol, and several indigenous herbs. He also requests that the doctor insert an I.V. The doctor refuses. The potion does not cure Gonzalo.

I mention the ingredients to Doña Victoria. She says that her cure for the kharisiri is cream of tartar, bicarbonate of soda, corn starch, lime, wine, and aspirin, but never alcohol, because alcohol is not fresca, and the kharisiri is a fresca disease and must be treated with the opposite, things caliente. Victoria says, "This is crazy, I know, Libbet. But what is really crazy is that it works." The yatiri, however, never returns to complete the cure.

Saturday, March 3: Gonzalo's white blood cell count returns to normal.

Sunday, March 4: For a week now, Gonzalo has lain at the hospital, and Daneri has kept a twenty-four hour vigil by his bedside. He washes him, feeds him, cares for him. He wears a perpetually cheerful smile and looks a little daffy, but is as consistent, efficient, and reliable as a doting mother. Even Doña Soña respects Daneri because he works so hard and so well. To cover Gonzalo's expenses at the clinic, Daneri takes the laundry job that Antonia refused when they lowered her wages.

Daneri tells me that if I take Gonzalo to La Paz, he will walk the five days to a secret place he knows of where he can mine gold to pay for Gonzalo's medical bills. He also tells me he never sleeps. He says proudly that he is not afraid of anything and can walk all night with neither fatigue nor fear. He will meet up with other travelers, he says, and walk with them to keep watch over them all night, because he is special, he says, and no harm can come to him. Daneri is very proud to tell me that once a group of travelers was very grateful to him for keeping watch and warning them when someone approached.

Gonzalo has not received any sedatives now for three days. He lies in bed and stares at nothing, although his eyes change position occasionally. Sometimes he wears a worried expression. Occasionally he turns to me with an initially hopeful expression that quickly vanishes into nothingness. Occasionally he looks mad.

His hair is disheveled. His breath carries the putrid smell of the kharisiri solution that did not work. It is nearly impossible to realize that barely two weeks earlier, this pathetic and helpless, nearly lifeless form, sat at my table singing along with the rest of us at the top of his lungs, animatedly unraveling extravagant tales of fantasy, and full of life.

At 10:00 P.M. when the kerosene lamp begins to flicker, I send Daneri out to buy himself a candle, and I replace him in the vigil over Gonzalo. Gonzalo stares at me, but will not answer me. Sometimes it seems as if he sees me. At other times I move and his eyes do not follow. When I touch him, his eyelids flicker, or he blinks; I know, then, that he at least knows we are there.

When Daneri returns I get up to leave, and put my hand on the bed to touch Gonzalo as a form of good-night, and discover that the bed is soaking wet. Gonzalo has become incontinent.

At that time I had lived in Kachitu for a year and invested a great deal of myself in it. For all of their arguments, I had grown to love these people very much. I was even fond of Doña Soña's husband, whose harsh words were the deployment of a strategy that masked a well-meaning soft heart in his own way. And I had a great deal of respect for Doña Teresa who, for all her condescension, was a strong and successful woman and thus an example for future women. When Gonzalo's condition deteriorated to the extent it did on March 4 I felt that what happened to him affected me and fell prey to my own ethnocentricity. I determined to take him to La Paz if his family wished it.

Gonzalo was interned in the Hospital de Clinicas, the public hospital affiliated with Bolivia's medical school, on Wednesday, March 7. He remained there for four months, during which time the doctors could find no evidence of organic pathology except a metabolic imbalance of the brain which, his doctors explained, might have been brought on by the high doses of valium and librium he received in Kachitu. He was switched from psychiatry to neurology. After several months he was sent back to psychiatry and locked in a cell after he ran way repeatedly and was found in the street with nothing on but an open bed shirt. Gonzalo was released on July 2, 1978, because Mario and Daneri requested it and because the hospital could provide nothing but custodial care. Gonzalo returned to Kachitu, where he subsisted on town charity. Two months later he disappeared.

CHAPTER 12

Culture, Ideology, and Hegemony, and the Meaning of Medical Pluralism

Two analytically identifiable processes are occurring in Kachitu, one social, the other medical. A dialectic between the two affects both and contributes to a transformation of social relationships and hence to social change. Essential to this dialectic is medical pluralism.

In Kachitu, what were once understood clearly as two separate ethnic groups have been transformed into multiple social classes in a changing, amorphous world defined by more than four hundred years of an irrational economy, a national revolution, a subsequent peripheralization of the region surrounding Kachitu, and national political instability. What once clearly demarcated "ethnic" boundaries on the basis of "race" has overtly dissolved into competition for social class membership. Kachituños resort to ethnicity or to religion to identify themselves, to secure a social class position. However, as fortunes change, social positions are also renegotiated. Few people in Kachitu are secure in a social class, and as the revolution and subsequent years of economic contraction destroy one social order after another (e.g., since 1980 a new order has been emerging around the cocaine economy), the very foundations of social class are transient. For some, membership in the Methodist church is a means of upward mobility. For others authority in the vecindario is a means of maintaining an image of social position that is economically eroding. For yet others, acceptance in the Aymara community constitutes downward mobility but nonetheless provides access to desperately needed resources. Different strategies are employed in different contexts, for membership or affiliation in different groups. This process is charged by the fact that what it means to be Aymara, mestizo, or Methodist is also uncertain and subject to negotiation. Thus individuals reconstruct and negotiate their cultural identities, and their strategies are subject to the economic and political position of the individual within the community.

A principal means by which people negotiate identity and shift affiliation is through medicine. Marisol's yatiris taught us this lesson: that medical pluralism helps create and regulate power within and between class relations, particularly between oppressor and oppressed groups. Gonzalo tragically taught us the alternate side of the same principle: though a mestizo, the universal understanding of him as an Indian as stipulated by the consensus that he suffered an Aymara illness, resolved the problem brought on by the fact that there was no social place for him in town. Illness mediated his social dilemma.

Three questions remain: how do people do this, what is the significance of this model, and what are its practical applications. In other words, so what?

HOW PEOPLE NEGOTIATE IDENTITY AND SHIFT MEMBERSHIP THROUGH MEDICINE

People negotiate identity and shift membership from one group to another through the process of diagnosis. Contrary to the assumption underlying decision-making models, the three medical traditions available in Kachitu do not compete for patients with the same illness, but are seen as necessary alternatives that etiologically recognize different types of illnesses. All things being equal, if one has tuberculosis, one goes to the physician at the Methodist clinic; if one suffers from the khan achachi, one goes to the yatiri; if one has a stomach upset, one resorts to medicinas caseras. Choice of resource depends on diagnosis. It is in the domain of diagnosis that all things are rarely equal, and the notion of medical efficacy becomes problematic, subject to cultural context. We assume medical efficacy is the basis of medical decisions as people try to choose the most appropriate resource for a given disease or illness. The process of diagnosis, however, is not only highly subjective, but subject to cultural and social definition as well.

Diagnosis is problematic on three counts. First it depends upon a variety of social factors at least as much as symptomatology. This is so because social factors inform the perceptions and interpretations of symptoms. They also affect the interpretations of opinions offered in the course of medical dialogue about the diagnosis. The degree of trust in the available practitioner, for example, plays a major role in the interpretation of possible diagnoses, as does the relationship between all participants in the dialogue. Diagnosis is molded by individual perception and advice.

Second, diagnosis derives from medical traditions which themselves are value laden (e.g., Frake 1961). Those values take on concrete meaning within their cultural and social contexts. In the social context in which it is deployed, medical discourse is infused with meaning over and above the medical. Thus it informs the diagnosis that is pursued through it. Medical pluralism creates a specific discourse because decisions may be drawn on all available medical ideologies: in Kachitu it permits a dialogue armed with the values inherent in all three medical traditions.

Third, even within the confines of the medical staff in a teaching hospital in New York or Boston, diagnosis is a finely tuned, problematic art. In any complex medical case, even when the most sophisticated technology is available, the physician usually does not know the full, holistic answer to the medical problem. His training permits him to generate a diagnosis based on symptomatological information, not ecological, epidemiological, social, psychological, judicial, or political information that may be variables in the illness. Unfortunately poverty, stress, political strife, migration, and chaos, not to mention downward social mobility, also impinge on health. The physician's diagnosis is meant to lead to a therapeutic intervention that is curative, not to social engineering, economic management, judicial protection, or political realignment that might be critical variables in the reestablishment of health. Furthermore, a physician's cure is dependent on both a correct diagnosis and on technical and chemical support. For the vast majority of the world's population, even adequate cosmopolitan chemical and technical support are unavailable. This in turn has negative implications for the hegemonic goals of cosmopolitan medicine.

Cosmopolitan medicine, itself the product of a historical context, contains its own values that contrast with those of other systems. It too is subject to "magic."[1] The relevance of the Kachitu materials, however, is not the link between history and ideology, and hence the essentiality of "magic," to any medical system, but rather the synergistic coexistence of several medical systems for social ends. In an environment in which there are several medical traditions, the art of diagnosis, which is problematic under any conditions, is given greater flexibility by the culturally defined differential perceptions of the prevailing medical ideologies, regardless of the accessibility of cosmopolitan medicine. So many factors not identifiable by cosmopolitan medicine affect illness and disease that, outside a totalitarian state, neither cosmopolitan nor any other type of medicine is able to monopolize medical authority.

Diagnosis is subjected to dialogue; dialogue opens diagnosis to debate. In the course of a given illness in Kachitu, all three medical systems may be consulted, and great debate may take place across ethnic and religious (that is, social-class) lines. Culturally defined perceptions are also subject to negotiation that in turn is further complicated when the content of cultural identity is itself open to negotiation and change. In Kachitu, as in much of the rest of the world, the content of cultural identity is very much open to negotiation. In the process of debate, participants express values. These values are reinforced or changed by the cultural groups encompassed within the medical dialogue. Indeed, what is positively valued by one group because of its history of dominating another can be appropriated through medical dialogue and result in shifts in medical belief by the other at specific points in time to reverse the relationship and effect social change. By serving as a social idiom for the expression of values, the three medical traditions are as much a dynamic element of Kachitu as are other aspects of culture, such as the economic, political, legal, and religious processes that inform them and are transformed by them. Through medical dialogue, participants often switch ethnic and religious allegiances and improve their class status or their material well-being. The physicians in Kachitu demonstrated as much as anyone else that through medical dialogue, shifts in medical beliefs are frequently made, and as a result, nonmedical ends are achieved.

This matrix of simultaneous or differential reliance on multiple medical traditions by different ethnic and religious groups (or social classes) to redefine cultural identity occurs in Kachitu because all three social groups in fact acknowledge the same etiological beliefs. This is possible because, contrary to the notion of ethnicity and race that Kachituños so often use to support their own social positions, everyone in town shares confluences of the same culture. In today's world, it would be hard to locate any ethnic group that does not share confluences of the national domain of which it is a part, or of other social groups with whom it articulates. In Kachitu, an individual's concept of his own ethnic or religious identity, however, may require that he resort to different curative treatments in an attempt to negotiate his cultural identity with other Kachituños. Different curative traditions are options for social negotiation with members of one's own or other ethnic and religious groups. Joan Koss (1975, 1980) in her discussion of *espiritismo* in

Puerto Rico and Margaret Clark (1959) in her work among Mexican Americans have, along with a myriad of others working with other cultural groups, long insinuated this position. In Kachitu over time, as social, economic, and political conditions of Kachitu's history change, so does the very content of the three medical ideologies. This, too, is not a new idea, as Paul Unschuld working in China (1975, 1979, 1985), or Michel Foucault with Western medical thought (1965, 1973), or Paul Starr with medicine in the United States (1982) have shown. What it means is that in spite of scientific evidence to the contrary, people do what is meaningful for them, and what is meaningful depends on where a person is situated socially, economically, and politically. As material conditions and power structures change throughout history, so does what is meaningful. Medicine is a domain critical to our sense of selves, infused with enormous power, and riddled with different paths that access material and nonmaterial wealth. Thus it is a domain in which meaning is created and negotiated and reformed. It structures social life as much as it is structured by it. As a primary resource, people are empowered by it and thus change their social, economic, and political conditions.

THE SIGNIFICANCE OF THE MODEL
BEING APPLIED TO KACHITU

Most of these ideas are built on earlier work. They are here put together with new material. Two principal concepts being advanced are the simultaneous maintenance of medical beliefs that are seemingly contradictory by Western logic, and the relegation of medical efficacy as it is understood in cosmopolitan medicine to a secondary role in medical choice. These contradict decision-making models and the concept of patient as rational in the economic sense.

Following Allan Young's critique of decision-making models (1982), Janzen's study of medical-resource choice among the Kongo in Lower Zaire (1978) is one of a number of excellent works (e.g., Comaroff 1980; Leslie 1975; Lock 1980; Low 1985) illustrating the link between simultaneous maintenance by patients of seemingly contradictory beliefs and the sociocultural context in which the different beliefs derive. He further clarifies the fact that the indigenous social environment is not fully responsible for the nearly ubiquitous rejection of the request for total monopoly over health care that cosmopolitan medicine makes. The nature of cosmopolitan medical ideology and the historical context from which it derives also play a role. Janzen thus demonstrates the merit of medical pluralism to respond to the complex biological and social etiology of illness and disease. In most cases examined in Kachitu, however, a cure was not the only issue at hand; the efficacy of a specific therapy was not the principal motive underlying shifts in medical ideology, be they Dr. Sabas's and Dr. Acietuno's or Eva's and Marisol's. Thus, if we assume that conflicting medical ideologies can be held simultaneously in order to negotiate the environmental, biological, and social elements of illness, and that such ideologies exist in sociohistorical contexts that inform them, we can further refine the question to include nonmedical factors in order to broaden the scope of our investigation and resolve the riddles of choice in Kachitu. This is easily expedited by conceiving of medicine—medical resources, practices, ideologies, and dialogue—as having a significance greater than simply the medical, particularly in a culturally complex—multiclass, multiethnic, and multireligious—and medically plural environment.

Fabrega and Silver's work in Mexico (1973) is a fine example of earlier work that suggests a similar thesis, but within a functionalist paradigm. They argue that use of indigenous medicine in Mexico served judicial needs where the state judicial system was ineffective or lacking. In fact, beyond rational decision-making models (e.g., Paul 1953; Press 1969; Rubel 1960; Simmons 1955), the persistence of indigenous medicine in the service of latent functions, such as social engineering (Clark 1959) or political realignment (O. Lewis 1955), has been the primary explanation for medical pluralism in Latin America until the mid-1980s (Turner 1964, 1969 is renowned for his discussion of the relationship between medical systems and political process among the Ndembu in Africa). Besides broadening the focus of medicine itself, these models also accommodate the involvement of more individuals than the patient and healer in the case. A functionalist model, however, cannot accommodate change beyond the stipulated function, and as so often happens in Kachitu, medical dialogue and medical decision often involve a change in social relations that may significantly affect the whole community of Kachitu.

Change in social relations can be accommodated by the perception of medicine as a primary resource deployed in order to obtain secondary resources of which a cure is only one possibility. Choice of a specific type of medicine when several alternatives are available can restructure social relationships. Medical decisions are made in political, economic, and social contexts that form and inform the behavior of not ony patient and healer, but the community at large. Those behaviors in turn restructure social relationships between different healers and between everyone involved in the same social space. Opinions about health are social commentary about multiple facets of the life of the person under discussion. Opinions are also a dimension of their author's self; they tell other people more about the

author than about the subject being discussed. And they are developed in a historical context. In the backwaters of Bolivia, as well as in professional centers of New York, people compete and negotiate to monopolize the control of the consumption of opinions and thereby gain some power, which can later be used to get something else: resources, legal protection, loyalty, or security. As diagnostic opinions are articulated, as debate ensues, and as curative strategies are developed, people express and negotiate values. No place has this been more evident in contemporary United States than in the debate over AIDS.

A given medical dialogue may draw on only one ideological tradition, and in so doing, make a statement about the other ideologies excluded from discussion. In Kachitu, medical dialogue is both a reflection of what goes on in town and of political and economic processes, as well as a means of altering what goes on to the

benefit of those participating in the dialogue. Medical dialogue is particularly potent as a mechanism for empowering individuals, creating alliances, and instigating change because its subject is overtly and concretely the individual, while the
real object of the dialogue is covertly and abstractly social relations. In medical
dialogue in Kachitu, metaphors of victimization and exploitation which emerged
from a history of political hegemony and oppression can be appropriated and
transformed into mechanisms of empowerment, as we saw, for example, in the
various versions of Gladis's death. Through the idiom of medicine as a primary
resource, people communicate information about themselves, their relationships
to others, and their intentions, in order to obtain secondary resources, restructure
social relations, and create social change. Medical dialogue is most effective as a
primary resource when it is public, and the manner in which medicine is used
as a primary resource is related to the nature of both the medical pluralism and
social pluralism that pertain in a given environment.

Meanwhile, social, economic, judicial, and political pressures or interests frequently result in a shift in the medical beliefs entertained by patients and by medical practitioners, and eventually shifts occur in the very bodies of medical ideologies held by a given population. For those of us accustomed to viewing health-care
resource use through the popular world view informed by cosmopolitan medicine
and the biomedical model, this process is easier to identify in exotic contexts such
as the one in Kachitu. Michael Taussig's work along the Putamayu (1987) has
melded history and the dialectics of colonial and ethnic identity to reveal that the
power of shamanism emerges from the very dialectic between the colonizer and
the colonized and the colonizer's perception of the colonized's perception—as the
whites form their obsession with shamanism through their conception of what
they think the Indian thinks the white thinks the Indian thinks about the white.
However, this process is not limited to environments where cosmopolitan resources are scanty (e.g., Felker 1983; Frankenberg 1981). So accustomed are we in
the West, however, to thinking of medicine as amenable to evaluation solely in
terms of biomedical measures of curative efficacy, that we often neglect to expand
our inquiry into other salient domains.

Medical pluralism is significant because alternatives create the possibility of
the use of medicine—of medical dialogue and clinical choice—as a social idiom
through which cultural identity negotiation takes place. Through the negotiation
of such identities, social relations and access to resources are established, restructured, or destroyed. Because medicine becomes an effective idiom in a medically plural environment, everyone involved in discussion, not simply the patient, healer, or therapy management group, participates in secondary resource
acquisition.

Medical pluralism is thus significant for reasons political. Paul Unschuld has
argued that the absence of medical pluralism is only obtainable within totalitarian

states. Marjorie Balzer's work on the Shanti in Siberia (1987) demonstrates that even under sovietization, Shanti shamanism could not be eradicated. It simply went underground. This is because, like religion, to which medicine has always been so closely connected in the anthropological literature, medicine can mobilize resources, particularly social relations and power.

This model departs from the Marxist model that emphasizes the hegemony of cosmopolitan medicine and the consequential subjugation of indigenous systems to it. What is hegemonic is the world market and power structures that facilitate it. But as that hegemony peripheralizes and marginalizes vast domains of the world's populations, medicine is one powerful mechanism by which individuals meaningfully situate themselves in a constantly changing environment.

APPLICABILITY, OR SO WHAT?

In Bolivia, where crises are endemic, and epidemic during the 1980s, and where life is so fragile that it renders impotent all the beneficial power of modern economic, political, and technological science, the khan achachi gathers considerable power. We must not, however, be sidetracked into thinking that science will eliminate the khan. Indeed, kin to the khan walk the halls of Bellevue and the Massachusetts General hospitals. But that is not the point. The point is that physicians, mestizos, Methodist Aymara, and Aymara campesinos, as well as Italian Americans, Puerto Ricans, and middle-class Anglo-Saxons on the upper East Side of Manhattan, shift their medical beliefs because they can use them as primary resources through which they can get access to secondary ones. In Kachitu, through

medicine as a primary resource, people transform social relationships and cultural identities, and in so doing, acquire actual resources: land, agricultural goods, jobs, privileges, prerogatives, and power. Evaluation of medical efficacy takes place within the context of interests in such secondary resources. Thus choices between alternative medical resources and shifts in medical ideologies are made at least as much for social and political reasons as they are for advances in technological knowledge. And while this can be easily perceived in Kachitu, it is no less true for any other environment in which social pluralism and medical pluralism are found. As anthropology has propounded for all other forms of human behavior, medical practices and behaviors are also logical, regardless of their divergence from the opinion of the chiefs of staff at Presbyterian or Massachusetts General hospitals. History, social change, and political process, however, are essential to an understanding of them.

APPENDIX 1

The Scheduled Medical Interview

To assess any differences in health and disease notions among the cultural and religious segments of Kachitu which might affect medical dialogue and decisions, I administered a scheduled interview to thirty-eight individuals representing these social divisions. Significant disparities between groups would render the political interpretation of their discussions and actions false. The scheduled interview elicited responses on definitions, causes, symptoms, and cures of 110 illness and disease terms. Analysis of these responses indicates the range of agreement among and between members of the different social divisions and hence reaffirm the proposition that all Kachituños, whether mestizos, Aymara campesinos, or Aymara Methodists, acknowledge the same medical beliefs and, therefore, the same symbolic expressions of power, but that they manipulate them in different ways.

The analysis also reveals the extent to which members of the three social divisions differ in their belief in "magical" infirmities and cures as opposed to "natural" ones or in the extent to which they claim to rely upon physicians or yatiris.

The 110 disease and illness terms on the scheduled interview are those I had collected from conversations and observations over a period of a year and from the town death records; I had, therefore, determined these terms to be the major disease and illness terms in use in the village. Of these, 17 were eliminated from the analysis because no one responded to them.

All those interviewed were over twenty-five years of age. Individuals interviewed were chosen first on the basis of cultural identity as defined in Chapter 1: vecinos, Methodists, and campesinos. Because Methodists, however, are also distinguished religiously and economically and may also be referred to as cholos, an attempt was made to contrast them with Catholic cholos.

There are three campesino families in Kachitu which participate marginally in a commercial economy, dress their children in Western clothes, send their children to school or to the university in La Paz, and struggle to enter the cholo class rather than remain land based and campesino in identity. As their religious preference is Catholic, I distinguished them in the scheduled interview to contrast them

TABLE 1 Interviewees by Cultural and Social Segment

	Number Interviewed	Number of Adults in Kachitu
Vecinos	7	60
Catholic cholos	3	75
Methodists	3	7
Campesinos	11	60
Yatiris	14	60[a]

[a] Estimated number of yatiris from nearby communities that practice in Kachitu

with the Methodists on the one hand and with the completely land-based campesinos on the other. Members of this fourth group are referred to as Catholic cholos.

A fifth group, Aymara yatiris, was also interviewed. Although yatiris do not monopolize knowledge, they do monopolize access to ritual, power that has social implications. Thus they are included as a distinct segment. The yatiris are, of course, Catholic and campesino. As none live in Kachitu, those interviewed were selected from the yatiris who serve the Kachitu population and who live in the nearby communities.

Therefore, the scheduled interview contrasts vecinos, Methodists, Catholic cholos, campesinos, and yatiris.

After administering the initial scheduled interview, a sample was selected for intensive interviewing. This group was drawn largely on the basis of willingness to undergo what proved to be an ordeal.

As respondents were self-selecting rather than chosen at random from each strata, the data from the five groups are somewhat uneven and may not be truly representative in an exact, statistical sense (see Table 1).

DEGREE OF NOSOLOGICAL AGREEMENT

In order for members of different cultural groups to negotiate cultural identity through the diagnostic and curative decisions, they must agree to some extent upon nosology. That is, while interviewees might suggest varying treatments and cures, they ought to agree about what each disease and illness actually is. Nosological agreement was determined by the definition of the illness term in symptomatological terms.

In the field I compared the qualitative responses provided in the scheduled interview—that is, those that provide more information than a claim to ignorance or disbelief—and then determined through further extended interviews the common definition of each illness and disease term. To determine the degree to which members of the different cultural groups agree upon nosological definitions I compared the qualitative responses providing nosological definitions in terms of symptomatology in the scheduled interview with each other and with the determined common definitions. The results of this analysis are presented in Table 2.

I determine sufficient agreement to exist among members of the same cultural group when over 50 percent of the qualitative responses provided the same description or symptomatological identification of each disease or illness term.

Agreement within each cultural group is indicated in Table 2 with a "+." Disagreement over nosological identification between 50 percent or more of the interviewees within an ethnic or social group is indicated with a "−." Disagreement resulting from lack of information, as in the case when all interviewees claimed ignorance or disbelief, or when only one interviewee provided an informative response and that response corresponds to the "actual definition," is indicated with an "O." Sufficient agreement is assumed to exist between all cultural groups when sufficient agreement existed among members of four of the five cultural groups.

TABLE 2 Agreement of Nosological Definitions Between Cultural Groups and Yatiris

Nosology	Vecino	Catholic Cholo	Meth-odist	Cam-pesino	Yatiri	Agreement
Lowland Diseases						
bosio	+	+	+	+	−	yes
c'oto	+	+	−	+	+	yes
chujchu	+	+	0	+	+	yes
paludismo	+	0	0	0	0	no
terciana	+	+	+	+	+	yes
Infectious Diseases						
alfombrilla	+	+	0	+	+	yes
amalloque	+	+	+	+	+	yes
angina	+	−	+	+	+	yes
berrugas	+	+	+	+	+	yes
chojri	+	+	+	+	−	yes
ch'upu	+	+	+	+	−	yes
coqueluche	+	+	+	+	+	yes
costado	+	+	+	+	+	yes
curmi	+	+	−	+	+	yes
disenteria	+	+	+	+	+	yes

TABLE 2 (continued)

Nosology	Vecino	Catholic Cholo	Meth-odist	Cam-pesino	Yatiri	Agreement
enfriamiento	+	0	+	+	+	yes
erisipelas	+	0	0	0	0	no
escarlatina	+	+	+	+	+	yes
fiebre	+	+	+	+	+	yes
gangrenado	+	0	+	0	0	no
gripe	+	+	+	+	+	yes
hinchazon	+	+	+	+	+	yes
infeccion	+	+	+	+	+	yes
insolacion	+	0	+	+	+	yes
kustipa	+	+	+	+	+	yes
kutupi	+	+	0	+	+	yes
mal de urin	+	+	+	+	+	yes
mallcu	+	+	0	+	+	yes
mal interior	−	0	0	+	+	no
mal tratadura	+	0	+	+	+	yes
maripichupichu	0	0	0	0	+	no
meningitis	+	0	0	0	0	no
negrotewartillu	+	0	0	0	+	no
neumonía	+	0	0	0	0	no
otitis	+	0	0	0	0	no
paperas	+	0	+	+	+	yes
paralysis	+	0	+	0	0	no
peste	−	−	0	−	−	no
piampia	+	0	+	+	+	yes
pulmonía	+	+	+	+	0	yes
quebracion	+	0	0	+	+	no
reuma	+	0	+	+	+	yes
sarampion	+	0	+	+	+	yes
sinusitis	+	0	0	0	+	no
sopladura	+	0	+	+	−	no
taaya	+	+	0	+	+	yes
tabarstillo	−	0	0	+	0	no
tesis	+	0	0	−	0	no
tifus	+	0	0	0	+	no
tosferina	+	0	0	0	+	no
tuberculosis	+	0	+	+	+	yes
umamausa	+	0	0	+	+	no
Noninfectious Diseases						
aire	+	−	0	0	+	no
anemia	+	+	+	0	0	no
ataque cardiaco	+	0	+	+	+	yes
colico	+	+	+	+	+	yes
debil	+	+	+	+	+	yes

TABLE 2 (*continued*)

Nosology	Vecino	Catholic Cholo	Meth- odist	Cam- pesino	Yatiri	Agreement
epilepsia	+	0	0	0	0	no
gusanera	+	0	+	+	+	yes
hemoragia de sangre	+	0	+	+	+	yes
hernia	+	0	+	0	0	no
kepu	+	+	+	+	+	yes
mal parto	+	+	+	+	+	yes
raquitismo	−	0	0	0	0	no
reumatismo	+	0	+	+	+	yes
senectud	0	0	0	0	0	no
sirk'i	+	+	+	+	+	yes
sisu	+	0	0	0	+	no
tullimiento	+	0	0	0	0	no
ulcera	−	0	0	0	0	no
ventosidad	+	0	+	+	+	yes
Magical and Psychological Illnesses						
ajayu	+	+	0	+	+	yes
amartillo	+	+	+	+	+	yes
anchanchu	+	+	0	+	+	yes
arrebato	+	+	+	+	+	yes
ataques	+	+	+	+	+	yes
chullpa	+	+	0	+	+	yes
colerina	+	+	+	+	+	yes
cumena	−	0	0	0	0	no
embrujada	+	0	0	0	0	no
khan achachi	+	+	0	+	+	yes
kharisiri	0	+	+	0	0	no
lampara	+	0	0	0	0	no
lari lari	−	0	0	+	+	no
larpa	+	+	+	+	+	yes
limpu	+	+	0	+	+	yes
malos demonios	0	0	0	0	0	no
qate qate	−	0	0	0	0	no
saliwa	−	0	0	0	0	no
sirena	+	0	0	−	−	no
tericia	−	0	0	+	+	no
la viuda	0	0	0	−	−	no
waj waj	+	0	0	0	0	no

Table 2 demonstrates that Kachituños share a high degree of agreement between cultural and social groups concerning nosological identifications which contributes to the premise that all Kachituños share the same medical beliefs and are able therefore to negotiate cultural identity through the use of these beliefs. More specifically, Table 2 indicates that of ninety-three disease and illness terms, at least 50 percent of all social groups agreed upon the symptomatological identification of fifty-three nosological terms, and that they disagreed upon the symptomatological identification of three nosological terms: *peste*, or plague, which is not endemic to the altiplano, and *sirena* and *la viuda*, or two demonic spirits (of Hispanic, not Aymara derivation). Responses for forty terms did not provide sufficient information pertaining to nosological identification to warrant analysis.

"MAGICAL," "NATURAL," AND "PSYCHOLOGICAL" ETIOLOGIES AND CURES

The number of responses to the scheduled interviews identifying "magical," "natural," and "psychological" causes and cures is tabulated in Table 3 by cultural group and compared to reveal differences in general reliance upon "magical," "natural," and "psychological" etiologies and cures between these groups.

I isolated a "psychological" category because it had been suggested by a few Kachituños and in isolating it I could determine if such a distinction were common among the population.

I determined causes to be "natural" if they contained no "supernatural" agent from my ethnocentric point of view: epidemics brought by wind, sunstroke, excessive heat or cold, eating unfit foods, and poor nutrition constituted my conception of "natural."

I determined causes to be "magical" when a supernatural agent was explictly mentioned, such as one of the innumerable demonic beings that infest the Kachitu universe, or when I could not understand from my own ethnocentric background a natural cause-and-effect relationship between the agent of disease and disease itself. For example, *chupu* and *saliwa*, both tumorous rashes, are commonly believed to be infirmities caused by hurting but not killing a toad, frog, rat, or similar small animal. This belief could possibly contain a natural element if, though no one was able to explain it to me, some natural element or pathogen in the animal is transferred to the human. Kachituños explain that the source of infection stems from the animal's excretions: saliva, vomit, sweat, and so on. The cure for this, however, is usually to find the animal and kill it. I allowed this sort of cause to be magical and determined its cure to be magical as well, as the "cure" is administered to the frog, not the patient.

I determined a cause to be psychological only when the respondent specifically identified it as such—that is, when the informants perceived of the cause as psychological from their point of view: sorrow, preoccupation, and grief.

In certain cases I found it difficult to determine whether an explanation of cause or cure was magical, natural, or psychological. Some infirmities could be caused by *either* magical or natural elements or by *either* psychological or natural elements. In such cases, I chose to identify the cause to be both. However, these differences suggested that further analysis of these partially magical and partially natural causes and cures might reveal further information about how Kachituños negotiate cultural identity through medical beliefs (see Tables 8–11).

I determined cures to be natural when they involved any type of treatment that did not include supernatural intervention or the use of items that had specific symbolic significance associated with the supernatural. These natural treatments included herbal teas, massages, sweat baths, poultice plasters, and the like. Any cure that involved either the intervention of the supernatural, such as demonic beings, or the use of natural items of supernatural symbolic significance, I determined to be magical. Many of the cures for magically caused illnesses involve natural items of doubtful but yet possible medicinal value: excrement, fetuses, placentas, and old spiders' webs "with lots of bugs in them." Informants defined cures as being of psychological value, such as throwing urine in a child's face to cure him of amartillo or malaise caused by grieving over an absent loved one.

Again, however, problems in analysis arose. Often a respondent did not know a cure and referred the infirmity to the care of a physician, yatiri, or pharmacy only. Such responses are tabulated separately and not subsumed under magical, natural, or psychological categories.

The analyses in Tables 6 through 11 that pertain to magical, natural, and psychological categories, then, are based upon causes and cures of these diseases and illnesses. All causes and cures of more than one category are assigned in the first series of analyses below to a single category according to the criteria outlined above.

None of the interviewees knew all the terms asked in the scheduled interview. Occasionally respondents claimed not to know a disease or illness when other indicators (gossip, slips of the tongue on other occasions, or considerable knowledge in related areas) suggested that they did indeed know but preferred to impress me with their non-Indianness, their nonsuperstitiousness, their "educated Westernness," or the fact that they were "civilized" by claiming ignorance. At other times, respondents chose to deliver such impressions with a flat denial in belief. "I don't believe in that," or "That is an old Indian belief," they would say. Such disbelief, however, referred to Spanish terms such as *embrujada* (to be ill by witchcraft), *la viuda* (the enchanted widow), or *sirena* (a demonic mermaid), as well as to certain Aymara terms. Such disbeliefs were most often expressed by Evangelicals who deny existence of magic according to church doctrine.

TABLE 3 Number of Possible and Actual Responses to Scheduled Interview by Cultural and Social Group

Number of Interviewees by Cultural or Social Group		Possible Number of Responses	Actual Responses
7 vecinos	× 93 terms	651	553
3 Catholic cholos	× 93 terms	279	184
3 Methodists	× 93 terms	279	274
11 campesinos	× 93 terms	1023	900
14 yatiris	× 93 terms	1302	1072
38 TOTAL INTERVIEWEES	× 93 terms	3534 TOTAL POSSIBLE RESPONSES	2983 TOTAL ACTUAL RESPONSES

However, ignorance of certain terms was obviously related to lack of experience with certain illnesses. For example, respondents' knowledge of goiter and malaria, which are endemic only in the lowlands and are perceived to be magically caused, became a general indicator of extended experience in the lowlands. Likewise, those groups who have greater access to education, the clinic, and the city have a greater command of Western scientific medical terms than those who do not. This was obvious in the case of Methodists and vecinos.

On the other hand, there were occasional Aymara terms that few or no respondents claimed to recognize *except* vecinos. All of those terms were magical: *cumena*, or illness caused by not offering alcohol and wine to the Pachamama and the Condor Mamani during August to protect the house; *lampara*, or witchcraft done by oneself without the aid of a witch against a lover; *qate qate*, or a magical bird that steals children's souls; and the *waj waj*, or malevolent spirit that enchants its victims to their deaths. That is, extent of knowledge of Western scientific disease or illness terms is not necessarily indicative of greater reliance upon natural as opposed to magical categories.

Tables 4 and 5 indicate how many responses claim either ignorance or disbelief. These facts must be taken into consideration in the remaining tables. Table 3 shows the ratio of claims to ignorance and disbelief to the entire number of responses received. In Table 5, claims are broken down by linguistic origin of the term asked, and the ratio of claims to ignorance and disbelief are percentages of the total number of Spanish and then Aymara terms asked. These figures are contrasted with the entire number of elicited responses, and then with the number of elicited responses that provided information about the illness or disease terms.

Tables 6 and 7 indicate the number of responses by cultural group that provide etiological and curative information based upon natural, magical, and psycho-

TABLE 4 Percentages of Responses Providing Information, Claiming Disbelief, and Claiming Ignorance

CULTURAL GROUP	TOTAL NUMBER ELICITED RESPONSES		TOTAL NUMBER RESPONSES PROVIDING INFORMATION		TOTAL NUMBER RESPONSES CLAIMING DISBELIEF OR IGNORANCE		PERCENTAGE OF ALL ELICITED RESPONSES CLAIMING IGNORANCE: Spanish Terms		Aymara Terms		PERCENTAGE OF ALL ELICITED RESPONSES CLAIMING DISBELIEF: Spanish Terms		Aymara Terms	
	N	%	N	%	N	%	N	%	N	%	N	%	N	%
Vecino	553	100%	399	72%	154	28%	63	11%	67	12%	13	2%	11	2%
Catholic Cholo	184	100%	108	59%	76	41%	60	33%	13	7%	1	.5%	2	1%
Methodist	274	100%	136	50%	138	50%	71	26%	52	19%	6	2%	9	3%
Campesino	900	100%	359	40%	541	60%	347	39%	171	19%	12	1%	11	1%
Yatiri	1072	100%	487	45%	585	55%	420	39%	153	14%	7	.7%	5	.5%

TABLE 5 Percentages of Responses Providing Information, Claiming Disbelief, and Claiming Ignorance, Broken Down by Linguistic Origin of Terms

CULTURAL GROUP	TOTAL NO. ELICITED RESPONSES		in Spanish		in Aymara		CLAIMS TO IGNORANCE: Spanish Terms		Aymara Terms		CLAIMS TO DISBELIEF: Spanish Terms		Aymara Terms	
	N	%	N	%	N	%	N	%	N	%	N	%	N	%
Vecino	553	100%	362	65%	191	35%	63	17%	67	35%	13	4%	11	6%
Catholic Cholo	184	100%	124	67%	60	33%	60	48%	13	22%	1	.8%	2	3%
Methodist	274	100%	186	68%	88	32%	71	38%	52	59%	6	3%	9	10%
Campesino	900	100%	612	68%	288	32%	347	57%	171	60%	12	2%	11	4%
Yatiri	1072	100%	720	67%	352	33%	418	58%	152	43%	7	1%	5	1%

	RESPONSES PROVIDING INFORMATION: in Spanish		In Aymara		RESPONSES CLAIMING DISBELIEF OR IGNORANCE: in Spanish		in Aymara	
	N	%	N	%	N	%	N	%
Vecino	286	79%	113	59%	76	21%	78	41%
Catholic Cholo	63	51%	45	75%	61	49%	15	25%
Methodist	109	59%	21	31%	77	41%	61	69%
Campesino	253	41%	106	37%	359	59%	182	63%
Yatiri	295	41%	195	55%	425	59%	157	45%

TABLE 6 Elicited Responses Providing Information About Magical, Natural, and Psychological Etiologies

CULTURAL GROUP	MAGICAL ETIOLOGIES		NATURAL ETIOLOGIES		PSYCHOLOGICAL ETIOLOGIES		TOTAL
	N	%	N	%	N	%	N
Vecino	78	20%	287	72%	34	8%	399
Catholic Cholo	26	24%	72	66%	10	9%	108
Methodist	15	11%	112	82%	9	7%	136
Campesino	39	11%	294	82%	26	7%	359
Yatiri	87	18%	353	72%	47	10%	487

logical categories. Chi square analysis of statistical dependence based on the tabulations in Tables 6 and 7 established comparative relationships between the different cultural groups.

Numerical tabulations were established in the following manner: as there are ninety-three terms on the scheduled interview and thirty-eight interviewees, there is a maximum of 3,534 possible responses. Divided by cultural and social group, then, there is a maximum of 651 possible responses from vecinos, 279 from Methodists, 279 from Catholic cholos, 1,023 from campesinos, and 1,302 from yatiris. The actual number of responses in each category is somewhat less because interviewees frequently did not address a question for various reasons. There is a total of 2,983 responses: 553 from vecinos, 184 from Catholic cholos, 274 from Methodists, 900 from campesinos, and 1,072 from yatiris. Tabulations in Tables 4 and 5 are based upon all responses offered from individuals within each social and cultural category.

Many responses indicated that an infirmity belonged within one curative domain, such as of a yatiri or physician, even though the informant did not know the cause or cure. Consequently, the actual number of responses that provide etiological and curative information for analysis is less still and is indicated in Tables 6 and 7. Tabulations, then, are based upon the number of responses and not upon the number of respondents.

When the causes and cures of the illness and disease terms on the scheduled interview are organized according to magical, natural, and psychological categories as divined above, the result is the percentages of elicited responses providing information about such terms that are shown in Tables 6 and 7.

Etiologies. Each cultural or social group was compared by means of chi square tests of statistical dependence with every other cultural or social group with respect to reliance upon magical, natural, and psychological etiologies. The numer-

TABLE 7 Elicited Responses Providing Information About Magical, Natural, and Psychological Curative Treatments

Cultural Group	Magical Cures		Natural Cures		Psychological Cures		Pharmaceutical Drugs Only		Physician Only		Yatiri Only		Total Cures
	N	%	N	%	N	%	N	%	N	%	N	%	N
Vecino Catholic	46	9%	265	53%	9	2%	18	4%	135	27%	27	5%	500
Cholo	17	14%	74	62%	3	2.5%	6	5%	17	14%	3	2.5%	120
Methodist	7	4%	92	55%	1	.6%	13	8%	53	32%	2	1%	168
Campesino	58	13%	258	59%	8	2%	34	8%	79	18%	0	—	437
Yatiri	120	22%	350	64%	5	1%	39	7%	34	6%	0	—	548

ical data are presented in Table 6. On the basis of these tests (using P = .01 as level of significance), no significant differences between cultural or social groups were evident, except between campesinos, on the one hand, and vecinos, Catholic cholos, and yatiris, on the other. This significant difference occurs in that vecinos, Catholic cholos, and yatiris, rely much more heavily upon magical etiologies than do campesinos. Yatiris also rely much more heavily upon psychological etiologies than do campesinos. However, there is no significant difference between vecinos, Catholic cholos, yatiris, and Methodists in reference to reliance upon magical and psychological etiologies. On the basis of my experience with the campesinos in Kachitu, however, I suspect that this difference stems from their reluctance to admit to me their credence in magical etiologies.

Cures. All respondents tended to be more open in their discussion of cures. Using the chi square test of statistical dependence (using P = .01 as level of significance), I compared the data from the scheduled interview of each cultural or social group with the data of every other cultural or social group with respect to reliance upon magical, natural, and psychological cures. The numerical data are presented in Table 7. The number of curative categories was increased to differentiate the sole reliance upon the yatiri, physician, or pharmaceutical items. These six categories are mutually exclusive. The chi square tests revealed a variety of significant differences between cultural or social groups.

Vecinos and yatiris differ significantly in reference to use of a physician. Vecinos claim to resort to the physician roughly four times more frequently than do yatiris. In reference to all other curative resources and domains, however, there is no significant difference between vecinos and yatiris.

Vecinos and campesinos also differ significantly in reference to use of a physician and in reference to the use of pharmaceutical items. Vecinos resort to the physician significantly more often than do campesinos, while campesinos resort to pharmaceutical items roughly twice as often as do vecinos. In reference to all other curative resources and domains, there is no significant difference between vecinos and campesinos.

Vecinos and Methodists differ significantly in reference to the use of magical cures, psychological cures, use of the yatiri, and use of pharmaceutical items. Vecinos resort to magical cures more than twice as often as do Methodists, to psychological cures roughly three times as often, and to yatiris more than four times as often. Methodists, on the other hand, resort to pharmaceutical items roughly twice as often as do vecinos.

Vecinos and Catholic cholos differ significantly in reference to the use of magical, psychological, pharmaceutical, yatiri, and physician cures. Catholic cholos resort significantly more often to the use of magical, psychological, and pharmaceutical cures; vecinos resort to the physician and to the yatiri roughly twice as often as do Catholic cholos.

Between Catholic cholos and yatiris there is no significant difference in the use of any type of curative resource. Between Catholic cholos and campesinos there is no significant difference in the use of any type of curative resource. Catholic cholos and Methodists, however, differ significantly in the use of magic, physicians, yatiris, and psychological cures. Methodists rely on the physician roughly twice as often as do Catholic cholos, on yatiris roughly half as often, on magic roughly a third as often, and on psychological cures roughly a fourth as often as do Catholic cholos.

Methodists and yatiris also differ in the use of magical cures and physicians. Yatiris rely on magical cures over four times as often as Methodists, and Methodists resort to the physician over five times as frequently as do yatiris.

Methodists and campesinos differ as well in reference to magical, psychological, and physician's cures. Campesinos rely upon magical cures roughly twice as often, and upon psychological cures roughly three times as often as do Methodists, while Methodists resort to the physician roughly twice as often as do campesinos.

Lastly, campesinos differ significantly from yatiris in the use of magical and physician's cures. Yatiris rely upon magical cures almost twice as often as do campesinos and upon physicians about a third as often.

Taken together, the chi square tests of statistical dependence on the numerical data presented in Tables 6 and 7 demonstrate that, with the one possible exception of campesinos, there is no significant difference between cultural groups in their reliance upon magical, psychological, and natural etiologies, but there are many significant differences in the curative strategies the different cultural groups use. No group, however, consistently denied the use of any one resource, except the yatiris, who never recommended yatiris (they presumed that the scheduled interview with them was requested because of their professional status), and campesinos who also did not recommend yatiris but who did recommend magical cures as often as any other group. I suspect campesinos were reluctant to discuss yatiris with me rather than that they do not use them.

There is a roughly equivalent degree of use among all groups of magical cures except among Methodists, as can be seen in Table 7. Methodists, however, deny the use of or belief in magic as part of their religious doctrine. Even though they resort to magic as a curative resource less often than any other group because of their religious doctrine, they do not differ significantly from any other group in their reliance upon magical etiologies. That is, the chi square tests demonstrate that Methodists in Kachitu do share the same etiological beliefs as the rest of the Kachituños. Their heavy reliance upon physicians and pharmaceuticals is a medical strategy that plays a major role in their cultural identity; their lack of reliance upon magical cures is an idiom of Methodist identity and ideology. It is not indicative of independence from the Kachitu medical beliefs, or from the continuing processes of victimization of the individual and ritual inversion as the individual's most effective response to it.

Other significant differences in the use of magical cures that can be seen in Table 7 were the greater reliance upon them by Catholic cholos than by vecinos. Likewise, yatiris relied more upon magical cures than did campesinos. These differences are not surprising, as I have already discussed possible reasons why campesinos might respond in this way (I suspect they were reluctant to discuss magical cures with me), and to the yatiri, magic is the basis for his profession.

There is no significant difference between any social or cultural group in the use of natural cures. All individuals in Kachitu, regardless of cultural identity, have a wide range of herbal knowledge and attempt to cure the vast majority of illness events in the home. Only when these attempts fail, or when the infirmity as diagnosed is one which falls within the curative domain of a yatiri or physician, do Kachituños abandon their reliance upon medicinas caseras and turn to a medical practitioner.

On the subject of psychological cures, it was noted that only Methodists relied upon them significantly less than any other group, though Catholic cholos relied upon them significantly more than vecinos. That is, except for Methodists, all groups resorted to psychological cures to a roughly equivalent degree. I propose that Methodist reluctance to resort to psychological cures is related to their reluctance to resort to magical cures, and that magical and psychological phenomena are recognized by them to share some common causes and processes. Methodist doctrine, as taught in Kachitu by Herrick and adopted by the Aymara converts, is a demanding, materialist work ethic with little room for self-indulgence. Nevertheless, between Methodists and all other groups, there is no significant difference in the use of psychological etiologies (see Table 6).

Use of pharmaceuticals is roughly equivalent among all groups, with significantly less use by vecinos. I believe this difference is related to vecino use of physicians, a point which is discussed below (see Table 7).

Use of the yatiri differs significantly among Methodists and vecinos. Methodists, for all the reasons outlined above, resort less often than any other group to yatiris as a curative resource. Vecinos, however, turn to yatiris significantly more often than any other group (see Table 7). They recognize, as do all other groups, specific disease or illness terms that fall within the domain of yatiri care, and, at least during the past twenty years, they have tended to be more susceptible to these diseases and illnesses—specifically, soul theft by demonic spirits—than any other group. Likewise, vecinos also explained to me that they turn to the yatiri and the physician simultaneously when medicinas caseras prove ineffective. This simultaneous use derives from the inability to determine a diagnosis and the resultant anxiety that all possible resources should be mustered.

Significant differences in the use of the physician by all groups suggests an association of the user. But the qualitative data and the associations outlined above do not support this interpretation. While all groups use the physician, members of certain groups tend to resort to the physician for different reasons. The yatiris refer to the physician less often than any other group (6 percent) while the Methodists refer to the physician most often (32 percent). Vecinos also rely heavily upon physician care (27 percent; see Table 7).

Methodists, however, tend to resort to the physician on principle; the church runs the clinic and use of Western medical care is advocated by the church authorities as responsible Protestant behavior. Their response to many disease terms was that they fell within the domain of the physician and that the interviewee knew neither the cause nor the cure.

Vecinos are the only group to explicitly claim to resort to the physician when all other resources fail. For many diseases and illnesses vecinos offer a variety of herbal treatments, and they refer to the physician should these herbal treatments yield no results. The vecinos, however, dislike going to the clinic and prefer in the case of a serious illness needing treatment by a physician to go to La Paz. Or, having diagnosed a disease demanding a physician's care, they go to the clinic to buy specific drugs that they then administer at home. They expressed dislike for the clinic because it is run by the Methodists. The doctors who come to serve there are outsiders, represent church authority, and are consequently perceived as suspected enemies of the vecino class. The clinic was established for, and is now run by, Methodist Aymara. Hence actual vecino use of the clinic is far less than use by any other group. During the eighteen months of field research and out of the canton population of approximately 16,000 potential users of the clinic, of which approximately 15,500 are Aymara and approximately 500 mestizos (Paredes 1955), 4,153 visits were recorded at the clinic. Of these visits, only 91 were made by 18 Kachitu vecinos. Of these 91 visits, 68 were to buy medicines only.

Yatiris, campesinos, and Methodists claim to resort to physicians for specific diseases, diseases that they claim are most effectively treated by the physician. Certain diseases are perceived by members of all groups, however, as requiring the aid of a physician, specifically: tuberculosis, dysentery, cardiac arrests, whooping cough, epilepsy, erysipelas, gangrene, hemorrhage, difficult pregnancies and stillbirths, pneumonia, mumps, paralysis, ulcers, and measles.

Analysis of all cures taken as a whole reveals that yatiris do not have wider curative medical knowledge than lay people in that they cannot cure a wider variety of infirmities, although they frequently do have a greater repertoire of magical and herbal cures. This substantiates data collected among shamans and laymen in

Zanacantan by Fabrega and Silver (1973 : 102) and supports the position that the value of the yatiri lies not in his medical knowledge but in his power to converse with the supernatural and divine in the coca. Both yatiris and campesinos, however, not only have a greater repertoire of remedies than do vecinos, cholos, and Methodists, but they express both a large number of symptoms and more severe symptoms as well.

Comparing causes and cures. Tables 8 through 11 separate causes and cures that are entirely and only magical from those which are partially magical and partially natural. This is done to overcome the problem of multiple causation and use of curative resources containing elements of two categories, magical and natural, or psychological and natural.

While Table 8 presents a comparison of etiologies and cures that are partially or entirely magical, Table 9 offers a comparison of etiologies and cures that are only magical. Table 10 presents data on a comparison of etiologies and cures that are entirely natural, and the last table, Table 11, offers a comparison of etiologies and cures that are partially or entirely psychological. The data for each ethnic group in Tables 8, 10, and 11 are, when added together, the total number of etiological and curative responses proffered which provided qualitative information. Curative resources designated as yatiris, on the one hand, and as physicians and pharmaceuticals, on the other hand, in Table 7, are subsumed under entirely magical in Table 8, and under entirely natural in Table 10, respectively. These causes and cures are then compared with one another to reveal further strategies in Kachitu medical resources use.

Interviewees in all groups described natural cures for magically defined diseases and illness, and less often, magical cures for naturally defined infirmities. Much of the latter might be explained by the above-mentioned reluctance to admit credence in magically caused beliefs. However, it would appear the concepts of

TABLE 8 Comparison of Etiologies and Cures That Are Partially or Entirely Magical

CULTURAL GROUP	CAUSES			CURES		
	N	(100%)	%	N	(100%)	%
Vecino Catholic	399	78	(20%)	500	100	(20%)
Cholo	108	26	(24%)	120	23	(19%)
Methodist	136	15	(11%)	168	9	(5%)
Campesino	359	39	(11%)	437	58	(13%)
Yatiri	487	87	(18%)	548	120	(22%)

TABLE 9 Comparison of Etiologies and Cures That Are Only Magical

Cultural Group	Causes			Cures		
	N	(100%)		N	(100%)	
Vecino Catholic	399	69	(17%)	500	63	(13%)
Cholo	108	21	(19%)	120	7	(6%)
Methodist	136	14	(10%)	168	5	(3%)
Campesino	359	38	(11%)	437	27	(6%)
Yatiri	487	82	(17%)	548	44	(8%)

naturalness and magicalness are more complex than a simple unilinear causal relationship.

Tables 8 and 9 distinguish infirmities that are partially magically caused and those that are entirely magically caused. For example, goiter is seen as a disease caused by iodine deficiency, but a demonic spirit causes the iodine deficiency. Likewise, saliwa is a tumorous rash that is caused by the vomit or saliva of a rat, toad, frog, or a similar animal. But these excretions infect a person only if the animal is maimed; if the animal is killed the excretions have no effect.

Tables 8 and 9 also distinguish between infirmities that are partially magically cured and those that are entirely magically cured. Many entirely magically caused infirmities, such as insanity inflicted upon a victim by a malevolent spirit (khan achachi, anchanchu, and so on), are cured by burning mesas, excrement, dried snake and bat meats, fetuses, and placentas for the spirit to "eat." Naturally caused diseases, however, may be cured in part with natural treatments, such as herbal teas, massages, and even pharmaceutical items, as well as with magical treatments. Often salves must be administered with only black cloths, which are symbolic of magical power. A cure for temporary insanity requires that the patient eat the brains and blood of a dog, which symbolizes the patient's spirit and blood that a malevolent spirit has eaten, thereby curing the insanity. Brains and blood, however, have high concentrations of vitamin B and are effective in treating aberrant behavior due to vitamin B deficiency that tends to occur after week-long fiestas involving heavy drinking.

Often natural cures are accompanied by magical cures, such as offerings for the supernatural spirits to eat, as a solicitation of supernatural aid in the curing process. Furthermore, an individual may perceive an infirmity to be of natural origin, but perceive the patient to have been susceptible to the natural infirmity because the patient's soul had been stolen by a malevolent spirit. Hence a natural cure must be preceded in such instances by rituals for soul loss or soul theft.

TABLE 10 Comparison of Etiologies and Cures That Are Entirely Natural

CULTURAL GROUP	CAUSES			CURES		
	N	(100%)		N	(100%)	
Vecino Catholic	399	287	(72%)	500	418	(84%)
Cholo	108	72	(67%)	120	97	(81%)
Methodist	136	112	(82%)	168	158	(94%)
Campesino	359	294	(82%)	437	371	(85%)
Yatiri	487	353	(72%)	548	423	(77%)

TABLE 11 Comparison of Etiologies and Cures That Are Partially or Entirely Psychological

CULTURAL GROUP	CAUSES			CURES		
	N	(100%)		N	(100%)	
Vecino Catholic	399	34	(8%)	500	9	(2%)
Cholo	108	10	(9%)	120	3	(3%)
Methodist	136	9	(7%)	168	1	(1%)
Campesino	359	26	(7%)	437	8	(2%)
Yatiri	487	47	(10%)	548	5	(1%)

Tables 10 and 11 also compare the number of entirely natural and partially and entirely psychological etiologies and cures which were proffered by interviewees on the scheduled interview, with which Tables 8 and 9 are compared.

On the basis of percentages of all responses received per cultural group, Tables 8 through 11 demonstrate a series of variations. None of the variations are significant ($P = 44.01$) among cultural groups. These tables show, on the contrary, that all groups resort to entirely natural cures more often than they perceive of infirmities to be naturally caused. That is, magically caused diseases are often treated with entirely natural cures. Further, all groups tend to propose more partially magical cures for partially magical infirmities, as well as numerically more partially magical etiologies than entirely magical etiologies. This flexibility provides Kachituños with options both magical and natural when choosing etiology and curing strategies. A given case of illness may be diagnosed as partially magical to retain concepts of power and victimization and yet be treated with entirely natural cures as a means of making a statement about cultural identity.

Conclusion. The results of the structured interview support the proposition that all Kachituños, regardless of educational background, class, or cultural identity, share the same etiological beliefs. They agree according to criteria outlined above upon nosology and do not differ significantly in reliance on magical, natural, and psychological etiology.

The structured interview also outlines a flexibility inherent in the etiological and curative structure of Kachitu medical beliefs that would permit considerable manipulation of magical and natural etiological and curative strategies.

Most important, however, the structured interview supports the premise that Kachituños do not differ in curative behavior according to degree of orientation toward Western or cosmopolitan domains. In spite of the fact that pre-1952 vecino society attempted to emulate that of the Bolivian elite, vecinos recognized more magical disease terms of Aymara derivation in the scheduled interview than members of any other cultural or social group; they also resort to yatiri more often than any other group. Even Methodists, who disdain magical cures because of their doctrine, acknowledge magical etiologies as much as any other group.

Results of the Scheduled Interview

Thirty-eight interviewees were asked what each disease was and what was its symptomatology, its etiology, and its most effective cure. The disease or illness term is provided at the far left in Table 12. The linguistic derivation of the term is indicated by an *A* for Aymara or *S* for Spanish to the immediate right of the term. An *M*, *N*, or *P* to the immediate right of the linguistic indicator explains how I classified the term in analysis. Translations of the disease names are provided directly underneath the disease names. Symbols to the left of the / sign refer to responses given about the disease or illness etiology. Symbols to the right of the / sign refer to responses given about the disease or illness cure. The number of responses for each symbol is given underneath each symbol.

Symbols: N—"natural"
                  M—"magical"
                  P—"psychological"
                  A—Aymara; S = Spanish
                  !—interviewee didn't acknowledge as valid
                  ?—interviewee didn't know
                  MD—physician was specifically recommended
                  Y—yatiri was specifically recommended
                  D—pharmaceutical was specifically recommended
                  P or M—response involved both P and M, or M and N

TABLE 12

N = Natural cause/cure
M = Magical cause/cure
P = Psychological cause
A = Aymara; S = Spanish
! = Didn't believe
? = Didn't know
MD = Specifically recommends physician

Y = Specifically recommends yatiri
D = Specifically recommends some pharmaceutical
Any two symbols: M = possibly one or the other
Number of respondents = addition of numbers to the left of /.

Disease or Illness Term	Vecino	Catholic Chollo	Methodist	Campesino	Yatiri
1. Aire—S N bad air	M N N/MD,N,M 7/2,5,2	N,M/M,Y,N 1/1,1,1	M ?,N/N 2,1/1	?,N/N 10,1/1	M M P,?,N/N,M 1,11,2/2,1
2. Ajayu—A M soul loss	M/M 7/7	M/M,N 2/2,1	?,M/M,Y 2,1/1,1	?,M/M 1,10/10	M/M 14,14
3. Alfombrilla—S N measles	?,N/MD,N 3,4/1,4	?,N/N 1,1/1	? 3	?,N/N,MD 3,8/8,3	?,N/N 3,11/11
4. Amalloque—A N herpes foster	?,N,N/N,MD 2,1,4/4,1	N/N 2/2	?,N/N 2,1/1	?,N/N 3,7/7	?,N/N 1,13/13
5. Amarillo—S P nostalgia	P P/N 7/7	P P/N 3/3	P P/N,N 3/2,1	?,P/N,N 4,6/4,2	P ?,P/M 2,12/12
6. Anchanchu—A M demonic spirit	!,?,M/M,Y 1,5/5,2	N !,M/M,M 1,2/2,1	N ?,!,M/M 11,1/1	M 1,?,M/M,N 1,4,5/3,3	M 1,?,M/M,N 1,1,12,5,7
7. Angina—S N tonsillitis	N/N,MD 7/7,2	N/N 2/2	?,N/N 2,1/1	?,N/MD,N 5,6/1,6	?,N/N 12,2/2
8. Anemia—S N anemia	P N/N,MD 7/7,2	?,/MD 3/1	?,N,P/N,MD 1,1,1/3,1	?,N/MD 9,1/1	?,N/N 13,1/1

9. Arrebato—S P cold	M or N,N,M/N 1,3,3/7	N/N 2/2	N/N,MD 3/3,1	?,N/N 3/7/7	P ?,N,P/N 3,9,2/11
10. Ataques—S M P attacks	N or P,P,N/N,MD 3,1,1/5,3	M,P P,N/MD,N 1,1/1,2	N or P,?/MD 2,1/2	N M N or P,?,P/MD,N,N 3,5,2/3,2,2	P P or N,?,P,N/N 1,8,3,2/5
11. Ataque—S N heart attack	?,N/MD 3,3/3	?,N/N 1,1/1	? N/N,MD 1,2/1,1	N M ?,M,N,P/MD,N,N 8,1,1,1/2,1	?/P/N 7,2/2
12. Bosio—S N bosio = goiter	N/MD,N 7,2,3	?,N/N 1,1/1	?,N/N 1,2/2	?,N/N 10,1/1	?,O,N/N 1,2,1/1
13. Chojri—A N infected wound	M,?,N/MD,N 1,2,3/1,3	N/N,D 2/2,1	?,N/N,MD 1,2/2,1	N ?,N/N,M 2,8/8,1	?,N/N,MD 3,11/11,1
14. Chujchu—A N possibly TB	?,N,M/N,M,MD,Y,P 1,4,2/2,2,1,1,1	N,M/N,N,MD,Y 2,1/2,1,1	?/MD 3/2	?,M,N/N 8,1,2/3	N ?,M,N/N,M 6,1,7/6,3
15. Chullpa—A M TB (bone)	?,M/M,Y 4,2/2,1	M/M 2/2	?,! 2,1	N ?,M/N,M,MD,M 2,7/4,3,2,1	P M M,?,M/N,M,MD,D,N 1,1,12/6,3,1,1,4
16. Chupa—A N tumefaction, abscess, ulceration	?,N,M/N,MD 2,2,3/5,2	N,M/N,MD 1,1/2,1	?,M/N,MD 1,2/2,1	?,N/N 7,3/3	?,N/N 12,2/2
17. Colerina—S P bile	P/N,D,MD 6/5,2,2	P/N 2/2	N,P/N,MD,D 1,2/3,1,2	N,P/N,D 2,8/10,6	N or P,?,N,P/N,D 1,2,3,8/12,7
18. Colico—S P bad stomach	N/N,MD,D 7/7,6,3	N/N 2/2	N/N,MD,D 3/3,2,3	N ?,N/N,MD,D,M 3,7/6,1,4,1	M P or N,?,N/N,N,N,D 2,3,9/9,2,5
19. Coqueluche—S N whooping cough	?,N/N,MD 2,5/5,3	?,N/MD 1,1/1	N/MD 3/1	?,N/N,MD 5,6/6,4	?,N/MD/N 12,2/1,2

TABLE 12 (continued)

Disease or Illness Term	Vecino	Catholic Chollo	Methodist	Campesino	Yatiri
20. Costado—S N pleurisy	N/N,MD,Y 7/7,2,1	?,N/N 1/1/1	?,N/N,MD 1,2/2,1	?,N/N,D 3,7/7,2	?,N/N,D 2,12/12,3
21. C'Oto—A N goiter	N,M/N,M,MD,Y 5,2/4,2,1,1	N,M/N 1,1/2	?,N/N 2,1/1	?,M,N/N,M,MD 8,1,2/2,1,2	N ?,N,M/N,M 11,2,1/2,1
22. Cumena—A M magical illness	?,M/M 3,3/3	?,! 1,1	? 3	? 11	? 14
23. Curmi—A N TB	?,N/N,MD,M 4,2/2,2,1	N N,M/N,MD 1,1/2,1	?,N/MD 2,1/1	N ?,N/N,M 4,6/6,2	N ?,N/N,MD,M 2,12/12,2,3
Subtotal	N 147/158	N 48/46	N 66/51	N 230/142	N 303/184
24. Debil—S N debility	N/N,MD 7/7,2	N,P/N 2,1/2	N/N,MD 3/3,1	?,N/N,MD 7,3/3,1	?,N/N 12,2/2
25. Disenteria—S N dysentery	?,N/N,MD,D 1,6/6,2,1	N/N,D 2/2,1	N/N,MD,D 3/3,1,1	?,N/N,MD 3,8/4,4	?,N/N,MD 5,9/5,4
26. Embrujada—S M witchcraft	!,M/Y 3,3/3	? 1	!,M/Y,M 2,1/1,1	?,! 5,5	M !,?,M/Y 4,9,1/1
27. Enfriamiento—S N common cold	?,N/N,MD,Y 1,4/4,1,1	? 2	?,N/N,D 12/2,2	?,N/N,D 5,6/6,1	?,N/N 6,5/5
28. Epilepsia—S N epilepsy	?,P,N/MD,Y 2,1,2/3,1	? 2	?,N/MD 2,1/1	? 10	?,N/MD 10,1/1
29. Erisipelas—S N erisipelas	?,N/N,MD 3,3/2,2	? 2	? 3	? 11	?,N/N,MD 9,2/1,1
30. Escarlatina—S N scarlet fever	N/N,MD 5/5,3	N/N 2/2	?,N/MD 1,2/1	?,N/N,MD,D 2,7/7,3,1	?,N/N,D 2,8/9,1

31. Fievre—S N fever	?,N/N,MD 1,5/5,1	?,N/N,MD 1,1/1,1	?,N/N 1,2/2	?,N/N,M 5,5/4,1	?,N/N 8,3/3
32. Gangrenado—S N gangrene	?,N/MD 4,2/1	? 2	N/MD 3/3	?,N/MD 10,1/1	?,N/N,MD 9,1/1,1
33. Gripe—S N gripe	N/N,D 5/5,5	N/N,D 2/2,2	N/N,D,MD 3/3,3,1	?,N/N,D,MD 1,10/10,7,1	?,N/N,D 3,8/8,5
34. Gusanera—S N worms	N/N,MD,D 5/5,2,1	?,N/N,D 1,1/1,1	N/N,D 3/3,1	?,N/N 2,9/9	?,N/N,D 4,7/7,1
35. Hemoragia de Sangre—S N hemorrhage	M,N/N,MD 1,5/5,2	?,N/N,MD 1,1/1,1	N/MD,N 3/2,2	?,N/MD,N 5,6/5,1	?,N/N,M,MD 4,4/2,2
36. Hernia—S N hernia	N/N,MD 5/5,4	? 2	?,N/MD 1,2/2	?,N/MD 10,1/1	N ? 14
37. Hinchazon—S N swelling	?,N/N,MD 1,4/2,2	N/N,MD 2/1,1	?,N/N 1,2/1	?,N/N,MD 3,6/5,1	?,N/N,M,MD 2,8/5,3,1
38. Infeccion—S N infection	?,N/N,MD 1,4/4,2	N/N 2/2	N/N,MD 3/3,3	?,N/N,MD 3,7/7,5	?,N/N,MD 6,3/3,1
39. Insolacion—S N sun stroke	?,N/N,MD 3,2/2,1	? 2	N/N 3/3	?,N/N,D 3,7/7,2	?,N/N,D 2,7/7,1
40. Kepu—A N warts	?,N/N,MD 2,4/4,2	N/N 2/2	?,N/N 1,2/2	?,N/N 7,2/2	?,N/N 5,5/5
41. Khan achachi—A M demonic being	M ?,M/M,Y 2,4/4,4	M/M 2/2	?,!,M/N 1,1/1,1	M ?,M/M,N 5,4/3,1	M ?,M/N,M,N 3,7/2,4,1
42. Kharisiri—A M demonic being	M ?,!,M/N 2,2,2/1	?,M/N,N 1,2/1,1	!,M/N 1,2/2	?,! 5,4	?,!,M,N/N,D 62,1,1/2,1

TABLE 12 (continued)

Disease or Illness Term	Vecino	Catholic Chollo	Methodist	Campesino	Yatiri
43. Kustipa—A pleurisy	?,N/N 3,3/3	N/N 2/2	?,N/N 1,2/2	?,N/N 6,5/5	2,N/N 6,8/8
Subtotal	N 119/118	N 43/31	N 63/56	N 205/118	N 236/119
44. Kutupi—A N pleurisy	?,!,N/N,MD 41,2/1,2	N N,M/N,MD 1,1/2,1	? 3	N ?,N/N,M 6,3/1,2	N ?,N/N,M 3,7/3,4
45. Lampara—S M magical death	?,N,M/M 2,1,3/3	?,M/M 1,1/1	!,?,M/M 1,1,1/1	? 9	?,M/M 9,1/1
46. Lari Lari—A M demonic being	?,M/N 4,2/2	?,M,Y 1,1/1	? 3	M !,?,M/M,N 1,6,2/1,1	M ?,M/M,N,D 8,2/1,1,1
47. Larpa—A M anemia	M/M,N,MD,Y 6/2,3,1,2	M M/N,N 2/1,1	N !,M/M,N 12/1,1	M N,?,M/M,N 1,4/2,3	N ?,M,N/M,N 3,2,5/6,1
48. Limpu—A M magical death	!,?,M/M,Y 1,1,4/1,1	M,N/ 1,1/	!,?,N/N 1,1,1/1	M ?,N/N,N 7,2/1,1	N ?,N/N,M,D 7,3/1,2,1
49. Mallcu—A N measles	?,N/N 3,2/2	N/N 1/1	?,N/N 1,1/1	N ?,!,N/N,M 1,1,6/5,1	N ?,N/N,M 1,10/9,1
50. Mal de Urin—S N urinary infection	N/N,MD 6/6,3	?,N/N,MD 1,1/1,1	?,N/N,MD 12/1,1	?,N/N,MD 2,7/4,3	?,N/N 2,8/8
51. Mal Interior—S N Intestinal infection	?,N/MD 4,2/1	N ?,N/M 1,1/1	? 3	N ?,N/N,M,MD 1,9/7,1,1	?,N/N,MD 1,9/9,1

52. Mal Parto—S N Stillbirth or spontaneous abortion	N/N,M,MD 6/1,1,3	N/N,MD 2/1,1	?,N/MD 1,2/1	?,N/N,MD 5,6/3,3	?,N/N,MD 6,4/2,2
53. Mal Tratadura—S N Bruises	?,N,N/N,MD,Y 1,1,4/4,1,1	?,N/N 1,1/1	?,N/N 1,2/2	?,N/N,M,MD 1,9/7,1,1	?,N/N 1,9/9
54. Malos demonios— S M demonic being	!,M/Y 3,3/3	? 2	!,M/M 1,1/1	?,! 4,5	?,!,M 7,3,1
55. Maripichupichu—A N measles	? 5	?,N/N 1,1/1	? 3	?,1,N/N 6,1,1/1	?,N/N 7,3/3
56. Meningitis—S N meningitis	N ?,N,P/N,MD 2,2,2/1,4	? 2	?,N/MD 2,1/1	?,N/MD 9,1/1	? 14
57. Negrotewartillo—A N fever	?,N/N 4,2/4	?,N/N 1,1/1	? 3	?,1,N/N 5,1,1/1	?,N/N 7,3/3
58. Neomonea—S N pneumonia	?,N/N,MD,D 1,5/5,4,1	?,N/N 1,1/1	?,N/MD 2,1/1	?,N/MD 8,1/1	? 10
59. Otitis—S N ear infection	?,N/N,MD 2,4/4,2	? 2	?,N/MD 2,1/1	? 9	? 10
60. Paludismo—S N malaria	N/N,Y 6/5,1	?,N/N 1,1/1	?,M/N 2,1/1	?,N/N 9,1/1	? 10
61. Papera—S N mumps	N/N,MD,D 5/5,1,1	?,N/MD 1,1/1	?,N/MD 1,2/2	?,N/N,MD 4,4/3,1	N ?,N,M/N 7,2,1/3
62. Paralysis—S N paralysis	?,N/N,MD,D 2,4/4,3,2	?,M/ 1,1/	?,N/MD 1,2/1	?,N/MD 8,1/1	? 10
63. Peste—S N plague	?,N/N 1,5/3	N/N 2/2	? 3	?,N/N 9,1/1	?,N/N 13,1,1

TABLE 12 (continued)

Disease or Illness Term	Vecino	Catholic Chollo	Methodist	Campesino	Yatiri
64. Piampia—A N measles	?,N/N 2,3/3	?,N/N 1,1/1	?,N/N 1,2/2	?,N/N,MD 3,7/6,1	N/N 9/9
65. Pulmonea—S N pulmonary	N/N,MD 6/5,5	N/N,MD 2/2,1	?,N/N,MD 1,2/2,1	?,N/N,MD 6,4/2,2	?,N/N,MD 12,2/1,1
66. Qate, qate—A M demonic being	?,!,N,M/Y 1,1,1,3/1	?,M/ 1,1/	!,? 2,1	?,! 7,2	?,!,M 7,2,3
Subtotal	N 135/108	N 45/25	N 65/23	N 211/71	N 242/84
67. Quebracion—S N urinary infection	?,N/N,D 2,3/2,1	?,N/N 1,1/1	?,N/N 2,1/1	N/N,D 9/9,2	?,N/N,D 4,8/8,1
68. Raquetismo—S N rickets	M ?,N,M/N,N 2,2,1/2,1	? 2	? 3	? 8	? 11
69. Reoma—Sp? N nasal congestion	N/N,MD 4/4,3	?,N/N 1,1/1	?,N/N 1,2/2	?,N/N,MD 3,6/6,1	?,N/N 2,8/8
70. Reumatismo—S N rheumatism	N/N,MD 6/5,3	?,N/ 1,1/	N/N,MD 3/2,2	N/N,MD 7/7,2	?,N/N 4,6/6
71. Saliwa—A? M magical warts	?,!,N,M/N 1,3,1,1/2	?,M/N 1,1/1	!,?,N/N 1,1/1	? 9	? 10
72. Sarampion—S N measles	N/N,MD 6/5,2	?,N/N,MD 1,1/1,1	?,N/N,MD 1,2/1,1	?,N/N,MD 1,7/4,4	?,N/N,MD 1,8/7,1
73. Senectud—S N senility	?,N/ 4,1/	? 2	? 3	? 8	? 10
74. Sinusitis—S N sinusitis	?,N/N,MD 1,5/5,3	?,N/N,D 2,1/1,1	?,N/MD 2,1/1	?,N/N 8,1/1	?,N/N,D 6,2/2,2

Disease					
75. Sirena—Sp M magical mermaid	?,!,M/ 1,1,4/	? 1	!,!,M/M 1,1,1/1	M ?,!,M/M,N 4,1,4/3,1	N ?,M/M,M 3,6/2,4
76. Sirk'i—A N warts	N/N,MD 7/6,4	N/N 2/2	N/N 3/3	M N,M/N,N 6,2,1/2,1	N ?,N,M,NorM/N,M,M 2,2,2,4/8,1,2
77. Sisu—A N warts	?,N/N,MD 2,4/4,1	?,N/ 1,1/	?,N/MD 2,1/1	?,N/N 10,1/1	?,N/N,D 6,4/4,4
78. Sopladura—S N strong cold?	?,N/N,Y 2,2/2,1	?,N/N 1,1/1	?,N/N 1,2/2	?,N/N 8,2/2	?,N/N 6,3/3
79. Taaya—A N common cold	?,N/N,D 3,3/3,1	N/N 2/1	? 3	?,N/N,D 7,3/3,1	?,N/N 8,6/6
80. Tabarstillo—A N measles	?,N/N 5,1/1	? 2	? 3	?,N/N 8,2/2	?,N/N 8,1/1
81. Terciana—S N malaria	N/N 6/6	N N M/M 1/1	?,N/N,MD 1,2/2,1	?,N/N 6,2/2	N ?,N/N,M 3,5/3,2
82. Tericia—S terciary fever	M P,N,!/N,N,MD 3,1,1/2,1,1	M P/N 1/1	?,P/N 2,1/1	?,P/N,N 4,6/4,2	P ?,P/M 2,12/12
83. Tesis—S N TB	?,N/MD 3,3/3	?,N/MD 1,1/1	?,N/MD 2,1/1	?,N/MD 9,1/1	? 10
84. Tifus—S N typhus	?,N/MD 1,5/3	? 2	? 3	?,N/MD 10,1/1	?,N/N 8,3/3
85. Tosferina—S N whooping cough	N/N,MD 5/5,3	? 2	?,N/N,MD 1,2/1,1	?,N/MD 5,4/4	?,N/N,MD 5,5/4,1
86. Tuberculosis—S N tuberculosis	N/MD,N 7/7,1	?,N/MD 1,1/1	N/MD 3/3	N/MD 10/10	?,N/MD 3,7/2

TABLE 12 (*continued*)

Disease or Illness Term	Vecino	Catholic Chollo	Methodist	Campesino	Yatiri
87. Tullimiento—S N debility	?,N/N,P 3,3/1,1	? 2	? 3	? 11	? 14
88. Ulcera—S N ulcer	N ?,N/N,MD 2,4/2,2	? 2	?,N/N,MD 1,2/1,1	?,N/N,MD 9,2/1,1	?,N/MD 11,1/1
89. Umamausa—A N fever	?,M,N/N,M,M,MD,Y 3,12/1,1,2,2	? 1	? 3	N ?,N/N,M 4,6/6,2	N ?,N/N,MD,M 2,12/12,2,3
90. Ventosedad—S N colic	N/N,MD 5/4,1	N/N 1/1	N/N,MD,D 2/2,2,1	N ?,N/N,MD,D,M 3,7/6,1,4,1	P M ?,N,N/N,N,D 3,2,9/9,2,5
91. Verugas—S N warts	?,N,M/N,MD 2,3,1/4,1	N/N 2/2	N/N 3/3	N ?,N/N,D,M 8,2/2,2,2	N N,M/N,M 7,7/14,5
Subtotal	N 142/115	N 46/18	N 74/38	N 236/104	N 272/155
92. La Viuda—S M demonic being	! 5	? 1	!,? 1,1	?,!,M/M 5,1,3/2	N ?,M/M,M,M,N 4,6/4,1,1
93. Waj Waj—A M demonic being	!,M/M 3,2/1	? 1	!,? 1,1	? 9	?,M 8,1
TOTAL N	553/500	184/120	274/168	900/437	1072/548

Notes

INTRODUCTION: Locating a Theoretical Perspective

1. After the revolution of 1952, the word *Indian* or *Indio* was replaced by the term *campesino*, as *Indio* was considered derogatory. Thus the use of the word *Indian* is, in this book, limited to contexts that refer to periods before 1952. Indians in Bolivia were primarily Aymara and Quechua. The Aymara and Quechua are, in most contexts, proud of their ethnic distinction and cultural differentiation from non-Indian or non-campesino domains. Thus use of these terms continues. Today, however, Aymara and Quechua are *campesinos*.

2. Mestizos are individuals presumably of both Hispanic and Indian descent. In fact they are a social class that carried out the administrative powers vested in them by the elite over the Aymara and Quechua and other indigenous highland groups before 1952. They were the middlemen, the brokers between the elite and Indians. In this volume it is argued that they were often Indians who shed their Aymara or Quechua or other ethnic identity to enter the mestizo class, or were of Hispanic descent but land-poor.

3. According to Joseph Bastien, in 1989 there were actually fifty-six projects in Bolivia. If Bolivia's population statistics at that time (7 million) can be believed, and given the want of social services outside the cities, that leaves 125,000 Bolivianos to be served per project, or approximately 100,000 per project in rural areas.

4. The Methodist mission to Bolivia represents the progressive arm of the Methodist church and may differ from more conservative branches on this point.

5. These models are also based on a reified conceptualization of medicine as a science uninformed by political and economic factors which was appropriated by the development community after World War II. "Western medicine" as practiced by physicians was believed to be heading happily toward a monopolization of the world's health care. Only lack of access to it kept the masses of poor throughout the world, particularly in the developing countries, from replacing folk systems and shamans with it. Decision-making models, therefore, also included logistical elements of accessibility, including transportation, waiting time, costs, social distance, and cultural differences between providers and patients (e.g., Cañedo 1974; Foster 1951, 1952, 1958, 1966; Kane and Kane 1972; Paul 1953; Wellin 1955). But as access to cosmopolitan medicine has increased, so have alternative medical systems, and medical pluralism has proliferated, not disappeared.

6. I am using the term *reconstruction* as Ray Elling (1971, 1974, 1978, 1981), Ronald Frankenberg (1980, 1981), and Allan Young (1976, 1978) use it to refer to the duplication of a particular hierarchical relationship within the medical setting. The term contrasts with "restructuring" employed here as used by Marshall Sahlins (1981) and Jean Comaroff (1980) to refer to the creation of change in the structure of a relationship.

CHAPTER ONE: Medical, Ethnic, and Religious Pluralism

1. The term *dual use* was first coined by Irwin Press in his discussion of the use of shamans in Bogota by the middle classes as well as the indigenous population. See Press 1969, 1971.

2. The *vecindario* refers to the mestizo community that controlled Indian labor in the countryside. From the word *vecino*, the term separates these mestizos from the Indian population as a separate class endowed with political, economic, and judicial power. Rasnake's discussion of vecinos in the Yura community he studied (1988: 40–41) is the most recent description with which the Kachitu vecindario can be compared.

3. This and most of the town historical materials were derived from the town archives, particularly the minutes of the monthly meetings of the vecindario.

4. Sara Stinson (1978) found that the infant mortality rate for Kachitu was 121 per 1,000, most from weanling diarrhea. Simple childhood diseases such as measles and smallpox sweep through the altiplano in periodic epidemic waves that are fatal in children under five. The Methodist clinic made major progress in reducing mortality from childhood diseases through vaccination campaigns, but with few resources, these campaigns have been uneven. Today the Andean Rural Health Care project is undertaking the burden of this crusade.

5. Anthropologically speaking, race does not exist in the natural world; it is a cultural construct. Thus how it is constructed, understood, and used varies from one culture to the next. Most variable is the degree of membership flexibility. In the United States racial membership is rigid, defined by phenotypic characteristics. In much but not all of Latin America, particularly Bolivia, race is defined by language and social class, and membership is thus flexible, as Marvin Harris has explained (1964). In Bolivia, however, in spite of the etic accuracy of Harris's explication, language and social class are addressed as fixed and genetic; the concept of race is deployed as an inflexible category.

6. This thesis is presented on the assumption that two contrasting processes affect all medical systems, including cosmopolitan medicine. First, all medical systems are altered and reformed by culture and history. There is thus no such thing as "Western biomedicine." Rather, allopathic cosmopolitan medicine has become ubiquitous and hegemonic (Elling 1971, 1974, 1978, 1981), but its form, its bureaucracy, the way it is developed, and how it articulates with other medical systems and with political, economic, and other institutions and processes, including history, varies over space and time.

   Second, cosmopolitan medicine, because it is based on scientific technology that in turn requires a specific economic base of its own, is very much a part of the world economic system. Hence the term *cosmopolitan* (Dunn 1976). Much of its efficacy is dependent upon the extent to which it articulates with the medical metropoli of the world.

   These two facts render an understanding of cosmopolitan medicine as it is dispensed through various types of programs throughout the world, particularly in peripheral areas, highly relative to its local, national, and international environment. Hence they are embedded in two more processes common to all medical systems that give medical pluralism its greatest significance: the political and the economic.

7. *Medicinas caseras* among the people Joseph Bastien worked with differed considerably from that which I describe here. My data are considerably more hispanized. Similarly Kachitu is closer to La Paz than is the province of Bautista Saavedra where he did his work, and much more influenced by it. The difference emphasizes the variability within Bolivia.

8. Fictive kin ties with mestizos, such as having mestizo godparents for campesino children.

9. Bastien (1979) says that the Aymara believe marriage to be indissoluble, and also points out that compadrazgo obligations associated with marriage—obtaining godparents, and the godparents' responsibilities toward the couple—are too expensive for marriage to be considered more than once in a lifetime.

CHAPTER TWO: Working in the Field

1. Genara knows how to cure a large number of illnesses and diseases but is not a yatiri. She doesn't practice healing as a livelihood. However, she thinks she has as much power as a yatiri. Thus, she is, instead, a wise, elderly, lady.

2. Well, yes, I did get a job upon completing my dissertation. It didn't pay much though.

3. I greatly appreciated the concern my illnesses generated, but it was difficult to take a bath in someone else's collected urine to bring my temperature down and to drink my own urine to kill the pathogen. Neither idea, however, is outlandish: both have a modicum of sense to them.

CHAPTER THREE: The Historical Context

1. *Caciques* are Indian political bosses imbued with power by a loyal following based on the loyalties and obligations of patronage and clientage. Abercrombie 1986, Murra 1978, Platt 1978b, Rasnake 1988, and Stern 1982, are recent works that explore the history of the Aymara elites under colonial rule and their participation in it. For a comparison with the structure of cacique power under Inca rule that preceded colonialism see John Murra 1968 and Julien 1983.

2. See particularly the works of John H. Rowe.

3. Carter 1964; Malloy 1970; Klein 1969; on the nature of precapitalist agriculture and the link between the hacienda and the peasant economy see Gustavo Rodriguez O. 1980, and Antonio Rojas 1980 respectively.

4. No reference was made to the mestizo population.

5. An excellent analysis of the agrarian reform and its relationship to the world capitalist system can be found in Susan Eckstein 1979 and 1983.

6. In May of 1981, Brazilian police captured six mercenaries in the employ of Bolivian Minister of the Interior Luis Arce Gomez, in possession of a large quantity of cocaine, heavy weapons, and nazi insignia (Dunkerley 1984: 323).

7. The most comprehensive histories in English of these years are Klein's (1969, 1982).

8. In 1989 Cultural Survival invested $20 million in a program on the altiplano.

CHAPTER FOUR: The Ecology of Dependency

1. I have seen tapeworms only in the tiny *ispis*. Because the *ispis* are so small, the worms are easily detectable, and as they are fried crisp, should not pose much of a health problem. However, the infestation of tapeworms in human hosts is not uncommon in the population that relies heavily on the lake, i.e., the provinces of Omasuyus and La Paz.

2. The term *cholo* varies in usage throughout the Andes but on the southern altiplano it refers to those Aymara who have entered the cash market. Cholo women identify themselves by wearing factory-made, rather than homespun, traditional clothing, but cholo men are "vestido"; that is, they wear Western clothes. Cholos principally act as wholesalers or run the black market. On market women see Judith-Marie Buechler (1979). In Kachitu, however, the cholos happen to be mostly Methodists. Perhaps because that is the case, Kachituños are reluctant to use the term in town where it is considered derogatory.

3. The early history of the Methodist mission in Bolivia is available in Copplestone 1973*a* and *b*. Undoubtedly drawing on many data from the same archives I reconstructed—the body of correspondence reserved at the mission in Kachitu—this history from 1907 to 1939 differs substantially from mine because of its focus. Copplestone was interested in the politics within the Methodist church itself. The early mission supported the interests of the elite classes in La Paz and Cochabamba in an era when the Protestant presence in Bolivia was of dubious legality, and attention to the Indians was considered subversive. Thus he rightfully draws a picture of Herrick as being almost saintly in his determination to defend the Indians. If my rendition of Herrick is of someone who was somewhat less praiseworthy it is because I am focusing on the politics of Kachitu itself. This shift in focus requires that Herrick's saintliness be reconsidered in light of its moralistic ethnocentrism. It is not my intention to detract from Herrick's due praise, but rather to understand his actions within the social space in which both vecinos and Aymara interacted.

4. Less than $20.00 U.S. a month by official rates, about $11.00 U.S. on the black market, according to Pick.

5. About $12.00 U.S. official rate, $7.00 U.S. on the black market, according to Pick.

6. Before 1952 what is now chola dress was the attire of rural mestizo women, further evidence of confluences of shared culture and shifts in social class.

7. A single generation ago, before the burgeoning of the cholo classes after 1952, manufactured dresses and bowler hats were proper attire for mestizo women, especially in the countryside. In the 1950s cholas emerging from the Indian classes appropriated the attire, as young mestizo women turned to Western dress and became *vestidas*. Thus Leonora de Ugalde and her counterparts never changed their attire. The significance is that everyone else did except the campesinos.

CHAPTER FIVE: Indigenous Medicine

1. The disease does not have a term of its own, and is referred to as "kharisiri," the name of its mode of transmission. Bastien discusses the concept of fat essential to it in Kallawaya medicine (1987:71). The phenomenon appears in almost all the literature on the Andes, most recently in Abercrombie 1986:269–270 in which priests and white people transform the fat from Indians into money in machines in La Paz.

2. El Tio does not correspond to the Christian Devil in indigenous Bolivian ideology and corresponds more closely to the trickster and maternal uncle. June Nash's (1979) and Michael Taussig's (1980) analyses of the relationship between the conceptualization of El Tio and the imposition of class relations in the Bolivian mines elaborate this concept more fully. Dillon and Abercrombie 1988, and Abercrombie 1986, analyze the concept as a syncretism that emerges from its historical context as a new form of protest, resistance, and empowerment.

3. Available at any tienda, a dulce mesa consists of pairs of candies (so both the Pachamama and Condor Mamani can partake) in the form of animals, squares with pictures on them, representations of the necessities of life (e.g., two houses), festive articles, and items representing wealth (a horse, gold and silver paper).

4. Available in any tienda, a chiuchi mesa consists of little lead figures of people and animals, and little slips of colored paper.

5. For extensive studies on the use of coca in Bolivia see Carter and Mamani (1978), and Carter, Mamani, Morales, and Parkerson (1986).

6. Although asymmetrical power relations disappear when people drink, awareness of those relations and animosity do not. Thus it is a good time to argue and does not constitute *communitas*.

CHAPTER NINE: Medical Metaphors and Political Strategies

1. Cold baths during the menses can produce endometriosis, which can develop into a serious disease. The water pushes shedding but still viable cells of the uterine lining backwards and upwards through the fallopian tubes into the peritoneal cavity where they become implanted on the peritoneum and bowel. This causes pain and obstruction of either the bowel or ureter. According to contemporary cosmopolitan medical research, women with this condition are frequently diagnosed as borderline psychotics. They may be further incapacitated at the time of menses, which may either become excessive or cease altogether, and severe dyspareinia occurs.

2. Runaway and emancipated African slaves integrated themselves into Quechua-speaking communities in the Yungas; however, their contemporary numbers are very few.

3. Upon hearing the case, a U.S. physician suggested Gladis may well have had a severe case of endometriosis, fatal because it went untreated and led to complications.

CHAPTER TWELVE: Culture, Ideology, and Hegemony

1. Daniel Moerman 1983 and Romanucci-Ross and Moerman 1988 on the magic inherent in cosmopolitan medicine are two of a number of works that expose the myth of value-free scientific medicine, thus revealing the link between culture, history, and medical beliefs.

Glossary

Achachillas. Supernatural beings that live in all major geological formations.

Aguayu. Shawl, or handwoven cloth, in which women carry babies and goods on their back. Market women also lay them on the ground and spread their wares on them for display and sale.

Ahijado. Godson.

Ajayu. Soul; one of three, according to Aymara ideology.

Alacitas. An Aymara fair in La Paz at which miniatures are bought and blessed in hopes of receiving the genuine article in the following year; the term means "buy from me."

Alcaldes comunarios. Local Aymara authorities on the hacienda.

Alma. Soul; one of three, according to Aymara ideology.

Amartillo. Hispanic folk disease caused by the loss of a beloved.

Anafri. Kerosene cooking burner.

Anchanchus. Supernatural beings that drive people mad.

Animu. Soul; one of three, according to Aymara ideology.

Año de provincia. Year of medical or educational service in the rural countryside required by the government.

Apachitas. Piles of rocks formed at mountain passes by offerings made to the supernatural by travelers as a protective measure.

Ataques de cabeza. Literally, attacks to the head.

Ayllu. Extended kinship organization that involves reciprocal obligations, especially *ayni*, and mutual support.

Ayni. "Traditional" system of cooperative labor based on kinship obligations.

Bichu. A disgusting insect.

Caciques. Aymara chiefs.

Calor. Heat. Used in dialogue about health in reference to an essential quality of foods and illnesses: that they are hot, instead of cold or fresh.

Camba. Lowlanders who claim in general to be of European ancestry.

Campo. The countryside.

Caudillos. Regional strong men.

Caya. Type of tuber.

Chacras. Fields.

Chagas. Trypanosomiasis, related to African sleeping sickness, caused by a protozoa carried by the reduviid bug that lives in thatch, and endemic throughout much of the slopes of the Andes. As of 1987 there was no satisfactory treatment, and organ damage was irreversible.

Challar. An offering to the Pachamama in which a portion of whatever liquid is being consumed is shared with her by being sprinkled on the ground.

Chamakanis. Specialists who have the power to talk to spirits both living and dead, and thus provide clients with information.

Charango. A ten-stringed mandolinlike instrument made out of the back of an armadillo.

Chiuchi mesa. Little lead figurines; people buy them to use as offerings to the supernatural.

Cholo, chola. Men and women who maintain their Indian ethnicity but work in the cash market, particularly the informal market or "black market" in the urban areas.

Chuño. Type of freeze-dried potato.

Compadrazgo. Godparenthood.

Compadres. People who stand in parent-godparent relationship to each other.

Comunidad. Community.

Copa. A small glass.

Cordillera. Mountain range.

Corregidor. An authority in the municipalidad of the canton who resolves disputes pertaining to laws of the state.

Criollos. Spanish who were born in the New World.

Curandero. Someone who cures or heals.

Despedida. Farewell party.

Dulce mesas. Imprinted and shaped candies that are bought to use as offerings to the Pachamama.

Empacho. Impacted stomach.

Envidia. Envy.

Finca. Small farm.

Fresca. Fresh.

Hacendados. Patrónes, or hacienda owners.

Hacienda. Ranch to which a population of peons are attached.

Hilacatas. Aymara authorities, democratically elected.

Ispis. Tiny edible fish that carry tapeworm.

Jach'a tata. Indigenous Andean healer.

Junta de vecinos. The body of mestizo residents who govern the town.

Kharisiri. Disease caused by the theft of the fat from Indians' kidneys.

Kolla. The indigenous highland population.

Kolliri. Indigenous Andean healer.

Kuraka. Indigenous leaders, chiefs, or kings during the precolonial and colonial eras; currently the term is sometimes employed to indicate elected leaders in Aymara communities.

Kustipa. A deady condition that befalls one who is drunk and falls asleep in the sun.

Latifundio. Large landholding.

Latifundista. Owner of a latifundio.

La Viuda. An evil spirit in the form of an enchanted widow.

Limpu. An illness visited upon the campesino witness to a stillbirth.

Madrina. Godmother.

Maligno. An evil spirit.

Mate. Tea.

Mate de coca. Tea made from the coca leaf.

Medicinas caseras. Home remedies.
Mesa Negra. A preparation of vegetable and animal items with which one can perform black magic.
Mestizaje. The existence of mestizoness or the mestizo socioeconomic class.
Minifundios. Small farms.
Mit'a. Inca tax system.
Moiety. Kinship division into two exogenous groups.
Mozo. Male servant.
Municipio. Town and juridical center of a canton.

Oficio. Official request.

Padrino. Godfather.
Patrón. Person to whom one is indebted.
Pensión. Small hotel or restaurant.
Pongueaje. Personal services by Aymara peons to the hacendado, required by law.
Preste. Fiesta sponsor.

Rutucha. First haircut.

Sampoña. Windpipe.
Sayana. Individual landholding.
Sinapismo. A homemade compress.
Sindicatos. Unions.
Suerte. Luck.
Susto. Fright; soul loss.

Tari. A small woven cloth in which coca leaves are placed to divine.
Tienda. Small store.
Tonto. Dull witted.
Trucha. Salmon trout.
Tunta. Type of freeze-dried potato.

Vecindario. The mestizo population of the town.
Vecino. Spanish for "neighbor," it refers to a mestizo.

Waj waj. Supernatural being.

Yankha. Harmful and noxious.
Yatiri. Aymara healer.

References Cited

ABERCROMBIE, THOMAS
    1986   The Politics of Sacrifice: An Aymara Cosmology in Action. Ph.D. dissertation, University of Chicago.

ALBO, XAVIER
    1972   Esposos, seguros y padrinos entre los Aymara. Paper presented at the symposium on Andean kinship and marriage, at the seventy-first meeting of the American Anthropological Association, Toronto.
    1975   (1974–1976) La paroja Aymara: solidaridad y faccionalismo? Estudios Andinos (La Paz) 11 : 67–109.

ALLEN, CATHERINE J.
    1988   The Hold Life Has: Coca and Cultural Identity in an Andean Community. Washington, D.C.: Smithsonian Institution Press.

BALZER, MARJORIE
    1987   Behind shamanism: changing voices of Siberian Khanti cosmology and politics. In: Beyond the Cure: Anthropological Inquiries in Medical Theories and Epistemologies. Special Edition of Social Science and Medicine 24 : 12, Crandon, guest editor.

BARTH, FREDRIK
    1969   Introduction, in F. Barth, ed., Ethnic Groups and Boundaries. Boston: Little, Brown.

BARTON, ROBERT
    1968   A Short History of the Republic of Bolivia. La Paz: Editorial Los Amigos del Libro.

BASTIEN, JOSEPH WILLIAM
    1978   Mountain of the Condor: Metaphor and Ritual in an Andean Allyu. St. Paul, Minn.: The American Ethnological Society (Monograph), West Publishing Co.
    1979   Matrimonio e Intercambio en los Andes. Estudios Andinos 8(15) : 33–51. English version: Marriage and exchange in the Andes. In: Actes du LXII Congres International des Americanistes (Paris) 6 : 149–164.
    1987a   Cross-cultural communication between doctors and peasants in Bolivia. In: Beyond the Cure: Anthropological Inquiries in Medical Theories and Epistemologies. Special edition of Social Science and Medicine 24 : 12 : 1109–1118, Crandon, guest ed.
    1987b   Healers of the Andes: the Kallawaya Herbalists and Their Medicinal Plants. Salt Lake City: University of Utah Press.

BOLTON, RALPH
    1972   The marriage system of the Qolla. Paper presented to the seventy-first meeting of the American Anthropological Association, Toronto.

BOLTON, RALPH, AND CHARLENE BOLTON
    1975   Conflictos en la familia Andina. Cuzco: Centro de Estudios Andinos.

BOLTON, RALPH, AND ENRIQUE MAYER, EDS.
    1977   Andean Kinship and Marriage. Special Publication of the American Anthro-
            pological Association, no. 7.

BONACHICH, EDNA
    1972   A theory of ethnic antagonism: the split labor market. American Socio-
            logical Review vol. 37.

BROWMAN, DAVID L.
    1980   El manejo de la tierra árida del Altiplano del Peru y Bolivia. América Indí-
            gena 40(1): 143–159.

BRUSH, STEPHEN
    1976a   Cultural adaptations to mountain ecosystems, introduction. Human Ecology
            4(2): 125–166.
    1976b   Man's use of an Andean ecosystem. Human Ecology 4(2): 147–166.

BUECHLER, HANS C., AND JUDITH-MARIE BUECHLER
    1971   The Bolivian Aymara. New York: Holt, Rinehart and Winston.

BUECHLER, JUDITH-MARIE
    1979   The dynamics of the market in La Paz, Bolivia. Urban Anthropology
            7(4): 343–360.

BURKE, MELVIN
    1971   Land reform in the Lake Titicaca region. In: Beyond the Revolution: Bolivia
            Since 1952, James Malloy and Richard Thorn, eds. Pittsburgh: University of
            Pittsburgh Press, pp. 301–339.

CAMPBELL, LEON G.
    1979   Recent research on Andean peasant revolts, 1750–1820. LARR 14:1:3–50.

CAÑEDO, LUIS
    1974   Rural health in Mexico? Science 185:4157:1131–1137.

CARTER, WILLIAM
    1958   Kachitu: Change and Conflict in a Bolivian Town. Unpublished master's
            thesis. Burgess Library, Columbia University.
    1965   Aymara Communities and the Bolivian Agrarian Reform. Gainesville: Uni-
            versity of Florida Monographs, Social Sciences no. 24, University of Florida
            Press.
    1977   Trial marriage in the Andes? In: Andean Kinship and Marriage, Ralph
            Bolton and Enrique Mayer, eds. Washington, D.C.: Special publication of
            the American Anthropological Association, no. 7, pp. 177–216.

CARTER, WILLIAM E., AND MAURICIO MAMANI P.
    1978   Traditional Use of Coca in Bolivia. La Paz: Museo Nacional de Etnografia y
            Folklore.

CARTER, WILLIAM E., MAURICIO MAMANI P., JOSE V. MORALES, AND PHILLIP
PARKERSON
    1986   Coca in Bolivia. La Paz: Tutapi.

CHOQUE-CANQUI, ROBERTO
    1978   Pedro Chipana: cacique comerciante de Calamarca. Avances (La Paz) 1:
            28–32.

CLARK, MARGARET
    1959   The social functions of Mexican-American medical beliefs. California's Health 16:21:153–156.

COHEN, ABNER
    1969   Custom and Politics in Urban Africa: A Study of Hausa Migrants in Yoruba Towns. Berkeley and Los Angeles: University of California Press.
    1971   The politics of ritual secrecy. Man 6:427–448.
    1976   Two-dimensional Man: An Essay on the Anthropology of Power and Symbolism in Complex Society. Berkeley, Los Angeles, London: University of California Press.
    1981   The Politics of Elite Culture: Explorations in the Dramaturgy of Power in a Modern African Society. Berkeley, Los Angeles, London: University of California Press.

COMAROFF, JEAN
    1980   Healing and the cultural order: the case of the Baralong boo Ratshidi of Southern Africa. American Ethnologist 7:4:637–657.
    1981   Healing and cultural transformation: the Tswana of Southern Africa. Social Science and Medicine 15B:367–378.
    1985   Body of Power, Spirit of Resistence. Chicago: University of Chicago Press.

COOMBS-SHILLING, M. E.
    1989   Sacred Performances: Islam, Sexuality and Sacrifice. New York: Columbia University Press.

COPPLESTONE, J. TREMAYNE
    1973   History of Methodist Missions, vol. 4; Twentieth Century Perspectives: The Methodist Episcopal Church 1896–1939. New York: The Board of Global Ministries, United Methodist Church.
    1985   Misión Metodista en Bolivia (1907–1939), La Paz: Imprente Metodista.

COSMINSKY, SHEILA, AND SUSAN SCRIMSHAW
    1980   Medical pluralism on a Guatemalen plantation. Social Science and Medicine 14B:4:267–278.

CRANDON, LIBBET
    1987   Beyond the Cure: Anthropological Inquiries in Medical Theories and Epistemologies. Special edition of Social Science and Medicine 24:12, Crandon, guest ed.

DALENCE, JOSE MARIA
    1951   Bosquejo Estadistico de Bolivia. Chuquisaca: Imprenta de Sucre.

DANDLER H., JORGE
    1969   El Sindicalismo Campesino en Bolivia: Los Cambios Estructurales en Ucurena. Mexico: Instituto Indigenista Interamericano, Serie Antropología Social, no. 11.

DEWALT, BILLIE
    1977   The illnesses no longer understand: changing concepts of health and curing in a rural Mexican community. Medical Anthropology Newsletter 8:1.

DILLON, MARY, AND THOMAS ABERCROMBIE
    1988   The destroying Christ: an Aymara myth of conquest. In: Rethinking History and Myth, Jonathan Hill, ed. Champaign: University of Illinois Press.

DOUGLAS, MARY
  1966   Purity and Danger: An Analysis of Concepts of Pollution and Taboo. New
          York: Praeger.
DUNKERLEY, JAMES
  1984   Rebellion in the Veins: Political Struggle in Bolivia 1952–1982. London:
          Verso.
DUNN, FRED
  1976   Traditional Asian medicine and cosmopolitan medicine as adaptive systems.
          In: Asian Medical Systems, Charles Leslie, ed. Berkeley, Los Angeles, Lon-
          don: University of California Press, pp. 133–158.
ECKSTEIN, SUSAN
  1979   El capitalismo mundial y la revolución agraria en Bolivia. Revista Mexicana
          de Sociologia 41(2) : 457–478. Bolivia.
  1983   Transformation of a "revolution from below": Bolivia and international capi-
          talism. Comparative Studies in Society and History 25(1).
EHRENREICH, BARBARA, AND DIERDRE ENGLISH
  1973a   Complaints and Disorders: The Sexual Politics of Sickness. Old Westbury,
          N.Y.: The Feminist Press.
  1973b   Witches, Midwives and Nurses: A History of Women Healers. Old West-
          bury, N.Y.: The Feminist Press.
ELLING, RAY
  1971   Health planning in international perspective. Medical Care 9 : 214–234.
  1974   Case studies of contrasting approaches to organizing for health: an introduc-
          tion to a framework. Social Science and Medicine 8 : 263.
  1978   Medical systems as changing social systems. Social Science and Medicine
          12B : 107–117.
  1981   Political economy, cultural hegemony and mixes of traditional and modern
          medicine. Social Science and Medicine 15A : 2 : 89–99.
FABREGA, HORATIO, JR., M.D.
  1972   Concepts of disease: logical features and social implications. In: Perspectives
          in Biology and Medicine, Dwight J. Inge, ed. New York: Basic Books.
FABREGA, HORACIO, AND DANIEL B. SILVER
  1973   Illness and Shamanistic Curing in Zinacantan. Stanford, Calif.: Stanford
          University Press.
FARQUHAR, JUDITH
  1987   Problems of knowledge in contemporary Chinese medical discourse. In:
          Beyond the Cure: Anthropological Inquiries in Medical Theories and
          Epistemologies. Special edition of Social Science and Medicine 24 : 12 :
          1013–1022.
FELKER, MARCIA ELLIOTT
  1983   Ideology and order in the operating room. In: The Anthropology of Medi-
          cine, Romanucci-Ross, Moerman, and Tancredi, eds. South Hadley, Mass.:
          Bergin and Garvey.
FOSTER, GEORGE
  1951   A Cross Cultural Anthropological Analysis of a Technical Aid Program.
          Washington, D.C.: Smithsonian Institution.

1952   Relationships between theoretical and applied anthropology. Human Organization 31:5–16.
1958   Problems in Intercultural Health Practice, pamphlet no. 12. New York: Social Science Research Council.
1966   Social anthropology and nutrition of the pre-school child, especially as related to Latin America. Pp. 258–266 in: Pre-school Child Nutrition. Washington, D.C.: National Academy of Sciences, National Research Council Publication 1282.

FOUCAULT, MICHEL
1965   Madness and Civilization: A History of Insanity in the Age of Reason. New York: Random House.
1973   The Birth of the Clinic: An Archaeology of Medical Perception. New York: Vintage.

FRAKE, CHARLES O.
1961   The diagnosis of disease among the Subanun of Mindanao. American Anthropologist 63:1:113–132.

FRANKENBERG, RONALD
1980   Medical anthropology and development: a theoretical perspective. Social Science and Medicine 14B:4:197–208.
1981   Allopathic medicine, profession and capitalist ideology in India. Social Science and Medicine 15A:2:115–124.

FREIRE, PAULO
1970   Pedagogy of the Oppressed. New York: Herder and Herder.

FRIEDLANDER, JUDITH
1975   Being Indian in Hueyapan: A Study of Forced Identity in Contemporary Mexico. New York: St. Martin's Press.

FURNIVAL, J.S.
1939   Netherlands India: A Study of Plural Economy. London: Cambridge University Press.
1948   Colonial Policy and Practice: A Comparative Study of Burma and Netherlands India. London: Cambridge University Press.

GEERTZ, CLIFFORD
1973   The Interpretation of Cultures: Selected Essays. New York: Basic Books.

GILL, LESLIE
1987   Peasants, Entrepreneurs, and Social Change: Frontier Development in Lowland Bolivia. Boulder, Colo.: Westview Press.

GOODRICH, CARTER
1971   Bolivia in time of revolution. Pp. 3–24 in: Beyond the Revolution: Bolivia Since 1952, James M. Malloy and Richard Thorn, eds. Pittsburgh: University of Pittsburgh Press.

HARRIS, MARVIN
1964   Patterns of Race in the Americas. New York: Walker.

HARRIS, OLIVIA
1978a   El parentesco y la economía vertical en el Ayllu Laymi (norte de Potosi). Avances (La Paz): Revista Boliviana de estudios históricos y sociales, no. 1:51–64.

1978b   Kinship and the vertical economy of the laymi ayllu, norte de Potosi. Actes du XLII Congres International des Americanistes (1976), vol. 4, Paris.

HUIZER, GERRIT JAN
    1972   The Revolutionary Potential of Peasants in Latin America. Lexington, Mass.: Lexington Books.

ISBELL, BILLIE JEAN
    1978   To Defend Ourselves: Ecology and Ritual in an Andean Village. Austin: Institute of Latin American Studies.

JANZEN, JOHN
    1978   The Quest for Therapy in Lower Zaire. Berkeley, Los Angeles, London: University of California Press.

JULIEN, CATHERINE J.
    1983   Hatunqolla, a View of Inca Rule from the Titicaca Region. Berkeley, Los Angeles, London: University of California Press.

KANE, ROBERT, AND ROSALIE KANE
    1972   Federal Health Care (with Reservations). New York: Springer.

KELLEY, JONATHAN, ET AL.
    1977   Movilidad social en Bolivia rural: comparacion con los Estados Unidos. Estudios Andinos (La Paz) 7(13): 183–191.

KELLEY, JONATHAN, AND HERBERT S. KLEIN
    1981   Revolution and the Rebirth of Inequality. Berkeley, Los Angeles, London: University of California Press.

KLEIN, HERBERT
    1969   Parties and Political Change in Bolivia 1880–1952. Cambridge: Cambridge University Press.
    1982   Bolivia: The Evolution of a Multi-Ethnic Society. Oxford: Oxford University Press.

KLEINMAN, ARTHUR M., M.D.
    1980   Patients and Healers in the Context of Culture. Berkeley, Los Angeles, London: University of California Press.

KOSS, JOAN
    1975   Therapeutic aspects of Puerto Rican cult practices. Psychiatry 38: 160–171.
    1980   The therapist-spiritist training project in Puerto Rico: an experiment to relate the traditional healing system to the public health system. Social Science and Medicine 14B: 255–266.

LARSON, BROOKE
    1979   Caciques, class structure, and the colonial state in Bolivia. Nova Americana 2: 197–235.

LAVAUD, JEAN-PIERRE
    1976   Compèrage, stratification sociale et rapports de pouvoir: un enquête à La Paz. Cahiers des Amériques Latines 13–14: 103–125.
    1977   La mobilisation politique du paysannes bolivien. Revue Française de Sociologie 18: (4): 624–649.

LEONS, MADELINE BARBARA
  1978   Race, ethnicity and political mobilization in the Andes. American Ethnologist 5(3) : 484–494.
LESLIE, CHARLES
  1975   Pluralism and integration in the Indian and Chinese medical systems. In: Medicine in Chinese Cultures: Comparative Studies of Health Care in Chinese and Other Societies, Arthur Kleinman, et al., eds. Washington, D.C.: U.S. Dept. of Health, Education and Welfare, Public Health Service, National Institutes of Health, DHEW publication no. (NIH) 75–653, pp. 401–417.
LOCK, MARGARET
  1980   East Asian Medicine in Urban Japan: Varieties of Medical Experience. Berkeley, Los Angeles, London: University of California Press.
LOSA BALSA, GREGORIO, M.D.
  1977   Esbozo de Medicina Aymara. La Paz: Mimeo, Facultad de Ciencias de la Salud, Universidad Mayor de San Andres.
LOW, SETHA
  1985   Culture, Politics, and Medicine in Costa Rica. New York: Redgrave.
McVAY, CYNTHIA, AND EVON VOGT
  1988   Some contours of social class in a southern Mexican town. Ethnology 27 : 1 : 27–44.
MALLOY, JAMES
  1970   Bolivia: The Uncompleted Revolution. Pittsburgh: University of Pittsburgh Press.
MOERMAN, DANIEL
  1983   Physiology and symbols: the anthropological implications of the placebo effect. Pp. 156–167 in: The Anthropology of Medicine: From Culture to Method, Romanucci-Ross, Moerman, and Tancredi, eds. South Hadley, Mass.: Bergin and Garvey.
MURRA, JOHN
  1968   An Aymara kingdom in 1567. Ethnohistory 15 : 2 : 115–151. Republished in: Formaciones Económicas y Políticas del Mundo Andino, 1975, Lima: Instituto de Estudios Peruanos.
  1972   El control vertical de un maximo de pisos ecologicos en la economía de las sociedades Andinas. Pp. 430–476 in: Visita de la Provincia de Leon de Huanuco, Tomo 2, Inigo Ortiz de Zuniga, ed. Huanuco, Peru. Republished in: Formaciones Económicas y Políticas del Mundo Andino, 1975, Lima: Instituto de Estudios Peruanos.
  1978   Aymara lords and their European agents in Potosi. Nova Americana 1 : 231–243.
  1980 (1956)   The Economic Origins of the Inka State: Research on Economic Anthropology, supplement no. 1. Greenwich, Conn.: JAI Press.
NALL, FRANK C., JR., AND JOSEPH SPEILBERG
  1967   Social and cultural factors in the responses of Mexican-Americans to medical treatment. Journal of Health and Social Behavior 8 : 4 : 299–308.

NASH, JUNE
  1979   We Eat the Mines and the Mines Eat Us. New York: Columbia University
          Press.
OBLITAS POBLETE, ENRIQUE
  1963   Cultura Callawaya. La Paz: Editorial Talleres Gráficos Bolivianos.
  1969   Plantas Medicinales de Bolivia. La Paz: Editorial Los Amigos del Libro.
  1971   Magia, Hechiceria y Medicina Popular Boliviana. La Paz: Ediciónes Isla.
PADI
  1983   Cronología: La Paz.
PAREDES, M. RIGOBERTO
  1955 (1934)   La Provincia de Omasuyu. La Paz: Ediciónes Isla.
  1968   Los Siñani. La Paz: Ediciónes Isla.
PARSONS, TALCOTT
  1968 (1937)   The Structure of Social Action (two vols.). New York: The Free
          Press.
PAUL, BENJAMIN
  1953   The cultural context of health education. Pp. 31–38 in: Symposium Pro-
          ceedings, School of Social Work, University of Pittsburgh.
  1955   Health, Culture and Community. New York: Russel Sage Foundation.
PICK, FRANZ
  1971   All the Monies of the World. With Rene Sedillot. New York: Pick Publish-
          ing Corp.
PLATT, TRISTAN
  1978a   Symétries en miroir. Le concept de yanantin chez les Macha de Bolivie. An-
          nales, E.S.C. (Paris) 33(5–6) : 1081–1107.
  1978b   Acerca del sistema tributario pre-toledano en el Alto Peru. Avances (La Paz)
          no. 1, pp. 33–46.
  1982a   Estado Boliviano y ayllu andino: tierra y tributo en el Norte de Potosi. Lima:
          Instituto de Estudios Peruoanos (Historia Andina 9).
  1982b   The role of the Andean ayllu in the reproduction of the petty commodity
          regime in Northern Potosi (Bolivia). In: Ecology and Exchange in the Andes,
          David Lehmann, ed., pp. 27–69. Cambridge: Cambridge University Press.
POOLE, DEBORAH ANN
  1984   Ritual-Economic Calendars in Paruro: The Structure of Representation in
          Andean Ethnography. Ph.D. dissertation, University of Michigan.
PRESS, IRWIN
  1969   Urban illness: physicians, curers, and dual use in Bogota. Journal of Health
          and Social Behavior 10 : 3 : 209–218.
  1971   The urban curandero. American Anthropologist 73 : 741–756.
RASNAKE, ROGER
  1982   The Kurakhuna of Yura: Indigenous Authorities of Colonial Charcas
          and Contemporary Bolivia. Ph.D. dissertation in anthropology, Cornell
          University.
  1988   Domination and Cultural Resistance: Authority and Power Among an An-
          dean People. Durham, N.C.: Duke University Press.

REBEL, HERMANN
  1989   Cultural hegemony and class experience: a critical reading of recent
          ethnological-historical approaches. American Ethnologist 16:2:350–365
          (May).

RIVERA, SILVA
  1978   El mallku y la sociedad colonial en el siglo XVII: el caso de Jesus de Machaca.
          Avances (La Paz) 1:7–27.

RODRIGUEZ O., GUSTAVO
  1980   Original accumulation, capitalism and precapitalistic agriculture in Bolivia
          (1870–1885), tr. by L. M. Costs and D. T. Robman. Latin American Per-
          spectives 7(4):50–66.

ROJAS, ANTONIO
  1980   Land and labor in the articulation of the peasant economy with the hacienda.
          Latin American Perspectives 7(4):67–82.

ROMANUCCI-ROSS, LOLA, AND DANIEL MOERMAN
  1988   The extraneous factor in Western medicine. Ethos 16:146–166.

ROWE, JOHN H.
  1951   Colonial portraits of Inca nobles. Pp. 258–270 in: The Civilizations of An-
          cient America, Sol Tax, ed. New York: Cooper Square Publishers.
  1954   El Movimiento nacional Inca del siglo XVIII. Revista Universitaria
          107:17–47 Cuzco. Also in: Tupak Amaru II–1780, A. Flores Galindo, ed.,
          1976, Lima: Retablo de Papel.
  1957   The Incas under Spanish colonial institutions. Hispanic American Historical
          Review 37:2:155–199.
  1961   The chronology of Inca wooden cups. In: Essays in Pre-Columbian Art and
          Archaeology, Samuel K. Lothrop et al., pp. 317–341; 473–475; 498–500,
          Cambridge: Harvard University Press.

RUBEL, ARTHUR
  1960   Concepts of disease in a Mexican-American culture. American Anthropolo-
          gist 62:795–814.

SAHLINS, MARSHALL
  1981   Historical Metaphors and Mythical Realities: Structure in the Early History
          of the Sandwich Islands Kingdom. Association for the Study of Anthropol-
          ogy in Oceania, Special Publication no. 1. Ann Arbor: University of Michi-
          gan Press.

SALLNOW, MICHAEL J.
  1987   Pilgrims of the Andes: Regional Cults in Cusco. Washington, D.C.: Smith-
          sonian Institution.

SCHNEIDER, JANE, PETER SCHNEIDER, AND ED HANSEN
  1972   Modernization and development: the role of regional elites and noncorporate
          groups in the European Mediterranean. Comparative Studies in Society and
          History 14:328–350.

SHARON, DOUGLAS
  1978   Wizard of the Four Winds. New York: The Free Press.

SIMMONS, OZZIE G.
    1955   Popular and modern medicine in mestizo communities of coastal Peru and
            Chile. Journal of American Folklore 68 : 57–71.
SMITH, ANTHONY
    1981   The Ethnic Revival in the Modern World. Cambridge: Cambridge Univer-
            sity Press.
SMITH, JOEL, AND ALLAN KORNBERG
    1969   Some considerations bearing upon comparative research in Canada and the
            United States. Sociology 3 : 341–357.
SMITH, M. G.
    1965   The Plural Society in the British West Indies. Berkeley and Los Angeles:
            University of California Press.
    1984   Culture, Race, and Class in the Commonwealth Caribbean. Mona, Jamaica:
            Dept. of Estra-Mural Studies, University of the West Indies.
SMITH, STEPHEN M.
    1977   Labor exploitation on pre-1952 haciendas in the lower valley of Cochabamba,
            Bolivia. Journal of Developing Areas 11(2) : 227–244.
SONTAG, SUSAN
    1977   Illness as Metaphor. New York: Farrar, Straus, Giroux.
SPALDING, KAREN
    1973   Kurakas and commerce. Hispanic American Historical Review 53 : 581–599.
    1984   Huarochiri: An Andean Society Under Inca and Spanish Rule. Stanford,
            Calif.: Stanford University Press.
STARR, PAUL
    1982   The Social Transformation of American Medicine. New York: Basic Books.
STEIN, STANLEY J., AND BARBARA Y. STEIN
    1970   The Colonial Heritage of Latin America. New York: Oxford University
            Press.
STERN, STEVE J.
    1982   Peru's Indian Peoples and the Challenge of the Spanish Conquest: Huamanga
            to 1640. Madison: University of Wisconsin Press.
STINSON, SARA
    1978   Child Growth, Mortality, and the Adaptive Value of Children in Rural
            Bolivia. Unpublished Ph.D. dissertation, University of Michigan.
    1980   Child growth and the economic value of children in rural Bolivia. Human
            Ecology 8(22) : 89–104.
    1982   The interrelationship of mortality and fertility in rural Bolivia. Human Biol-
            ogy 54 : 299–313.
    1983   Socioeconomic status and child growth in rural Bolivia. Ecology of Food and
            Nutrition 13 : 179–187.
STRICKEN, ARNOLD, AND SIDNEY GREENFIELD, EDS.
    1972   Structure and Process in Latin America: Patronage Clientage and Power Sys-
            tems. Albuquerque: University of New Mexico Press.

TAUSSIG, MICHAEL
  1980   The Devil and Commodity Fetishism. Chapel Hill: University of North
          Carolina Press.
  1987   Shamanism, Colonialism and The Wild Man: A Study in Terror and Heal-
          ing. Chicago: University of Chicago Press.

THIBODEAUX, BEN H.
  1946   Economic Study of Agriculture in Bolivia. Unpublished Ph.D. dissertation,
          Harvard University.

THOME, JOSEPH R.
  1966   Problems Which Obstruct the Process of Title Distribution Under the Boli-
          vian Agrarian Reform. Preliminary report, USAID contract. Land Tenure
          Center, University of Wisconsin.

THOMPSON, E. P.
  1979   Folklore, anthropology and social history. In: Studies in Labor History, J. L.
          Noyce, ed. Brighton: Noyce.

TSCHOPIK, HARRY
  1947   Highland Communities of Central Peru: A Regional Survey. Washington,
          D.C.: U.S. Government Printing Office.
  1951   The Aymara of Chuquito, Peru. New York: Museum of Natural History.

TUMIRI APAZA, JULIO, ED.
  1978   The Indian Liberation and Social Rights Movement in Killasuyu (Bolivia).
          Copenhagen: International Work Group in Indigenous Affairs, no. 30.

TURNER, VICTOR
  1964   A Ndembu doctor in practice. In: Magic, Faith and Healing, Ari Kiev, ed.
          New York: The Free Press.
  1969   The Ritual Process. Chicago: Aldine.

UNSCHULD, PAUL
  1975   Medico-cultural conflicts in Asian settings: an explanatory theory. Social
          Science and Medicine 9:303–312.
  1979   Medical Ethics in Imperial China; A Study in Historical Anthropology.
          Berkeley, Los Angeles, London: University of California Press.
  1985   Medicine in China: A History of Ideas. Berkeley, Los Angeles, London: Uni-
          versity of California Press.

VAN DEN BERGHE, PIERRE
  1983   Class, race, and ethnicity in Africa. Ethnic and Racial Studies 6:2:221–236.

VARGAS, EDGAR SOLIZ
  1979   La colonización y el desarrollo rural en Bolivia. Antropologia. Revista del
          Instituto Nacional de Antropologia (La Paz) 1(1):33–51.

VINCENT, JOAN
  1971   African Elite: The Big Men of a Small Town. New York: Columbia Univer-
          sity Press.
  1974   The structure of ethnicity. Human Organization 33:4:375–379.

WACHTEL, NATHAN
  1977   The Vision of the Vanquished. New York: Barnes and Noble Imports.

WAGLEY, CHARLES, AND MARVIN HARRIS
    1958   Minorities in the New World. New York: Columbia University Press.
WEBER, MAX
    1961   Ethnic groups. In: Theories of Society, Talcott Parsons, Edward Shils, Kaspar
            Naegele, and Jesse Pitts, eds., chapter 1. New York: The Free Press.
WELLIN, EDWARD
    1955   Water boiling in a Peruvian town. In: Health, Culture and Community,
            Benjamin Paul, ed. New York: Russell Sage Foundation.
WOLF, ERIC
    1982   Europe and a People Without History: Berkeley, Los Angeles, London: Uni-
            versity of California Press.
WRIGHT, PETER, AND ANDREW TREACHER
    1982   The Problem of Medical Knowledge: Examining the Social Construction of
            Medicine. Edinburgh: University of Edinburgh Press.
YOUNG, ALLAN
    1976   Some implications of medical beliefs and practices for social anthropology.
    1978   Mode of production of medical knowledge. Medical Anthropology 2 : 2.
    1982   Rational men and the explanatory model approach. Culture, Medicine and
            Psychiatry 6 : 1 : 57–71 (March).
YOUNG, JAMES C.
    1981   Medical Choice in a Mexican Village. New Brunswick, N.J.: Rutgers Univer-
            sity Press.
ZUVEKAS, CLARENCE, JR.
    1977   Unemployment and Underemployment in Bolivian Agriculture: A Critical
            Survey of the Literature. Washington, D.C.: Agency for International De-
            velopment, Bureau for Latin America, Rural Development Division.
    1979   Measuring rural underdevelopment in Bolivia: a review. Inter-American
            Economic Affairs 32(4).

Index

Designer: Linda M. Robertson
Compositor: G & S Typesetters, Inc.
Text: 10/12 Aldus
Display: Futura Medium
Printer: Bookcrafters, Inc.
Binder: Bookcrafters, Inc.